# Business Strategy Formulation

# Business Strategy Formulation

## Theory, Process, and the Intellectual Revolution

Anthony W. Ulwick

QUORUM BOOKS
Westport, Connecticut • London

**Library of Congress Cataloging-in-Publication Data**

Ulwick, Anthony W., 1957–
    Business strategy formulation : theory, process, and the
intellectual revolution / Anthony W. Ulwick.
        p.   cm.
    Includes bibliographical references and index.
    ISBN 1–56720–273–X (alk. paper)
    1. Strategic planning.   I. Title.
HD30.28.U44   1999
    658.4'012—dc21          99–13714

British Library Cataloguing in Publication Data is available.

Library of Congress Catalog Card Number: 99–13714
ISBN: 1–56720–273–X

First published in 1999

Quorum Books, 88 Post Road West, Westport, CT 06881
An imprint of Greenwood Publishing Group, Inc.
www.quorumbooks.com

Printed in the United States of America

The paper used in this book complies with the
Permanent Paper Standard issued by the National
Information Standards Organization (Z39.48–1984).

10 9 8 7 6 5 4 3 2 1

Dedicated to my wife, Heather Lee, and our son,
Anthony—my sources of love and inspiration.

# Contents

Contents

# Preface

When joining IBM in 1980, I was proud to be associated with such a respected and profitable organization. Working in the personal computer division was especially exciting as we were breaking new ground. The IBM PC was one of the biggest success stories of the decade. After its release, we worked on the development of other IBM products. They became known as PCjr, PS2 with Micro Channel Architecture and OS2. As you might guess, after putting in long hours over many years, we were sickened by the fact that these products were dismal market failures. I found it hard to believe that IBM's product and business strategies could be so incredibly flawed. Costly mistakes like these should never be made. As a result, I began to inquire as to how IBM's PC strategies were formulated and was shocked to find out what little effort was put forth in this area. It was apparent, however, that IBM was not alone. Many organizations failed to put enough concentrated effort into their strategic planning and product planning processes and often faced unfortunate results. The 1980s gave way to many strategic failures including New Coke, the NeXT desktop computer, Pepsi AM, dry beer and others. It was obvious that businesses could operate much differently. It was at that point that I made a commitment to myself to find, or create, a strategy formulation process that would prevent organizations from making such costly strategic errors.

Over the next five years I spent most of my time studying the theories, ideas and methods that shaped the field of strategy formulation. I studied the works of experts in the field including Michael Porter, Gary Hamel, C. K. Prahalad, Kenchi Ohmae, Igor Ansoff, Ken Andrews, Alfred Chandler, Henry Mintzberg and others. I studied various approaches to qualitative research, quantitative research, market segmentation, decision making and total quality management. After five years of intense study, I concluded that, although the experts knew the benefits of having a good strategy and knew what a good strategy was supposed to accomplish, there was no real "process" for creating a breakthrough strategy. In fact, I found that most strategists believed then, and many still do today, that a process for strategy formulation could not exist. Interestingly enough, it was thought that the complexities associated with strategy formulation were too numerous to control and that strategy formulation was, and would continue to be, an elusive art form that only a few gifted individuals could master.

I set out to prove that this thinking was incorrect. With a background in Neuro Linguistic Programming (NLP), I knew that any set of activities or behaviors could be modeled, including the formulation of successful strategies and solutions. So I set out to create a strategy formulation process that would generate a breakthrough strategy in every situation in which an organization attempted to formulate a business, product or operational strategy. The first step in this effort was to uncover the universal principles that were applied by organizations as they successfully created breakthrough strategies. To accomplish this task, I applied pattern detection techniques that are often used in physics, NLP and other behavioral sciences. After years of observation, I was able to detect a pattern that proved to be the impetus for the creation of a universal structure for strategy formulation. Through ongoing testing, it was verified that this pattern existed in every situation in which an organization created a successful strategy. It was at this point that I knew a strategy formulation process would evolve.

From that point on, many other obstacles were overcome on the way to creating an advanced strategy formulation process: the essential elements of strategy formulation were defined; methods for gathering pertinent information were established; advancements were made in the field of "requirements" gathering, benchmarking and positioning; and the tools required to process this information were created. During this period, I left IBM and became a consultant to mostly *Fortune* 100 companies. Since that time, my colleagues and I have completed strategy formulation projects with Allied Signal, Hewlett-Packard, IBM, Johnson & Johnson, Medtronic, Motorola, Pacesetter, Pfizer, Southcorp, Telectronics, Teledyne, Telematics, United Technologies and many other organizations. Our strategy formulation process evolved quickly as we constantly focused on making improvements, and today we have in our possession possibly the most advanced and complete strategy formulation process in the world.

Many of our clients have received tremendous benefits as a result of applying this process. One such client is Motorola. As a result, Motorola technologist Robert Pennisi, Ph.D., offered to make the following contribution. Dr. Pennisi writes:

When formulating company and product strategies, organizations may choose to take the same actions that have made them successful in the past. They may choose to react to complaints that have been made by existing customers, or respond to new products from competitors that have resulted in good press or in the loss of a traditional customer. Organizations may base their company and product strategies on internal goals such as cost reduction or quality improvement. They may choose to react to managers who believe the organization must simply do something different.

Given the increasingly competitive nature of most businesses and the advent of global markets, a reactive approach to strategy formulation may be a recipe for failure. Which organizations will be best positioned for the future? Will it be those who base their company and product strategies on past successes, customer complaints, competitors' actions, internal objectives or a desire to do something different? Or will it be those who systematically use facts, structure and process to formulate strategies and solutions that address the unique aspects of their situation and enhance their ability to create customer value?

Motorola has put forth a tremendous effort in past years to improve its internal processes. Our six-sigma initiative has become the cornerstone for many continuous improvement programs. After making vast improvements in our overall operational efficiency, we recognized that the future success of our organization is dependent on its ability to choose which markets, products and actions to pursue and which technologies to invest in. The ability to effectively strategize, plan and position has become the critical path to success.

Historically, organizations have pursued the development of multiple strategies, products, services and technologies knowing that only a few of them will succeed, but never knowing which of them will succeed. As a result, organizations were forced to nurture multiple opportunities until the obvious winners emerged. As competition stiffens and resources become more constrained, we want to be certain that we are only investing in, developing and backing the strategies, products, services and technologies that will ultimately win out. Financial and resource investments made in opportunities that ultimately fail must be avoided. Non-value producing investments and activities must be eliminated. Achieving this objective greatly reduces expenses and overhead while dramatically improving time to market, customer satisfaction and overall profitability.

In our quest for improvement in this area, we benchmarked many approaches to the process of strategy formulation. The process introduced in this book describes the most advanced approach to strategy formulation that could be found.

This process has provided us with a clear understanding of what our existing and potential customers value. As a result, we have been able to focus on systematically creating and delivering that value. We have been able to create low-cost product platforms and highly valued segment specific solutions. We have been able to rank existing and prospective technologies for their potential to satisfy future market opportunities. We have uncovered value producing product features that would have otherwise been undiscovered or ignored.

In addition, this process and the theory behind it have taught us many valuable lessons. For example, we have discovered that breakthrough products and services can be developed with current, off-the-shelf technologies and do not always require new technology. We have learned that traditional approaches to market segmentation rarely provide the best view of the market, since individuals across industry, geography and price point often share a common set of desired outcomes. We have proven that traditional approaches to strategy formulation typically produce concepts that deliver incremental rather than breakthrough improvement. And finally, we have proven to ourselves that breakthrough strategies and solutions can be created consistently and systematically, thereby accelerating the creation of customer value.

Over the past three years, the use of this process has enabled us to make decisions that are based on statistically supported facts rather than relying on subjective information, personal or political motivations or intuition. Individuals within our organization have come to realize the importance of having the right information to make and influence decisions. We have been able to use this information as a basis for agreement and as a means by which to gain consensus from cross-functional teams.

The strategy formulation process and theory introduced in this book provide structure to what was once the unstructured world of strategy formulation. As organizations prepare themselves for the future, they must be able to identify what their customers and potential customers value most. They must be able to successfully uncover areas of opportunity. They must be able to quantitatively determine which strategies, technologies, products and activities to pursue. They must ensure their employees have access to technologies that enable them to make customer-driven, value generating decisions. Organizations that successfully achieve these objectives will be well positioned for the future. The advanced strategy formulation process introduced in this book makes it possible to achieve these and other objectives.

Through first-hand experience, many of our clients have come to know the benefits that can be received from applying this advanced strategy formulation process. This process, which has been improved continuously since its initial application, will continue to evolve over the coming years. We are focused on ensuring this process is flawless and on improving the tools that simplify its application. These tools are being created by Strategyn.com.

This process is being made available to internal and external consultants, executives, managers, strategists and planners, change agents, academicians and others who are involved in the field of strategy formulation. This book describes where this process is today, how it has evolved, how it has rewritten the rules of strategy formulation and how it can be used immediately to create value for organizations and their customers.

# Acknowledgments

Many individuals have influenced the thinking that ultimately led to the creation of this advanced strategy formulation technology. Published authors who have devoted their lives to the study of strategy formulation, although too many to mention, have made lasting impressions. Peers and colleagues that have made contributions to this process include Robert Hales, Andrew Tiede, Wil Wengert, Dr. Ed Herrero, Bill Nordeen, Michael Walker, Dr. Edmund Dolfen, Kurt Hofmeister, Ray Leon, Tom Murphy, Mitch Auran and Gary Ekstrom.

As projects were executed for companies around the world, many company employees made contributions that led to improvements of the process. They include Dr. Bob Pennisi, Jim Clossick, Mark Nevins, Steve Golton, Mike Clouthier, John Brooks, James Busse, Rick Korchak, Ted Fluchradt, Andi Champagne, Chris Pike, Joseph Rexroad, Ron Varney, Dave Sapuppo, Pete Shaw, Rick Faleschini, Philip Smith, Theresa Bradshaw, Jill Ernst, Brent Jacobsen, Gary Kaiser, Linda O'Brien and David Ramsay.

I would also like to thank Jeff Herman, my literary agent; John and Joyce Eisenhauer, my assistants; and Alan Sturmer of Greenwood Publishing Group for their efforts and support in editing and publishing this book.

# Introduction

This book is written for individuals who are prepared to engage themselves and their organizations in an Intellectual Revolution: a revolution in which organizations create their own futures, encourage change and focus on the creation of value; a revolution in which organizations understand what their customers value and use that information as the basis for their actions; a revolution in which an organization of any size can possess the structure, information and processing power required to formulate strategies and solutions that will strengthen its strategic position.

This revolution is the result of breakthrough ideas and theories that have evolved the process of strategy formulation from an art to a science. With the use of this advanced process, organizations have the power to consistently and effectively anticipate future opportunities; make value-generating investment decisions; and determine which products and services concepts to pioneer, which core competencies to build, which alliances to form, which activities to pursue and which trade-offs to make. In short, this book introduces an advanced strategy formulation process that is not only fueling an Intellectual Revolution, but a process that provides organizations with the power to systematically accelerate the creation and delivery of customer value.

This advanced strategy formulation process has been developed and proven over the past seven years. It is being used effectively in organizations such as Pfizer, Hewlett-Packard, United Technologies, Medtronic, Motorola, Johnson & Johnson and other companies in the United States, Pacific Rim and Europe. Its use often results in strategies and solutions that have been documented to deliver up to 10 times more value than those derived through the use of traditional strategy formulation methods. This degree of improvement has been made possible through a unique integration of structure, information and processing power.

Organizations are using this process to harness their collective knowledge and wisdom, to make fact-based decisions and to create the strategies and solutions that are required to overcome their biggest challenges. This process is being used to formulate overall company strategies, product and service strategies and strategies that evolve an organization's operational, support and management processes. It is enabling organizations to put into practice the theories espoused by strategists and academics such as Michael Porter, Gary Hamel, C. K. Prahalad, Peter Senge, Kenichi Ohmae and a host of others.

This book is intended to help organizations unravel the mystery surrounding the concept of strategy and the process of strategy formulation. It unveils a structure that addresses the complexity of strategy formulation, planning and decision making without generalizations, deletions or oversimplification. It defines the essential elements of strategy formulation and will change forever the way organizations think about customer "requirements," measurement systems and competitive analysis. It explains precisely why most organizations fail to understand what their customers value and demonstrates why this phenomenon is a root cause of failure in most strategy formulation processes. It reveals technological advancements that are making it possible for any organization to possess the capability to effectively formulate breakthrough strategies and solutions.

In his article titled "Killer Strategies" (1997), strategist Gary Hamel asks, "Can we do anything to increase the fertility of the soil out of which strategy grows? One good place to start is to develop a deep theory of strategy creation." The aim of this book is to provide the business world with not only a deep theory of strategy creation but also a process that enables the application of this theory. A process that integrates facts with methods for non-linear thinking, the type of thinking that is often required to produce breakthrough strategies.

The advanced strategy formulation process introduced in this book combines many discoveries and innovations with unique applications of ideas and theories from different fields and disciplines. It is this unique combination of ideas and theories that has given birth to the science of strategy formulation. This book explains this new science and describes how it can be applied by organizations around the world to formulate strategies that consistently produce breakthrough results.

Many of the concepts presented in this book are new, challenge existing assumptions and are viewed as counterintuitive. As a result, many company executives, managers, internal and external consultants and others will be forced to question what they once thought to be true.

Those of you, who are ready to challenge your thinking strategies and are willing to leave the comfort of your existing paradigms, will learn to engage your mind, yourself, and your organization in an Intellectual Revolution.

Let your journey begin—now.

# Chapter 1

# The Intellectual Revolution

In the late eighteenth century, society witnessed the start of the first modern-day business revolution—the Industrial Revolution. Fueled with new technologies, such as power-driven machinery, the Industrial Revolution brought about dramatic increases in productivity, output and economic growth.

In the early 1920s, new manufacturing technologies enabled the mass production of a wide variety of products. The 1950s brought the computer and the space age. In 1969, man first landed on the moon. Again, new technologies resulted in dramatic increases in worldwide productivity, output and economic growth.

Since that time, we have entered into the Information Age—an age in which "information is power." With the advent of computers, the Internet and on-line services, individuals have access to a tremendous amount of information on literally thousands of subjects. We must ask: Does this information alone make us powerful? Or does the power really lie in our ability to use this information to create value for ourselves and others?

Imagine how powerful we would be if we could possess and structure all the information that is required to create value generating strategies and solutions. Imagine how powerful we would be if we could then take all that information and immediately process it to uncover the strategy or solution that would generate the most value for all those involved in a given situation. Imagine if we could consistently create strategies and solutions that delivered up to ten times more value than those that are normally created. If organizations possessed the capability to generate breakthrough ideas, strategies and solutions, it is argued that they would create another revolution—an Intellectual Revolution. Such a revolution could again bring about dramatic increases in productivity, output and economic growth.

The world is on the brink of an Intellectual Revolution.

Many aspects of strategy formulation, planning and decision making have been transformed from an art to a science. This transformation is evolving the ability of many open-minded organizations to create breakthrough strategies and solutions. It is providing them with a means to overcome their most important business challenges.

The objective of this book is to introduce the process that is being used to make this transformation possible. Through the application of this advanced strategy formulation process, many organizations will, for the first time, be able to take the steps that are required to create breakthrough strategies and solutions. They will be able to participate in the future of strategy formulation as they engage themselves in the Intellectual Revolution.

This book describes the science of strategy formulation, planning and decision making, a science which many have yet to acknowledge. Many individuals and strategists believe that the complexities associated with strategy formulation are too numerous to control and that a systematic approach to strategy formulation could not exist. Most strategy formulation processes to date have failed to successfully integrate logic, analysis, creativity and innovation. As a result, strategists such as Henry Mintzberg have concluded that the process of strategy formulation cannot be formalized. The truth is, the process of strategy formulation can be formalized if the applied process does not limit creativity and innovation or limit the strategic options that are considered. This book introduces such a process and explains how it can be used by any organization to formulate the strategies and solutions that will accelerate the creation and delivery of customer value.

In contrast to most books written on the subject of strategy, this one does not address why it is important to formulate effective strategies. The importance of effective planning and positioning is well recognized within most organizations. Instead, it is focused on describing how an organization can put into practice the theories that are espoused by some of the world's leading strategic thinkers.

In *Competitive Advantage* (1985), for example, Michael Porter stresses the importance of creating a unique and valued competitive position. In *Competing for the Future* (1994), Gary Hamel and C. K. Prahalad advise organizations on the importance of changing the rules of the game. In *Commitment: The Dynamic of Strategy* (1991), Pankaj Ghemawat emphasizes the importance of sustaining a competitive advantage. Simply stated, the goal of this book is to introduce a process that organizations such as Medtronic, Motorola, Pfizer, Hewlett-Packard, Teledyne, Johnson & Johnson and others are already using to achieve these and dozens of other strategic objectives.

To create this advanced approach to the process of strategy formulation, many barriers to effective planning were addressed. This book discusses these barriers and how they were overcome. It introduces new ways to think about the concept of strategy and the process of strategy formulation. It addresses the issues that have for years prevented organizations from understanding what their customers truly value.

The concepts introduced throughout this book are built on a strong foundation. To ensure that foundation is understood, it is prudent to start at the beginning. Let's start with a look at the definition of strategy.

## WHAT IS STRATEGY?

As a wise person once told me, "definitions of strategy are like vitamins, you get one-a-day and most of them are hard to swallow." Over the years, how many different definitions of the word strategy have you been exposed to? The definition of strategy is the subject of many articles and the cause of many debates. The word strategy is a vague statement that means different things to different people at different times. Much of the cause for debate can be explained as follows:

> Many definitions of strategy not only attempt to define what a strategy is, but they also contain information regarding how a strategy is created, and what a strategy is expected to achieve.

For example, Michael Porter, in his article titled "What Is Strategy?" (1996), states that "strategy is the creation of a unique and valued position, involving a different set of activities." Kenichi Ohmae, in his article titled "Getting Back to Strategy" (1988), states that strategy means "working hard to understand a customer's inherent needs and then rethinking what a category of product is all about." In his article titled "The Origin of Strategy" (1989), Bruce D. Henderson states that strategy is "a deliberate search for a plan of action that will develop a business' competitive advantage and compound it." In his book titled *Strategy and Structure* (1962), Alfred Chandler defines strategy as "the determination of the long-term goals and objectives of an enterprise, and the adoption of courses of action and the allocation of resources necessary for carrying out those goals." Notice that each of these definitions of strategy address *how* a strategy is created or *what* a strategy is expected to achieve.

Historically, hundreds of strategists and organizations have used many different approaches to strategy formulation to achieve a variety of strategic objectives. As a result, organizations, consultants and academicians have, over time, given the concept of strategy literally hundreds of different situation specific definitions. The definitions may be appropriate given the specific situation, but rarely does one definition fit all situations.

To overcome the confusion created by this phenomenon, it is important to draw a clear distinction between a strategy, the process by which a strategy is created and its expected results. The distinctions can be drawn as follows.

## A Strategy

A strategy is simply a plan. It is an executable plan of action that describes how an individual or organization will achieve a stated mission. A strategy is often perceived as being intangible, as there is nothing to touch and feel—there are no physical attributes associated with a strategy. A strategy is simply a plan—a plan that describes what an organization proposes to do to achieve a stated mission. Organizations often formulate company strategies, product and service strategies and strategies that drive operational, support and management processes.

## Creating a Strategy

The process by which a strategy is created is referred to as a strategy formulation process. A strategy formulation process results in the strategy, plan or solution that is to be implemented. Such a process defines the steps to take to formulate what will hopefully be the optimal strategy or solution. The concept introduced in this book is classified as a strategy formulation process. It defines the steps that must be taken in order to produce breakthrough strategies and solutions. An effective strategy formulation process should enable an organization to create strategies and solutions that will strengthen its strategic position.

When individuals define strategy as ''the art of devising plans toward a goal'' or ''the deliberate search for a plan of action,'' for example, they are defining the process by which a strategy is created. They are not defining what a strategy is, they are defining the process of strategy formulation. It is for this reason that many individuals have difficulty distinguishing between a strategy as a plan and ''strategy'' as a series of actions that yield a plan.

## The Expectations of a Strategy

The expected results of a strategy are dependent on the strategist, the organization and the situation for which the strategy is required. Strategies are intentionally developed for many different purposes and under a variety of conditions or situations. The desired results are expected to be different in each unique situation. For example, a strategist or organization may require a strategy that will ensure the organization achieves its desired competitive position, lowers its product cost, increases customer satisfaction, creates a sustainable competitive advantage, increases revenue or market share or accelerates the pace at which it delivers value. An organization may formulate a strategy for the purpose of improving company policy, a product family, a specific product or service or an internal process. In a non-traditional sense, a strategy may be required for hiring new employees, improving the product development process, pricing products and services, or selecting a target market or improving relations with suppliers or distributors. The expected results of a specific strategy are not mutually exclusive and depend on what is important to the strategist and the organization at the time the strategy is being contemplated. A company, in effect, executes a variety of strategies at many levels of the organization to serve a variety of purposes.

When individuals define strategy as "an attempt to develop a competitive advantage" or "an effort to ensure an organization's ongoing profitable growth," for example, they are actually defining the results that they expect to receive from a strategy that is effectively created and implemented for their organization at that time. They are not defining what a strategy is; they are defining what they would like the strategy to help them achieve. This is the reason why many individuals have difficulty distinguishing between a strategy as a plan and "strategy" as the outcome of effectively executing the plan.

Making these distinctions when analyzing various definitions of strategy helps to clarify how a specific organization, consultant or academician perceives the role of strategy. The definition of strategy that is used by an individual provides insight into *how* they think the strategy should be created and *what* they expect the strategy to help them achieve in that situation.

Regardless of the definition of strategy that is used, an organization's ability to strengthen its strategic position is dependent on one important factor—its ability to create the strategies that produce the desired results. An effective strategy formulation process is a prerequisite for success. An organization's strategy formulation process, whether it is formal or not, is the mechanism by which its actions, investments and decisions are determined. This ultimately controls the amount of value an organization creates for its customers, stakeholders, stockholders and others. An ineffective strategy formulation process negatively impacts an organization's rate of growth and overall competitive position. An effective strategy formulation process may in itself become a competitive advantage. This book is focused on the process of strategy formulation—a process that, when executed effectively, produces a plan that enables an organization to achieve its stated mission.

Over the years, organizations have learned to recognize the importance of creating competitive advantages and core competencies, competing on time, migrating value, crossing chasms and creating strategic intent. Organizations know what they need to accomplish. But what happens when an organization actually attempts to formulate a strategy, define a plan or make a complex decision? Organizations may know what results they are attempting to achieve, but do they know how to create breakthrough strategies and solutions that will enable them to achieve those results?

Ask yourself, within your organization, what processes are used to formulate strategy? How was the strategy formulation process developed or selected? Is a formal process used? What steps are taken to create a strategy? Do different parts of the organization define the concept of strategy differently? Do they have different strategy formulation processes? Are they effective? Do they consistently produce breakthrough strategies?

Since breakthrough strategies and solutions are not all that common, it is logical to conclude that something is preventing organizations from consistently creating them. What are the inhibiting factors? What obstacles are encountered when formulating an effective strategy or plan? What would happen if the obstacles were identified and overcome? We will soon find out. First, let's examine the barriers that are preventing the consistent creation of breakthrough strategies and solutions.

## NATURAL BARRIERS TO CREATING BREAKTHROUGH STRATEGIES AND SOLUTIONS

Recall the last time that you were involved in formulating a company, product or service strategy. Did you conclude with what you would consider a breakthrough strategy or solution? Did it create tremendous value for your customers and your organization? Was everyone committed to the resulting plan or strategy?

Recall the process from a technical perspective. When going through the strategy formulation process, was the mission clear? Were all the appropriate customers considered? Were all their requirements properly captured and understood? Did everyone agree on the criteria that were to be used to evaluate each proposed strategy or solution? Were the decisions based on fact? How did the organization prevent personalities, politics, personal agendas and gut-feel from negatively impacting the chosen strategy? How did the organization prevent the chosen solution from being negotiated and compromised to the point where its value was diminished? Was everyone committed to the strategy? Was the chosen solution supported throughout its implementation? Was a large percent of the company's collective knowledge and wisdom infused in the strategy formulation process?

Many obstacles tend to stand in the way of creating breakthrough strategies and solutions, but what if those obstacles could be overcome? What if an organization could master its ability to consistently make the optimal choices and create the optimal strategies? How much more value would it be able to create for its customers and stockholders? If an organization could consistently create the optimal strategies, it would then be able to optimize its investment decisions, deliver the optimal products and services and achieve the optimal competitive position. This, in turn, would accelerate the organization's rate of growth and profitability.

What prevents an organization from consistently formulating the strategies and solutions that create the most value? The ability to formulate breakthrough strategies and solutions has been inhibited by what can be described as three natural barriers. They are natural barriers in that they result from limitations that are inherent to most individuals and organizations. Since they are natural barriers, they often go unchallenged and are typically accepted as insurmountable obstacles to success. These barriers were identified through qualitative and quantitative research that I conducted in companies around the world between 1985 and 1991. The barriers are defined as follows.

## Structure

First, organizations often lack a structure that will enable them to filter, organize, prioritize and manage all the information that enters into the strategy formulation process. This is a complex process. It involves the interaction of people and information. When formulating strategies and solutions, organizations must consider thousands of pieces of information from multiple sources. Customer requirements, regulatory issues, competitive data, manufacturing inputs, stockholder demands, resource constraints, stakeholder requirements, industry trends and other information must be considered. Information from customers, executives, managers, engineers, sales representatives, consultants and others must be evaluated. Organizations must be able to determine which information takes precedence and how one piece of information impacts another. In addition, they must be able to determine the order in which to process the information.

What happens when information cannot be structured in a meaningful way? How does that impact the dynamics of a strategy formulation session? Have you ever tried to obtain consensus on a strategy or solution when everybody is using different information as a basis for decision making? Without a structure to organize information, individuals involved in the strategy formulation process lack a solid basis for agreement or disagreement. As a result, they often fail to reach consensus or a conclusion and limit the possibility of creating a breakthrough strategy or solution. Without a solid structure for gathering and processing information, strategy formulation and planning sessions often become a forum for argument, debate, negotiation and compromise. Solutions are often negotiated and compromised to the point where they lack both value and commitment.

Who in your company filters, organizes, prioritizes and manages the information that is included in the strategy formulation process? How is the information filtered and organized? What methods are used to prioritize the importance of the information? Does a structure exist? A lack of structure is often accepted as a barrier that cannot be overcome. Top strategists rarely address this as a barrier to success, it is simply accepted as one of the complexities of strategy formulation.

What would happen to the quality of your strategies, plans and decisions if your organization could effectively structure all the information that enters the strategy formulation process? Would this be the first step toward an Intellectual Revolution?

### Information

Second, individuals often do not have the information they need, or know what information they need, to create breakthrough strategies and solutions. Sure, individuals have access to large amounts of information, much more than ever before. But they may not know which pieces of information are important, which pieces should be eliminated, which pieces are missing or how to obtain the information they need. For example, organizations often talk about providing strategies and solutions that satisfy their customers' desired outcomes, but how often do they know all their customers' desired outcomes? How often do they know which desired outcomes are most important? As a result of missing or inaccurate information, individuals often base their strategies, plans and decisions on an incomplete or inadequate set of facts. Ask yourself, when contemplating a business or investment strategy, defining a product or service plan or making a trade-off decision, how often do you have access to 100% of the facts? How many of your decisions are based on 100% of the facts? How often do you have access to 100% of your customers' prioritized desired outcomes, internal constraints and competitive positioning data?

The inability to capture all the information required to effectively formulate strategies and solutions is often accepted as a barrier that simply cannot be overcome. In *The Rise and Fall of Strategic Planning* (1994), Henry Mintzberg points out that ''much of what is considered as 'hard' data is often anything but.'' He goes on to say, ''there is a soft underbelly of hard data'' typified by the fallacy of ''measuring what is measurable.'' Many organizations simply use the information they have at hand to assist in strategy creation without questioning its value or relevance. This clearly contributes to the inefficiency of most strategy formulation processes and the ineffectiveness of the strategies they produce.

What would happen to the quality of your strategies, plans and decisions if they were based on 100% of the facts? What if you had access to all the prioritized desired outcomes of your internal and external customers, all the constrainst imposed on the solution and knew what competitive position you wanted to achieve? Would an Intellectual Revolution be closer at hand?

### Processing Power

Third, individuals must be able to simultaneously process literally hundreds of pieces of information when attempting to formulate strategies, define plans and make complex decisions. Unfortunately, the human mind is limited in its ability to know, remember, process and apply all the pertinent facts that are required when conducting these activities.

Psychological research suggests that individuals consider only a small number of variables when contemplating strategies, plans and decisions. Psychologists generally agree that individuals rarely consider more than five to nine pieces of information at a time. Howard Gardner, in *Frames of Mind: The Theory of Multiple Intelligences* (1983), for example, says that individuals often rely on ''a small set of human intellectual potentials, perhaps as few as seven in number.''

It follows that when formulating a strategy it would be nearly impossible for an individual to accurately define the optimal solution for any complex situation given that there are often hundreds of possible solutions from which to choose and over 100 different evaluation criteria that must be considered. As a result, individuals often fail to effectively process all the information that must be considered when attempting to formulate a breakthrough strategy. An analogy of this situation is as follows:

When solving a simultaneous algebraic equation, you may be asked, for example, to determine the values of $x$ and $y$ given that:

$2x + y = 3$, and $y = x + 1$

In this situation you are asked to solve this equation given two variables ($x$ and $y$) and the numerical constants. Most people cannot solve this relatively simple equation in their head. Now consider that in most strategic situations there may be over 100 solutions (variables) and between 50 and 300 evaluation criteria (constants) that must be considered to effectively formulate a strategy. Without the assistance of additional processing power, the probability of an organization choosing the strategy that will deliver the optimal results is near zero.

Despite this fact, businesses and individuals often rely on their internal decision-making capabilities to determine which strategy or solution will work best in a given situation. Some strategists encourage this behavior. As a result, strategies, plans and decisions are rarely optimized. This is an obvious barrier to the formulation of breakthrough strategies and solutions.

In his book titled *The Mind of the Strategist* (1982), Kenichi Ohmae states, ''Phenomena and events in the real world do not always fit a linear model. Hence, the most reliable means of dissecting a situation into its constituent parts and reassembling them in the desired pattern is not a step-by-step methodology such as systems analysis. Rather, it is that ultimate non-linear thinking tool, the human brain.'' This sounds great, but in the complex world of strategy formulation there are few people that can meet this mental challenge. It is true that strategy formulation requires non-linear thinking, but it is also true that the human mind requires assistance in processing all the information that is required to think in a non-linear fashion.

Ask yourself, how often do you rely on your internal decision-making capabilities to determine which strategy or solution will work best in a given situation? How many pieces of information can you process at one time? Do the processes you use alleviate any confusion that may be caused by attempting to simultaneously process hundreds of pieces of information? How many potential solutions are considered? How many potential solutions exist? At what point do you stop searching for a ''better'' solution? Does new information, when it becomes available, make you less confident in your chosen action?

The fact is that individuals seldom choose the optimal solution when contemplating strategies, plans and complex decisions. The structure, information and processing power that is required to choose the optimal solution is rarely available. Think back to the results of your last strategy formulation experience. How confident were you that the chosen solution was the optimal solution? Was the optimal solution ever even considered? Was the chosen solution reconsidered or changed prior to implementation?

The need to simultaneously process more than five to nine pieces of information at a time makes it difficult for any one person, or group of people, to create the optimal solution without additional processing capability. Obtaining the information that is required to uncover the optimal solution is often impractical as the required skills and resources are rarely available. Structuring all the information that is presented is difficult and time consuming. As a result, these inherent limitations are often simply accepted as insurmountable obstacles or natural barriers to greater success and inhibit the formulation of breakthrough strategies and solutions.

> Strategies and plans are often formulated without an information structure, or a basis for agreement or disagreement. Their formulation is often attempted without all the facts and without the processing power that is needed to simultaneously process all the required information.

Assume for a moment that the process of strategy formulation is comprised of only the three steps that have been mentioned: organizing the information in a structure, capturing the required information, and processing the information in an effective manner. If an organization is 80% efficient at structuring the information that is entered into the strategy formulation process, 80% efficient at obtaining the required information and 80% efficient at processing the information, then its strategy formulation process is about ($.8 \times .8 \times .8$) or 51% efficient. If each aspect is 60% efficient, then the overall process efficiency drops to just 22%. If each aspect is 50% efficient, the overall process efficiency drops to 13%. How efficient is your organization at executing each of these aspects of the strategy formulation process? Can it afford to be less than 90% efficient?

These barriers must be eliminated before organizations can dramatically increase the amount of value they create for themselves and others. This book describes how these barriers have been overcome. It describes what organizations must do to obtain the structure, information and processing power they require to consistently formulate breakthrough strategies and solutions.

## OVERCOMING THE NATURAL BARRIERS TO SUCCESS

Does your organization successfully anticipate future opportunities? Does it know which technologies to pursue, which core competencies to build, what product or service concepts to back, which alliances to form and what kind of people to hire? Does it know which investments, activities and actions will create and deliver the most value now and in the future? How does it choose what investments, activities and actions to pursue?

Organizations must constantly address a variety of complex strategic issues. Given the disparity between our inherent limitations and the desire to create strategies and solutions that deliver the greatest value, organizations have made many attempts to find simple ways to deal with complex realities. Despite the number of strategy formulation methods that exist, most have failed to eliminate the natural barriers to success.

In 1991, several emerging technologies from unrelated disciplines were integrated into a strategy formulation process by the principals of my consulting firm, The Total Quality Group. This process was the result of years of effort, research and study and was designed to specifically attack the three barriers that prevent the consistent creation of breakthrough strategies and solutions. Ideas, concepts and theories from disciplines such as statistics, communications, psychology, quality, business, mathematics and computer science were used to create this advanced strategy formulation process. It was apparent to us that strategy formulation was not simply a business ritual but a combination of many intricate activities that required intimate knowledge of many disciplines. Our knowledge was specifically focused on creating a strategy formulation process that would provide the world with:

1. A structure that enables organizations to successfully organize, filter, prioritize and manage the information that enters the strategy formulation process.
2. A process that enables organizations to capture, filter and sort requirements and other information that is required to create breakthrough strategies and solutions.
3. The tools that deliver the processing power that is required to simultaneously process all the information needed to uncover the optimal strategy or solution.

In short, the process resulting from our efforts provided the structure, information and processing power that is required to formulate breakthrough strategies and solutions. We have quantified that the strategies and solutions resulting from this process are "breakthrough" in the sense that they often deliver up to 10 times more value than strategies and solutions that are created through the use of traditional methods. This magnitude of improvement is accelerating the rate at which organizations create and deliver value to their internal and external customers. This explains why many organizations are using this process to replace or enhance their existing strategy formulation processes.

Since 1991, these ideas and theories have evolved into an advanced strategy formulation process that we now call The Customer-Driven Mission Achievement Process, or CD-MAP. This process is being used by *Fortune* 100 companies and other organizations around the world to create a broad array of company, product and operational strategies. For example, organizations are using this process to:

1. Devise company-wide and division-wide operating strategies.
2. Formulate short-term and long-term product and service strategies.
3. Create strategies that improve their value-added processes.
4. Formulate strategies that reduce time to market.
5. Optimize investment and trade-off decisions.
6. Identify and select target markets.
7. Optimize product and service concepts.
8. Improve many other operational, support and management processes.

This process has been used across many industries and for many purposes and consistently produces breakthrough results. For example, when using this process to improve the development and testing of composite materials, a *Fortune* 100 company discovered how to reduce the cost of development by over 80% while reducing development time by nearly 75%. A cardiac pacing system company used this process to create a product concept that offered the same function as a highly valued competitive product, but at 40% of the cost. A manufacturer of industrial packaging used this process to create a company strategy that increased their market share by 10% in an environment in which the top 10 players had less than 50% market share. A medical device manufacturer used this process to create a line of angioplasty balloons that took them from less than 1% market share to a market leadership position in just two years.

Organizations are effectively using this process to choose which markets, products, technologies, investments and activities to pursue to strengthen their strategic position. They are identifying value-producing activities that complement, reinforce and optimize one another. They are making discoveries that often form the basis for a distinctive and sustainable competitive advantage.

The following study gives you an idea of the degree to which this process has overcome the natural barriers to success. Approximately 60 individuals from organizations around the world, who have applied this process, were asked to compare their traditional strategy formulation process to the CD-MAP process. They were asked to respond, quantitatively, to a series of questions that offer insight into the effectiveness of the strategy formulation processes that they use. They were asked to compare the strategy formulation methods they typically use to the CD-MAP process for each of the stated criteria. The results of the survey are documented in Table 1.1. As you read through the questions, you

**Table 1.1**
**An Evaluation of the CD-MAP Process**

| Question: When formulating strategies, developing plans or making complex decisions... | Your Approach | Traditional Methods | CD-MAP |
|---|---|---|---|
| What percent of the decisions are based on 100% of the facts? | | Less than 10% | Over 90% |
| What percent of the customers' desired outcomes or "requirements" are captured and understood? | | Less than 20% | Over 90% |
| What percent of the chosen strategies and solutions are negatively impacted by politics, intuition or gut-feel? | | Over 90% | Less than 10% |
| What percent of those formulating the strategy or plan agree on the criteria used to evaluate each proposed strategy or solution? | | 20% - 30% | Over 90% |
| What percent of the proposed strategies or solutions are negotiated and compromised to the point where value or commitment is diminished? | | Over 90% | Less than 10% |
| What percent of those formulating the strategy or plan are committed to the chosen solution? | | 50% - 60% | Over 90% |
| What percent of the chosen solutions are re-thought or changed prior to implementation? | | 70% - 80% | 10% - 20% |
| What percent of the organization's collective knowledge and wisdom is infused in the process? | | Less than 10% | 80% - 90% |
| What percent of the chosen solutions are believed to be the optimal solution? | | 20% - 30% | Over 90% |

can evaluate the strategy formulation process used within your organization in the space provided.

Dramatic improvements have been made to the process of strategy formulation along each of these dimensions. Individuals using this process recognize that it dramatically reduces the percent of decisions that are negatively affected by politics, intuition and gut-feel. They also recognize that it reduces the percent of strategies that are negotiated and compromised to the point that they are void of value. At the same time, the users of this process recognize that it dramatically increases the percent of decisions that are based on 100% of the facts as it enables organizations to capture and understand what their customers value and define evaluation criteria that all can agree on. In addition, they recognize that it increases the number of individuals whose knowledge and wisdom are used to formulate the strategy. As a result, more people within the organization believe they have uncovered the optimal solution, and they are committed to the result.

This process is focused on ensuring organizations make the choices, formulate the strategies and define the plans that create the most value for their customers and investors. It empowers individuals—gives them the power—to effectively contemplate strategies, plans and decisions. It enables organizations to win today's battle for intellectual leadership so they will be likely to win tomorrow's battle for market leadership. It is a driving force behind the Intellectual Revolution.

## TERMINOLOGY

It is important to have a clear understanding of the terminology that is used to describe the concepts introduced in this book. Several concepts are described using words that may have other meanings. To reduce the time it will take to internalize the concepts that are put forth, several potentially ''vague'' words are defined below. The terms will only be used in the context in which they are defined.

*Breakthrough Solution*: A solution or strategy that satisfies over 50% of the customers' desired outcomes better than an existing strategy or solution. Breakthrough solutions often deliver up to 10 times more value than commonly implemented solutions and enable an organization to leapfrog their competition. Breakthrough solutions also often provide an organization with a unique and valued competitive position. A competitive advantage will often arise as a result of a breakthrough solution.

*Concept*: An idea, strategy or potential solution in its conceptual or theoretical stage.

*Customer*: An individual or group of individuals involved in, or affected by, the strategy, plan or decision that is being contemplated. As an example, if an organization wants to improve the process of surgery, the customers may include surgeons, support staff, hospital administrators, the manufacturer of the product and the individuals within the organization who are providing the solution.

*Desired Outcome*: A desired outcome is a statement, made by an individual involved in or affected by a strategy, plan or decision, that describes an important benefit they would like to receive from the strategy, plan or decision that is being contemplated. Desired outcomes are unique in that they are free from solutions, specifications and technologies, free from vague words such as ''easy'' or ''reliable'' and are statements that are stable over time.

*Mission*: A specific task or project with which an individual or organization is charged. A mission may include improving a surgeon's ability to conduct the process of surgery, improving an organization's ability to manufacture a product or improving an organization's ability to formulate a strategy. A mission may be large or small in scope.

*Optimal Solution*: The one solution or strategy that will satisfy the largest number of important desired outcomes given the internal and external constraints imposed on the solution and the competitive position that is desired. The optimal solution will also be the solution that delivers the most value for the least cost, risk and effort. The optimal solution is typically a breakthrough solution.

*Predictive Metric*: A parameter that can be measured today to ensure its corresponding desired outcome will be achieved in the future. A predictive metric is measured and controlled in the design of the solution and predicts the solution will satisfy one or more desired outcomes. A predictive metric may also be referred to as a predictive success factor (PSF).

*Process*: A series of activities, actions or events that produce a desired result. Examples of processes include conducting surgery, manufacturing a product, making an acqui- sition, developing a product and formulating a strategy.

*Solution*: A specific set of features that form the elements of a plan or strategy, and define how the desired outcomes will be achieved. A proposed solution is often re- ferred to as a plan or a strategy.

*Strategy*: A strategy is a plan. It is an executable plan of action that describes how an individual or organization will achieve a stated mission.

*Strategy Formulation*: The process of creating a strategy.

*Value*: The degree to which important desired outcomes can be satisfied while minimizing cost, risk and effort.

The language used throughout this book is precise. It may be helpful to ref- erence the definitions stated above, as required. A comprehensive list of com- monly used words and their meanings can be found in the Glossary.

## SUMMARY

In this chapter we have established the fact that a process for strategy for- mulation does exist and that it is capable of consistently delivering breakthrough results. This process was the result of years of effort and required the integration of knowledge from disciplines such as statistics, communications, psychology, quality, business, mathematics and computer science.

This strategy formulation process is focused on overcoming the barriers that typically stand in the way of formulating breakthrough strategies and solutions. The barriers are defined as structure, information and processing power. Struc- ture relates to the way information entering the strategy formulation process is organized, filtered and structured for use. Information relates to the types of data that are required for the successful execution of the process. Processing power relates to the power that is required to simultaneously analyze, calculate and process the information that has been gathered to deliver a breakthrough result.

Strategy formulation processes used by most organizations fail to provide the structure, information and processing power that is required to formulate break- through strategies and solutions. These barriers are often simply accepted as insurmountable obstacles to success. Organizations that have used our advanced strategy formulation process have been able to successfully overcome these ob- stacles. They have used this process to successfully formulate overall company strategies, product and service strategies and strategies that drive the improve- ment of operating, support and management processes. When applying this proc- ess, organizations have been able to consistently formulate strategies and solutions that deliver up to 10 times more value than those formulated using their existing strategy formulation methods.

This process embodies the science of strategy formulation. It has transformed the process of strategy formulation from an art to a science. Throughout this book, you are introduced to the concepts, theories and ideas that have made this transformation possible. You will learn why this process works and how to apply it. You will learn how it can be applied successfully in any organization, and you will learn how you and your organization can use this process to participate in the Intellectual Revolution.

# Chapter 2

# Transforming the Thinking Process

In his book titled *The Age of Unreason* (1989) Charles Handy writes, ''We are all prisoners of our past. It is hard to think of things except in the way we have always thought of them. But that solves no problems and seldom changes anything.''

Creating a strategy formulation process that integrates logic, analysis, creativity and innovation required new thoughts and new ways of thinking about strategy formulation. It required thinking differently about the very concept of strategy. As we studied the process of strategy formulation, we discovered that organizations around the world had adopted an unspoken high-level thinking strategy that guided their approach to strategy formulation. By high-level thinking strategy we mean the mental or subconscious logic that individuals apply when formulating a strategy. We discovered that individuals inherently follow this set logic, and it drives a natural sequence of activities that most organizations follow when attempting to formulate a strategy. This logic is based on our natural tendencies and instincts, and it is often executed without question. We found that this logic, although ineffective, is often simply accepted as a fundamental of strategy formulation. It has been accepted, without question, for hundreds of years, and until now, this logic has remained unchallenged.

We will introduce this logic and explain how for years it has undermined the process of strategy formulation and inhibited the creation of breakthrough strategies. We will then introduce a different, high-level thinking strategy that embodies the logic that organizations can use to formulate breakthrough strategies. This alternative logic resulted from the application of modeling and pattern detection techniques that were focused on improving the strategy formulation process. This new logic lays the foundation upon which the future of strategy formulation has been built.

## SOLUTION-BASED LOGIC

What actions do you and your organization take when formulating a strategy? How does the process begin? When offered the challenge of formulating a strategy, what is your first inclination? Do you instinctively start thinking about the process that you are going to follow, who is going to be involved or do you begin to brainstorm potential solutions? When the team responsible for formulating a strategy is gathered together and given their mission, what actions do they take? What becomes the focus? The process? Structure? Solutions? Let's say, for example, you were asked to improve your company's existing product line. What is your first thought? Do you think about several potential new product concepts? What is the first step you will take? Will you talk to customers to see what they want? What if you were asked to improve your company's order entry process? What is the first step you would take?

If you are like most individuals, the immediate focus when involved in formulating a strategy or plan of any kind is the brainstorming of potential solutions. We live in a solution-based world. Most people are solution oriented. From our earliest age, we are taught to find solutions to problems. We are taught to focus on solutions. We have created methods for brainstorming solutions. We are often rewarded for devising good solutions. When our business associates, peers or superiors present us with a problem we often take pride in offering solutions. We are motivated in many ways to focus on solutions.

This solution orientation has set the framework for the high-level thinking strategy that is typically used by organizations when they formulate strategies, define plans and make complex decisions. When attempting to find the best strategy or solution, organizations inherently follow a set logic or a natural sequence of activities. These activities are often executed subsconsciously and shape the organization's approach to strategy formulation.

The critical steps defining this logic are summarized as follows. Note the order of the steps.

1. First, individuals use various methods to think of alternative ideas and solutions. The methods may include brainstorming, research, talking to customers or other techniques.

2. Second, the individuals on the strategy formulation team discuss and evaluate each of the proposed solutions to determine which solution is best. The methods used to accomplish this task may include the review of supporting data and may involve debate. Intuition and gut-feel may affect the evaluation. Scientific methods such as concept testing, conjoint analysis, quantitative research or other methods may also be used in the evaluation process.

3. Third, the strategy formulation team considers the ideas that are presented and begins a process of debate, negotiation and compromise until the ''best'' solution is devised.

This logic dictates that individuals in the organization devise alternative solutions, evaluate each solution and then reach consensus on which solution is

**Figure 2.1**
**Solution-Based Logic**

best. Ask yourself, is this the logic that is followed by individuals in your organization when they are asked to formulate a company strategy, a product or service strategy or a strategy that is needed to improve an operating, support or management process?

The basic premise behind this logic is to first focus on the creation of the solution and to then focus on how well the solution meets the criteria that are being used to evaluate the solution. The key characteristic of this approach is that it starts with the creation of the solution.

In a typical strategy formulation scenario, for example, those responsible for creating a company strategy may be brought together for a series of strategy formulation sessions. Prior to the first session, the participants organize their ideas and solutions and prepare presentations that are intended to communicate their ideas to others and convince them of their value. As the sessions proceed, the participants present their ideas and solutions to the group. The group debates the value of each solution and the presenters defend and support their positions. Team members evaluate the proposed solutions using a variety of methods and criteria. The solutions are debated, modified and negotiated until consensus and agreement are reached.

The underlying logic here again is to devise alternative solutions, evaluate each solution and then reach consensus on which solution is best. This pattern reflects the traditional thinking strategy that is used by many organizations to formulate strategies, define plans and make complex decisions. We call this logic Solution-Based Logic in that it is focused on generating, evaluating and selecting solutions.

The elements of Solution-Based Logic are shown in Figure 2.1.

Solution-Based Logic defines the sequence of activities that are commonly performed by organizations when they execute their strategy formulation processes. The use of this logic is instinctive, it is often executed subconsciously.

This logic, or pattern, has been observed in individuals, organizations and cultures around the world. The use of this thinking strategy often goes unchallenged.

Does your organization inherently apply Solution-Based Logic when formulating its company, product, service and operating strategies? Is there an inherent focus on solutions? What problems, if any, does the application of this logic cause your organization?

We will show that the application of this logic, although pervasive, is destructive and prevents organizations from formulating breakthrough strategies and solutions. Challenging the use of Solution-Based Logic is a critical step in evolving the process of strategy formulation.

## APPLYING SOLUTION-BASED LOGIC

The application of Solution-Based Logic is found in most organizations today. People inherently talk about and focus on solutions. This includes executives, managers, employees, investors, customers, stakeholders and others. This fixation on solutions is what has caused most organizations and individuals to completely overlook the fact that a better way to formulate strategies may exist.

The use of Solution-Based Logic dictates the dynamics that most organizations experience when formulating strategies today. To gain some insight into these dynamics, recall the last time you were involved in an activity in which a strategy, plan or decision was being contemplated. How did the activity start? Did individuals propose solutions that they perceived to be best? Were they then required to convince others of the value of their proposed solution? Did they defend their proposed solutions with a complete set of facts? Were emotions involved? Did they want their solutions to win? Was power, position, recognition or peer acceptance at stake? How were the proposed strategies and solutions evaluated? Was the optimal solution created? Was the optimal solution chosen? What problems arose?

We will demonstrate that the use of Solution-Based Logic inhibits many organizations from formulating breakthrough strategies and solutions. Its use is responsible for the gross inefficiencies that exist in most strategy formulation processes today. Using the algebraic equation analogy, the use of Solution-Based Logic is like guessing the solution to a complex algebraic problem and then testing to see if you guessed the right solution. If you have ever attempted to use this approach when solving a complex algebraic equation, you've undoubtedly recognized that guessing is not an efficient approach to problem solving, and there is a good chance that you will never guess the optimal solution.

Most people underestimate the number of possible solutions that are technically possible when formulating a strategy in a given situation. Let's consider the following example. When formulating a company strategy you must make decisions regarding which market to target, which segment to target, how to position the product or service, which products and services to offer, how the offering should be priced, how to manufacture the product, how to distribute the offering, what the advertising message should be and how the offering should be promoted. Suppose, for the sake of illustration, that the company has only seven alternatives for each of the nine decisions. In reality, of course, there may be fewer than seven alternatives, but there may be more. If there are only seven alternatives for each of the nine decisions, how many different strategies are possible? The answer is not 7 times 9 or 63 different strategies. The answer is seven to the ninth power or 40,353,607 potential strategies. Among all these possible strategies, of course, some would be very successful and some would be disastrous, while most would fall somewhere in between. But what are the chances of an organization selecting the optimal solution from over 40 million possible alternatives? Statistically speaking, they approach zero, especially when you consider the fact that most organizations have a tendency to consider relatively few alternatives.

In *Human Performance Engineering* (1989), Robert Bailey summarizes his research on ineffective decision making and strategy formulation by stating that individuals involved in the strategy formulation process tend to:

1. Overaccumulate information.
2. Use a fraction of the available information.
3. Hesitate to revise their first options.
4. Consider too few alternatives.

This characterization of the strategy formulation process makes it obvious why most organizations fail to efficiently execute their strategic planning processes and formulate breakthrough strategies. Could these inefficiencies be linked to the use of Solution-Based Logic? As you will see, the answer is clearly yes.

Solution-Based Logic has at least three major drawbacks. These drawbacks affect the way a strategy is formulated and diminish the effectiveness of the resulting strategy. They negatively affect the dynamics between people within the organization. They are the cause of unnecessary friction and inhibit the creation of value. The three major drawbacks are defined as follows.

The first major drawback is that the use of this underlying logic and a fixation on solutions places people in a defensive position and prevents them from focusing on the creation of value. By definition, when using Solution-Based Logic, people first come up with solutions. Whether people are asked to propose an idea or solution, or if they propose one on their own, they know they will have to present their idea to others and convince them of its value. At this point, the act of simply proposing an idea or solution triggers an interesting but unfortunate set of dynamics. When proposing an idea or solution, individuals are put into a position where they must defend their proposed solution. As a result, not only will their ideas be judged, but they will be judged personally as well. Their proposed solution, and their ability to convince others of its value, now becomes a matter of personal concern. Many people believe that if their peers accept their proposed solution, it will signify they are competent, creative and deserving of respect. If it is not accepted, they may feel they have failed. Their ability to present and defend their proposed solutions suddenly becomes tied to protecting their own perception of self-worth.

As a result, people often do what they have to to defend their ideas. Individuals actively look for information that supports their proposed solutions. They may conceal information that refutes their position. They may use information out of context to support an idea.

People may even create or fabricate information that supports an idea or proposed solution. When people become defensive, they may not be focused on the prime objective of creating customer and stakeholder value. They are often more concerned with their careers and personal well-being. Being placed in a defensive position does not always bring out the best human qualities.

In some organizations, individuals intentionally pit people against other people or functions against other functions to see who can defend their position the best. The strategy that is defended the best often becomes accepted for implementation. This approach is unlikely to produce a breakthrough strategy, but it is likely to create bad feelings and deteriorate working relationships.

Why do organizations accept this somewhat barbaric approach to strategy formulation? What are their alternatives? Would organizations be better off if individuals worked toward the common goal of creating value without being subject to pressures that motivate them to behave in a defensive manner? A change in logic is required to make this possible.

A second major drawback of Solution-Based Logic is that it does not set out to create a basis for agreement. In fact, its use provokes unnecessary debate and causes disagreement when solutions are evaluated. The debate and disagreement occur because people are focused on solutions and rarely take the time to define and agree on the criteria that is to be used to evaluate the proposed solutions. As a result, they lack a basis for agreement. If an organization cannot agree on the criteria that should be used to evaluate the potential of a solution, then they will certainly not be able to agree on which solution is best. With a fixation on solutions and a motivation to quickly reach a conclusion, organizations rarely take the time to define and agree on the criteria that should be used to evaluate proposed solutions.

Again, think back to the last time you were involved in an activity in which a strategy, plan or decision was being contemplated. Did each person have their own criteria by which to evaluate proposed solutions? Did that criteria favor their proposed solutions? Did the organization take the time to gain agreement on which criteria should be used to evaluate the proposed solutions? Did each person in the room have a different understanding of what your customers valued, what constraints the company faced and what competitive position was desired? Did everyone agree on the criteria that were being used to determine which proposed solution was best? Were decisions based on facts? Was agreement reached on the chosen solution? Was consensus achieved? Was everyone committed to the solution?

The use of Solution-Based Logic does not provide an organization a basis for agreement. The criteria to be used to evaluate the potential of each solution are seldom agreed on. Instead, people have a tendency to use the criteria that support their position so the solution they are defending will win. They often define the criteria with this purpose in mind. Individuals present the benefits that their strategy will deliver and emphasize the importance of those benefits. They rarely identify other important requirements that the strategy will not satisfy. The criteria, or facts, that individuals use to support their proposed solutions may be incomplete, inaccurate or they may not be agreed on. These inefficiencies cause unnecessary debate and are not conducive to the formulation of breakthrough strategies and solutions.

When using Solution-Based Logic, how likely is it that consensus will be reached? More important, how likely is it that a breakthrough solution will be discovered? How can an organization expect to formulate a breakthrough strategy if it does not have or agree on the facts or criteria that should be used to evaluate the potential of alternative solutions? How will the organization ever know what solution is best?

Making decisions without a complete set of facts often results in failure. In his book titled *New Product Development* (1992), George Gruenwald states that "between one third and two thirds of all new products that are introduced result in failure." This does not include the hundreds of products that are developed but never introduced. Can this be any indication as to what percent of all strategies, plans and decisions result in failure? What is your organization's success rate? What, if any, was the cause of failure in any of your company's recent business, product, service or operational strategies? According to many sources, poor planning is cited as the single biggest reason for the failure of company, product, service and operational strategies. Poor planning often results from an organization's inability to gather, structure and process factual information. The use of Solution-Based Logic inhibits the effective execution of the planning process and can be cited as a cause of poor planning.

So why do organizations attempt to formulate strategies without having a basis for agreement? What are the alternatives? Would organizations be better off if individuals could work toward the common goal of creating value in an environment where everyone agreed on the criteria that is being used to evaluate the solutions that are proposed? Again, a change in logic is required to make this possible.

A third major drawback of using Solution-Based Logic is that it does not provide a means to quantify the potential of a proposed solution or enable an organization to determine if a breakthrough solution has been created. As a result, an organization may come across a breakthrough solution and never know it. They may unknowingly reject it in favor of a less attractive solution. This can happen because the individuals involved do not know what criteria define a breakthrough solution. They are focused only on defending the solutions they initially proposed and rarely know what constitutes value in the eyes of the customer or the company. As a result, they never know how much value a proposed solution is capable of delivering.

Recall again the last time you were involved in an activity in which a strategy, plan or decision was being contemplated. Did all those involved believe they had created a breakthrough solution? Did everyone know why one solution was better than another? Did everyone agree on how to make a solution better? At what point did you stop searching for a better solution? Was the optimal solution proposed? Would anyone have known if the optimal solution had been proposed? How did you set out to create the optimal solution?

The use of Solution-Based Logic often precludes the creation of the optimal solution. The criteria that define the optimal solution are often unknown. Therefore it is difficult, if not impossible, to know if the optimal solution has been created. To make matters worse, organizations tend to evaluate only a few alternative solutions out of the thousands or millions of potential solutions that exist. This makes the prospect of formulating a breakthrough solution even more unlikely.

How many alternative solutions did you consider in your last strategy formulation exercise? Five? Eight? A dozen? In any strategic situation, there may be hundreds, thousands or even millions of potential solutions in the universe of possible solutions. You know that the optimal solution does exist. But what is the chance that one of the dozen or so proposed solutions is actually the optimal solution? And if it was, how would you know? The fact is that the random creation and selection of the optimal solution is unlikely. It is as unlikely as guessing the answer to a complex algebraic equation.

The use of Solution-Based Logic is mainly focused on creating, defending and negotiating solutions. The use of Solution-Based Logic puts people in a defensive position, it does not provide a basis for agreement, and it does not provide a means to determine if a breakthrough solution has been created. These are just three of the major drawbacks of using Solution-Based Logic in the process of strategy formulation.

Before we continue, I would like you to contemplate the following. Unfortunately, many strategies are categorized as failures only after they have been introduced or implemented costing the company time, money and profits. But ask yourself the following question. If a strategy or solution can be classified as a failure after it is introduced, what is preventing an organization from knowing it is going to fail in advance of its introduction? According to what criteria did it fail? If those criteria were known, and used to evaluate the potential of the concept to begin with, could its eventual failure have been predicted in advance? Could the failure have been avoided altogether? Contemplate how this may be possible as we continue on with our explanation of Solution-Based Logic.

## TRADITIONAL STRATEGY FORMULATION SCENARIOS

The scenarios stated below highlight some of the activities that transpired during planning sessions that employed traditional strategy formulation methods. The scenarios, which are based on actual experiences in companies that will remain unnamed, demonstrate the application of Solution-Based Logic and its impact on the execution of the strategy formulation process. The drawbacks of using this approach are also described for each scenario.

### Scenario 1: Formulating a Division Strategy

Division management of a *Fortune* 100 company was given its annual task of formulating an operating strategy for the division. To ensure the participants remained focused on this important activity, the president of the division scheduled a three-day meeting at a resort hotel in Aspen, Colorado.

The president chaired the session. The vice-presidents of each major function were asked to attend along with the lab director and a legal advisor. The participants were asked by the president to present their ideas for a division strategy. As the session began, the president gave an overview of recent company performance and informed the team of his goal to increase division sales by 20% and profits by 10% per year for the next five years. The challenge to the 12-member team was to define and agree on a strategy that would enable the achievement of these goals.

Knowing what was expected, several participants were prepared to present their proposed strategies to the group on the first day. Four executives offered their ideas and proposed four alternative strategies. It became evident that the proposed strategies were not only devised to meet the presidents' objectives but were also intended to enhance the careers of those proposing the strategies.

Members of the group asked the presenters several questions regarding their proposals. Some questions were intended to clarify points. Other questions were intended to debunk, discredit and ridicule the strategies that were being proposed. After each presentation was made, the participants debated the merits of the proposed strategy. It was obvious that each participant evaluated the proposed strategies from a different perspective. Few positive comments were made as most of the effort was focused on finding the holes in the proposed strategies. The strategies that were proposed conflicted with each other. Each strategy was challenged. When questioned, the executives used whatever tactics they knew to defend their proposed strategies. They were well armed with financial data and used it to convince others that their proposed strategies would meet the aggressive financial objectives set by the president. They wanted to ensure the elements of their strategies were accepted. Each team member used different criteria to evaluate the potential of the proposed strategies. As a result, the strategies were debated, refined and negotiated in an attempt to obtain consensus. Participants with the most staying power, persuasive presentations and the loudest voice faired best in convincing the others of the merits of their proposed strategy.

For two and a half days, the various functions debated the value of each proposed strategy. Few new alternative strategies were introduced. The participants, however, had difficulty reaching an agreement. With three hours remaining on the third day, the president stepped in and made several key decisions that were required to break the remaining cross-functional deadlocks. Once these decisions were made, the participants, realizing that time was running out, worked together to gain consensus on a strategy. The chosen strategy was shown to meet the organization's financial objectives. It was to be documented over the following days and sent out for final review and signatures.

After the three-day session was complete, several team members spent a day or two skiing together. A couple of participants were overheard talking about proposing changes to the agreed-on strategy when it came around for final review.

### Analyzing Scenario 1

As stated by Gary Hamel and C. K. Prahalad in *Competing for the Future* (1994), "in many companies strategy means turning the crank on the planning process once a year." They go on to say that "typically, the planning process is more about making numbers add up.—This is the revenue and profit growth we need this year, now how are we going to produce it?—Than it is about developing industry foresight."

The example stated above is no exception. It was an attempt to formulate a strategy that would enable the organization to meet its financial objectives. In formulating this strategy, the participants followed the sequence of events dictated by Solution-Based Logic. Their first focus was to propose several strategies or solutions. The strategies were then discussed and evaluated using criteria that were incomplete and not agreed on. The strategies were then negotiated and compromised to reach a conclusion.

The participants did not agree among themselves on the criteria that define a breakthrough strategy. In fact, they never attempted to agree on a set of evaluation criteria. They spent most of their time defending their proposed strategies with the information they had prepared. The debate did not address which customers should be targeted, which customer requirements were most important or which competitive position they desired. They had access to financial information and used it to produce a financial-driven strategy. They did not have access to the information they needed to create a customer-driven strategy. As a result, the strategy they created was less than optimal at creating customer value. The team did not have all the facts that they required, nor did they establish a basis for agreement.

As time ran out, the proposed strategies were negotiated and compromised so that agreement could be reached. In reality, the strategies were negotiated and compromised to the point where they were void of true commitment. Each executive was forced to give up something they believed to be important. Politics, gut-feel and emotion drove the final result. Facts did not play a major role in supporting the chosen strategy. It is important to ask what percent of the decisions made in this process were based on 100% of the facts. In a subsequent conversation, several members confessed that maybe 10% to 20% of the decisions were based on 100% of the facts. Others suggested that it was less than that.

As stated by Bradley Gale in his book *Managing Customer Value* (1994),

> Management by fact is the path to competitive advantage. Yet, many companies cannot really manage by fact. Executives from different parts of the business speak different languages. The result: the team fails to achieve fact-based consensus, and the "boss" ultimately makes decisions based on his or her own subjective criteria.

The use of Solution-Based Logic often drives an organization down an unproductive path. The scenario stated above could be varied in numerous ways and still have many of the same limitations. Scenarios like the one stated above portray a real picture of how strategic planning activities are conducted in many organizations today. Organizations typically lack the structure, information and processing power that is required to formulate breakthrough strategies and solutions, and they inherently apply the use of Solution-Based Logic.

### Scenario 2: Formulating a Product Strategy

A product planning team in a *Fortune* 100 company was given the responsibility of defining a product strategy for its company's main line of products. The project manager chaired a series of product planning sessions that took place over a one-month period. The new products were required for introduction within 12 months.

The participants included planners, engineers, managers, sales people and, occasionally, company executives. Prior to the sessions, many of the participants talked to customers to obtain their requirements. These requirements, which included lists of solutions, features and specifications, were used by the participants as the basis for creating alternative product concepts.

A marketing executive came to the first session to propose a product concept that resulted from a conversation that took place with a potential customer on an airplane two weeks earlier. The potential customer told the executive that if his company's product had a specific feature set, it would be much more appropriate for use within his organization. The executive, acting with good intentions and focused on customer satisfaction, promised the potential customer that it would be resolved.

As the first planning session continued, the planners, engineers and others proposed the product concepts they believed would best satisfy the customers' requirements. Their concepts closely reflected the solutions that were requested by the customers to whom they had talked. It was found that the requirements captured by one participant often conflicted with requirements captured by other participants. Some customers wanted one solution, and others wanted alternative solutions. A large part of the planning activity involved the debate and discussion of these conflicts. They did not establish a basis for agreement but rather focused on defending the concepts they proposed.

As the second session began, the debate continued. The presenters were armed with new information and used it in an attempt to defend and gain support for their initially proposed solutions. The participants with the most staying power, political clout, persuasive presentations and the loudest voices faired best in convincing the others of the merits of their proposed product concepts.

After much debate and using subjective evaluation criteria, the group reduced the number of concepts under consideration to just three. Not everyone agreed that the best three concepts were selected. Unfortunately, for mostly political reasons the executive's proposed concept was accepted by the participants as one of the top contenders. At this point, the top three concepts were documented, prototyped and prepared for concept testing with customers in a focus-group environment.

Three weeks later, the three prototyped concepts were presented to the focus group participants, and they were asked to choose which one they believed delivered the most value. After concept testing was completed, the team members met to review the findings. Upon reviewing and debating the results, they chose to develop the concept that received the most favorable review. They then began to design and develop the concept.

In addition to concept testing, the planning team also elected to conduct conjoint analysis, which is a specialized form of market research that enables an organization to determine which combination of attributes are preferred by various segments of the population at various price points. Although it would take up to four months to complete this research, the results would be used to confirm the best concept had been chosen.

### Analyzing Scenario 2

The participants followed the sequence of events dictated by Solution-Based Logic. Their first focus was to propose several product concepts. The concepts were then debated, defended and were eventually negotiated and compromised to narrow the number of concepts under consideration to just three.

The participants used requirements they captured from customers as the basis for many of their proposed concepts. Many of the requirements that were captured simply described solutions and features that the customers requested. Unfortunately, customers are rarely technologists, engineers or strategists, and they seldom invent. Following their advice often leads to the creation of me-too products. In any case, the participants took the customers' words as gospel and fought to defend the solutions that they heard their customers request. Each proposed concept was defended with customer inputs. The debate often degraded to the point where participants tried to discredit a concept based on which customer the inputs came from.

To nobody's surprise, the marketing executive's idea was placed high on the list of valued solutions by the planning team. They felt politically obligated to do so. The solution that the executive supported may have taken care of the potential customer that made the suggestion; but many participants recognized that if it were developed, it would negatively impact other customers, curtail the company's production capabilities and impact the development of other offerings that were already planned. Many participants secretly hoped that this concept would not be selected. They admitted that it was not the first time that this executive reacted to comments made by a potential customer. The solution may have been promised by the executive with good intentions, but it worked its way through the product planning process for the wrong reasons. The team did not have the information it needed to refute the concept proposed by the executive; therefore, the team had little choice but to consider it as one of the top concepts.

The team failed to establish a basis for agreement, and they did not gain consensus on what the customers valued. As a result, they failed to agree on which concepts were best. The project manager ended up making a unilateral decision in selecting the top three concepts, but as he said, "that is why I get the big bucks."

Once the concepts were narrowed down to the top three, they were evaluated using concept testing. In conducting this test, customers were asked to evaluate three concepts out of thousands of possible solutions. They were asked to choose which of the three they perceived to be the best. It is possible that the customers were evaluating three highly valued concepts. It is also possible that they were evaluating concepts that were not valued at all, yet they were forced to choose the one they preferred. This type of testing may or may not result in the selection of a product that will be accepted in the market place. When conducted as stated, concept testing is a high-risk approach to product planning and strategy formulation. To make matters worse, several team members suspected that the concepts selected by the project manager for evaluation were pet projects that were easy to implement. They were not convinced that the decisions made to select the top three concepts were based on a complete and accurate set of facts.

The product planning team also elected to conduct conjoint analysis. As part of conjoint research, participants are asked to trade-off between several attributes that are part of a complete concept. The major drawback of conjoint analysis is that it assumes a solution and the attributes associated with that solution. It does not make provisions to determine if the solution that is assumed is a valued solution. An organization may be sorting out the best attributes for an eight-track tape player, while its competitors are developing a compact disc or DVD player. As another possibility, an organization may be focused on the right product, but may be evaluating unimportant or trivial attributes.

This scenario portrays a real picture of how product-planning efforts are conducted in many organizations today. The use of Solution-Based Logic makes people defensive, fails to establish a basis for agreement and makes it difficult to know if the optimal solution has been created or chosen. Combine this with the fact that most organizations also lack the structure, information and processing power they need to formulate strategies, and it is no wonder why most new product efforts fail. In fact, this characterization of the strategy formulation process puts into perspective why most organizations rarely formulate breakthrough strategies and solutions.

So why do organizations attempt to formulate strategies in an environment where people are defensive, lack a basis for agreement and do not know when they have created a breakthrough solution? What are the alternatives? Would organizations be better off if individuals could work toward the common goal of creating value without facing the complexities associated with the use of Solution-Based Logic? A change in the underlying logic that is commonly used to formulate a strategy is required to make this possible.

## DRIVING THE INTELLECTUAL REVOLUTION WITH OUTCOME-BASED LOGIC

We are only prisoners of our past if we let previous experiences limit our ability to accept new ideas and new ways of thinking. Sometimes, we must simply give ourselves permission to challenge our existing paradigms and recognize that change is exciting and can provide a source of energy, creativity and motivation. As we will see, changing the way we think about the process of strategy formulation offers many new opportunities. This transformation begins with the introduction of Outcome-Based Logic.

Outcome-Based Logic is an alternative high-level thinking strategy that offers a different approach to the process of strategy formulation. This approach challenges the use of Solution-Based Logic altogether. It redefines the sequence of activities that take place when formulating strategies and solutions. It enables an organization to overcome the limitations that are associated with Solution-Based Logic and breaks down the natural barriers that often stand in the way of creating breakthrough strategies and solutions. The discovery of Outcome-Based Logic resulted from the application of modeling and pattern detection techniques that I used to study the process of strategy formulation. We will discuss these techniques in more detail in the next chapter. This new logic was discovered after years of observation, and it lays the foundation upon which the future of strategy formulation has been built.

So, what is Outcome-Based Logic?

Simply stated, Outcome-Based Logic is a high-level thinking strategy that drives an organization to focus on outcomes rather than solutions.

The critical steps defining this logic are summarized as follows. Again, note the order of the steps.

1. First, individuals within an organization uncover, document and prioritize the outcomes they want to achieve. The outcomes are a list of criteria that describe what the organization would ideally like to achieve with the strategy or solution that is being contemplated. This may require them to consider the outcomes of the company and its customers, company constraints and competitive factors.

2. Second, individuals use the list of prioritized criteria to systematically create, brainstorm and develop alternative strategies and solutions. The same criteria are then used to evaluate the potential of each alternative solution.

3. Third, the results of the evaluations are used to optimize the already proposed solutions until the optimal solution is discovered. The result is often a breakthrough solution.

In contrast to Solution-Based Logic, which focuses on generating solutions first, Outcome-Based Logic focuses first on defining and prioritizing the criteria that will be used to create and evaluate any potential solution. It is important to emphasize that the first step does not involve the creation of solutions. The first step involves uncovering and prioritizing the criteria that will be used to create and evaluate the proposed solutions. The criteria that are established describe, in priority order, what outcomes the optimal solution would satisfy and the degree to which they would be satisfied.

Once the criteria are defined, the next step is to use them to assist the organization in systematically creating a number of alternative strategies or solutions. The concept is simple, if you know what outcomes the optimal solution must achieve, then it makes sense to use that information to create a solution that will produce the desired result. When formulating a company strategy, for example, if you know the optimal solution must enable the organization to minimize the time it takes to ship products, then it would make sense to formulate a strategy that would incorporate a mechanism that enables overnight shipment. Otherwise, the solution would not deliver the value that is desired—or achieve the desired outcome. Or when formulating a product strategy, for example, if you know that portable radio users want to minimize the number of unauthorized recipients who can intercept their communications, then it would make sense to devise solutions that prevent communications from being intercepted by any unauthorized individual. The point is that you know how value is defined. Efforts can then be focused on creating that value. So, once the criteria are uncovered, the objective is to define several alternative solutions that satisfy the stated outcomes. The criteria are used to guide the creation of the solutions.

Once several alternative solutions are defined, an organization can evaluate them against the same criteria to determine which proposed strategy or solution is best. The criteria provide a means to conduct an effective evaluation of each

**Figure 2.2**
**Outcome-Based Logic**

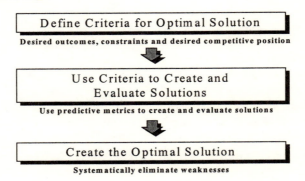

solution. The organization must simply determine the degree to which each proposed solution satisfies the stated criteria to determine which solution is best.

The third step in the application of this high-level thinking strategy is to use the results of the concept evaluations as a means to create the optimal solution. This concept optimization activity involves the proactive elimination of the weaknesses identified in any previously evaluated solution. For example, if a proposed solution is weak in a certain dimension, then other proposed solutions are analyzed to determine if they have the ability to overcome that weakness. The positive elements of each solution are systematically combined to create new solutions that possess even greater levels of value. After several iterations of improvement are completed, the optimal solution is identified.

The concept of Outcome-Based Logic can be summarized in Figure 2.2. It should be noted that this approach is different from Solution-Based Logic in that all the criteria that describe the optimal solution are first defined, and then the search begins to find or create the solution that will best satisfy that criteria.

> This is a transformation in logic in that it requires an individual to first define what outcomes the optimal solution must achieve, and then work to create it. It will be demonstrated that the use of this logic drives a set of dynamics that are conducive to the creation of breakthrough strategies and solutions.

Referring back to the algebraic equation analogy, the use of Outcome-Based Logic is like setting up a complex algebraic problem, plugging in the constants, and then systematically solving the equation. The optimal solution is discovered when the equation is solved.

## APPLYING OUTCOME-BASED LOGIC

The application of Outcome-Based Logic enables an organization to formulate breakthrough strategies and solutions as it eliminates the three major drawbacks associated with the use of Solution-Based Logic. Individuals no longer have to be defensive. It establishes a basis for agreement and it provides a structure by which the creation of the optimal solution can be verified. In addition, it enables individuals to work together to create value. This dramatically changes the dynamics that are involved in the process of strategy formulation. The discovery of this high-level logic was a major step toward the creation of an advanced strategy formulation process. Let's analyze the impact that this logic has had on the dynamics of the strategy formulation process.

First, the use of Outcome-Based Logic enables individuals to be inventive rather than defensive. It ensures that all the required criteria, or outcomes, are uncovered in advance of creating any potential strategy or solution. In other words, all the outcomes the organization wants to achieve with the optimal solution are known by all in advance of creating or evaluating a solution. For example, suppose that it is determined and agreed that a new company strategy must enable the organization to achieve the following seven outcomes. Of course, in the real world there may be up to 300 outcomes; but to illustrate this point, let's assume that the optimal strategy must enable the company to:

1. Minimize the time it takes to bring products to market.
2. Deliver products that are ordered by a customer faster than they could be delivered by any competitor.
3. Minimize the time it takes to respond to inquiries that are made by customers.
4. Improve the company's financial performance within 12 months.
5. Increase the production yield to 98%.
6. Improve overall employee satisfaction.
7. Offer products that provide more value than the products offered by any competitor.

If everyone knows that value can be created for the organization and its customers by formulating and executing a strategy that would enable the organization to satisfy the stated outcomes, then the efforts of individuals can be focused on devising such a strategy. The pressures that drive individuals to act in a defensive manner are eliminated because:

1. Contributors are asked only to document and submit their inventive ideas on how to satisfy the stated criteria.
2. The potential of each proposed strategy or solution is evaluated by individuals who honor the already-agreed-on evaluation criteria.
3. The evaluation phase does not necessarily require the presence of the individual proposing the solution.
4. Contributors are not judged on their ability to present and defend their solutions.
5. Contributors do not have to uncover new information to support their proposed solutions or hide information that may point out a weakness.

When using this thinking strategy, individuals are focused on the criteria that define the creation of value, and as a result they do not waste their time devising or defending solutions that satisfy other less important criteria. They can effectively focus their knowledge on being inventive. The proposal of an idea or solution no longer turns into a personal quest for approval and acceptance. Individuals can simply propose ideas for others to evaluate against criteria they all agree on. They are now free to create and test their own ideas against criteria that define the creation of value.

Second, the use of Outcome-Based Logic creates a basis for agreement. It has been established that when using this thinking strategy, all the criteria are known by all in advance of creating or evaluating a solution. As a result, the individuals proposing a solution and the people evaluating the solutions know what outcomes the solution is supposed to achieve. They know what criteria the solution must satisfy. They must then simply determine the degree to which a proposed solution satisfies the stated criteria. For example, if a proposed solution satisfies the two most important criteria to a great degree, then it will be considered better than a solution that satisfies two less important criteria to a moderate degree. All proposed solutions are evaluated against all criteria—no more, and no less—so their potential value can be determined objectively. The solution that best meets the stated criteria will likely be the chosen solution. Keep in mind that in a real world example, up to 300 criteria may be included in an evaluation. The criteria provide a foundation or basis for agreement. Individuals know if the criteria are satisfied then a highly valued solution has been proposed, and if they are not satisfied, the proposed solution is of less value. As a result, people can then work in an environment that is conducive to creating value and obtaining consensus. Individuals are less likely to argue and butt heads. The use of Outcome-Based Logic transforms a potentially hostile environment into one that is customer-driven and focused on the creation of value. It creates an environment in which individuals are creative rather than combative, as they are focused on a common goal of creating the optimal solution.

Third, the use of Outcome-Based Logic provides a means by which to create and verify the creation of the optimal solution. The application of this logic enables individuals to determine why one strategy or solution is better than another strategy or solution. It enables them to eliminate the weaknesses in a proposed solution. It drives them to keep searching for the optimal solution and makes it possible to know when the optimal solution has been defined. For example, if a proposed strategy or solution satisfies all the criteria to the greatest possible degree, then all those involved in the evaluation will know that the optimal solution has been discovered. It becomes obvious which solutions are best. It becomes less likely that politics, gut-feel and intuition will negatively impact the result, and it becomes easier to eliminate proposed concepts from the running—regardless of who proposed them. It provides the factual data that is required to convince the company president that his idea was not so good after all. When using Outcome-Based Logic, individuals are much more confident in their ability to create and select the optimal solution. They focus their collective knowledge on optimizing rather than compromising the creation of value.

So, organizations do not have to formulate strategies in an environment where people are defensive, lack a basis for agreement and cannot determine if they have created a breakthrough solution. An alternative does exist. But the discovery of Outcome-Based Logic was only the beginning. Several more discoveries were required before this high-level thinking strategy could be applied effectively. We still needed to uncover the structure, define the information and harness the processing power that would be required to make the execution of this thinking strategy possible.

## SUMMARY

As we studied the process of strategy formulation, we discovered that organizations around the world had adopted an unspoken high-level thinking strategy that guided their approach to strategy formulation. By high-level thinking strategy we mean the mental or subconscious logic that individuals apply when formulating a strategy. We discovered that individuals inherently follow this set logic, and it drives a natural sequence of activities that most organizations follow when attempting to formulate a strategy. This logic is based on our natural tendencies and instincts, and is often executed without question. We found that this logic, although ineffective, is often simply accepted as a fundamental of strategy formulation. It has been accepted, without question, for hundreds of years, and until now, this logic has remained unchallenged. We call this high-level thinking strategy Solution-Based Logic.

When applying Solution-Based Logic to the process of strategy formulation, organizations first devise alternative solutions, they then debate the value of each proposed solution and, as a third step, they decide which solution is best. The use of this high-level thinking strategy is mainly focused on creating, defending and negotiating solutions. Its application puts people in a defensive position, it does not provide a basis for agreement and it does not provide a means to determine if a breakthrough solution has been created. These are just three of the major drawbacks of using Solution-Based Logic to execute the process of strategy formulation. Its use rarely results in the formulation of a breakthrough strategy or solution.

To overcome the obstacles that are associated with the use of Solution-Based Logic, we applied modeling and pattern detection techniques that led to the discovery of an alternative high-level thinking strategy. We call this new thinking strategy Outcome-Based Logic. The application of Outcome-Based Logic dictates a sequence of actions that enable an organization to formulate breakthrough strategies and solutions. It can be applied effectively in any situation in which a strategy, plan or decision is being contemplated. It is applicable to the formulation of company and division operating strategies and product and ser-

**Table 2.1**
**Differences Between Solution-Based and Outcome-Based Logic**

| Solution-Based Logic | Outcome-Based Logic |
|---|---|
| Individuals are focused on defending the value of proposed solutions. | Individuals are focused on creating solutions that create value. |
| Forces people to defend their proposed solutions using any means at their disposal. | Provides the criteria that are required to evaluate all proposed solutions. |
| Allows gut-feel, emotion and politics to *negatively* impact the result. | Ensures all decisions are based on fact. |
| Allows debate, negotiation and compromise to diminish the quality of the solution. | Provides a basis for agreement and disagreement and is focused on creating value. |
| Prevents people from verifying the creation of the optimal solution. | Provides a means to create and verify the creation of the optimal solution. |

vice strategies. It can be applied to reducing time-to-market, value-added process improvement, the optimization of investment and trade-off decisions, the selection of target markets, the optimization of product and service concepts and to many other strategic activities.

The use of Outcome-Based Logic redefines how people use information to formulate strategies and solutions. Information is used as a starting point from which to create breakthrough strategies and solutions. It ensures that valued information is available to everyone and that decisions are based on fact. It provides a basis for agreement and consensus. The widespread use of valued information and a method to process it changes organizational dynamics, and, when used properly, it drives the creation of breakthrough strategies and solutions.

There are many clear differences between Solution-Based Logic and Outcome-Based Logic. The differences are summarized in Table 2.1.

As a result of applying Outcome-Based Logic, people focus their energy on being inventive, rather than defensive. They focus their intellect on being creative, rather than combative. They focus their collective knowledge on optimizing, rather than compromising. This new set of dynamics transforms the process of strategy formulation from a barbaric encounter to a civilized effort to create customer value. This new logic lays the foundation upon which the future of strategy formulation has been built.

Chapter 3

# Structuring the Process of Strategy Formulation

William Jennings Bryan once said, "Destiny is no matter of chance. It is a matter of choice." An organization's ability to make effective choices and control its destiny is dependent upon its ability to formulate effective strategies. But many organizations struggle to overcome the barriers that have long stood in the way of creating breakthrough strategies and solutions.

We have established that organizations often lack the structure, information and the processing power that is required to formulate breakthrough strategies and solutions. We have demonstrated that the inherent use of Solution-Based Logic undermines the effective execution of most strategy formulation processes. We have introduced an alternative high-level thinking strategy called Outcome-Based Logic that transforms the way organizations approach the process of strategy formulation. The discovery of Outcome-Based Logic was an important step in the evolution of strategy formulation, but many other discoveries were required before the use of this new thinking strategy could be made practical.

Once this high-level thinking strategy was discovered, we still needed to create the structure, gather the information and harness the processing power that would be required to effectively apply Outcome-Based Logic. More specifically, we recognized that we needed to:

1. Find or create a structure in which this logic could be organized.

2. Determine what types of information would be needed to apply this logic and then determine how to capture that information.

3. Decide how that information should be processed within the structure to effectively create, evaluate and optimize a strategy or solution.

We started by asking ourselves: Does a structure for strategy formulation exist? How have others created breakthrough strategies? What steps have they taken? Why do some succeed in creating successful strategies while others fail? We recognized that it was important to first define a structure for strategy formulation before we could focus on what information would be required and determine how that information should be processed.

We will describe the efforts that were undertaken to uncover a structure for strategy formulation—a structure that enables the effective execution of Outcome-Based Logic. We will explain how those efforts resulted in the discovery of a *universal* structure for strategy formulation. This universal structure is being used today as part of our advanced strategy formulation process to enable the formulation of breakthrough strategies and solutions.

## A UNIVERSAL STRUCTURE FOR STRATEGY FORMULATION AND PLANNING

Strategist Gary Hamel stated in "Killer Strategies" (1997) that "the dirty little secret of the strategy industry is that it doesn't have any theory of strategy creation." The complexities associated with the process of strategy formulation are generally thought to be overwhelming, and, as a result, many people believe the process of strategy formulation cannot be structured or formalized. As we looked for a structure, we too realized that a structure did not exist. So we set out to create a structure that would support the effective application of Outcome-Based Logic—a structure that would enable the formulation of breakthrough strategies and solutions in every instance in which an organization sought to formulate a company, product, service or operating strategy.

The first step in this effort was to understand why certain organizations managed to formulate breakthrough strategies while others failed altogether in their attempts at strategy formulation. The objective was to model the behaviors and actions that were taken by organizations capable of successfully formulating breakthrough strategies and solutions. To accomplish this task, we applied pattern detection techniques that are often used in physics, Neuro Linguistic Programming or NLP and other behavioral sciences. Pattern detection is often used as a means to uncover similarities that exist between seemingly unrelated activities. In the field of physics, for example, an idea known as topological quantum field theory allows physicists to find connections between seemingly unrelated equations. This pattern detection idea has earned Edward Witten, a renowned physicist, the Fields Medal, the mathematical equivalent of the Nobel Prize. In the field of NLP, pattern detection has been used to discover the cognitive patterns that are used by geniuses such as Albert Einstein, Wolfgang Amadeus Mozart and others. As stated by Robert Dilts in his book titled *Strategies of Genius: Volume II* (1994), "this gives us a way to look past the behavioral content of what people do to the more invisible forces behind those behaviors to the structures of thought that allow these geniuses to accomplish what they have accomplished.'' It is recognized across many disciplines that the detection of patterns often results in new insights, ideas, theories, models and concepts.

We applied pattern detection techniques to the field of strategy formulation in an attempt to find a pattern that offered insight into the formulation of break-through strategies. Literally hundreds of situations were studied across dozens of industries. After years of observation, we detected a pattern that proved to be the impetus for the creation of a universal structure for strategy formulation. Through ongoing testing, it was verified that this pattern existed in every situation in which an organization successfully formulated a breakthrough strategy. This pattern, in essence, defines the process of strategy formulation.

The discovery of this pattern has led to the creation of a universal structure for strategy formulation. In turn, this structure has made it possible to define the essential elements of strategy formulation—the types of information that must be available to formulate breakthrough strategies or solutions in *any* situation. This pattern defines what organizations are attempting to accomplish when formulating strategies and solutions. The pattern that was identified can be described as follows:

In every situation in which an organization was successful at formulating a breakthrough strategy or solution, it had searched through the universe of possible solutions in an attempt to find the one solution that would best satisfy the largest number of important desired outcomes, given the constraints that had been imposed on the solution and the competitive position that was desired.

This pattern indicates that when an organization is contemplating any strategy, plan or decision, it is attempting to achieve three major objectives. As the organization searches through the thousands of potential solutions in the universe of possible solutions, it is looking for the solution that will enable it to:

1. Satisfy the largest number of important desired outcomes. This ensures that the solution creates the maximum amount of value for those involved in or affected by the strategy, plan or decision. This, in turn, enables the organization to achieve high levels of customer satisfaction and obtain a reputation as a creator of value.

2. Honor any constraints that have been imposed on the solution. This ensures that the chosen strategy or solution is practical and can be implemented. Constraints result from a fixed or limited set of resources. If a solution were chosen that does not honor the constraints, its successful implementation would be unlikely.

3. Achieve their desired competitive position. This ensures that the chosen solution strengthens the organization's strategic position. It ensures the solution delivers more or different value than competing solutions and enables the organization to achieve a distinctive and sustainable competitive advantage.

**Figure 3.1**
**The Universal Strategy Formulation Model, or USFM**

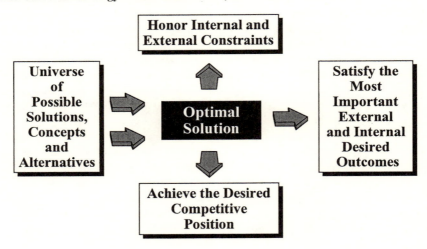

The one solution from the universe of possible solutions that will best meet all three objectives is called the optimal solution. Finding that solution is the challenge that all organizations face as they attempt to formulate their business, product, service and operating strategies.

Upon discovering this pattern, the elements were embodied into what we call the Universal Strategy Formulation Model, or USFM. This model, shown in Figure 3.1, describes the role that desired outcomes, constraints, the desired competitive position and the universe of possible solutions play in the formulation of optimal strategies and solutions. It illustrates how the optimal solution is the one solution from the universe of possible solutions that will best satisfy the largest number of important desired outcomes given the constraints imposed on the solution and the competitive position that is desired.

Although organizations may not be aware of it, they are *attempting* to exercise the USFM when they formulate a strategy or plan. This, of course, is assuming that they want to formulate a breakthrough strategy. They may not know about the model, or its elements, but when they are formulating a strategy, they are attempting to find the optimal solution. And the optimal solution can always be defined as the one that will satisfy the largest number of important desired outcomes given the imposed constraints and the competitive position that is desired. The attempted execution of this model reflects a universal pattern; a pattern that is common to every situation in which an organization has successfully formulated a breakthrough strategy.

Think back to the last several occasions in which you were involved in formulating a strategy. What were you attempting to accomplish? What information did you use? What steps did you take? Did you attempt to find out what desired outcomes were important to the affected internal and external customers? Did you consider the company's limitations or constraints? Did you spend time and effort analyzing the competition, benchmarking and deciding what it would take to make your organization more competitive? To gain a better understanding of the model, take the time to mentally apply it to several situations in which a strategy or plan was formulated in the past. Notice that regardless of the methods that may have been used, the overall objective was always the same.

Organizations are attempting to execute this model when they define their overall company strategies and new product and service offerings. They are attempting to execute this model when they evaluate which markets to enter, which investments to make and which activities to pursue. The methods used to attempt the discovery of the optimal solution may vary, but the overall objective remains the same in every situation.

> When formulating breakthrough strategies and solutions, organizations are attempting to find the one solution that will best satisfy the largest number of important desired outcomes given the constraints imposed on the solution and the competitive position that is desired.

The USFM describes a structure that addresses the complexity of strategy formulation, planning and decision making without generalization, deletions or oversimplification. The structure allows an organization to:

1. Determine what information is needed to create a breakthrough solution.
2. Organize information in a meaningful way so that its role and purpose is understood.
3. Properly consider and process information brought forth by any individual.
4. Filter out information that is not required.
5. Organize the information into a format that is suitable for processing.
6. Use all pertinent information to reach a conclusion.
7. Agree on the criteria to be used to create and evaluate potential strategies and solutions.
8. Reach consensus using facts as the basis for agreement.

Successful business leaders often have an inherent ability to exercise this model: they often possess keen insight into the outcomes they are trying to achieve; they know the constraints they face; and they have extensive knowledge of their competition. Steve Jobs and Steve Wozniak possessed great insight in these areas when they created the first Apple computers. Jan Carlzon possessed similar insights when he transformed Scandinavian Airlines (SAS) into a world class airline. Anita Roddick had a clear understanding of the elements in this model when she founded the Body Shop. Nicolas Hayek successfully worked the elements in this model when creating the Swatch. Applying pattern detection techniques to the strategy formulation processes used by these and other successful businesses is what led to the discovery of this model.

The USFM forms the foundation for a new approach to structured thinking. Each element plays a critical role in the strategy formulation process and in the creation of breakthrough solutions. The model is very powerful in that it applies to *every* situation in which individuals and businesses contemplate strategies, plans and decisions. It essentially defines the process of strategy formulation. Its applicability cuts across the boundaries that often limit the use of a strategy formulation process to a specific situation. It contains the essential elements of strategy formulation. As stated by Kenichi Ohmae in his book titled *The Mind of the Strategist* (1982), "In the construction of any business strategy, three main players must be taken into account: the corporation itself, the customer and the competition." This model integrates these main players into a systematic process for strategy formulation.

It has been established that in any situation in which a strategy is required, the optimal strategy or solution must satisfy important desired outcomes, honor constraints and enable an organization to achieve its desired competitive position. This implies that before the optimal solution can be discovered, an organization must have access to certain types of information. More specifically they must know:

1. Their customers' and potential customers' prioritized desired outcomes.

2. Any constraints imposed on the solution.

3. The competitive position that is desired.

4. The potential solutions that are available.

This information is critical to the success of any strategy formulation process. They are what we call the essential elements of strategy formulation. What follows is a description of each of these elements.

## DESIRED OUTCOMES

Organizations have long recognized that it is important to understand their customers' requirements. When formulating strategies, many organizations spend considerable effort attempting to find out what their customers value only to conclude that customers do not know what they want and that customer requirements change quickly over time. Desired outcomes are different from requirements—or at least how most people think of requirements. A desired outcome is a statement, made by an individual involved in or affected by a strategy or plan, that describes an important benefit they would like to receive from the strategy or plan that is being contemplated. Desired outcomes are unique in that they are free from solutions and specifications and are free from vague or ambiguous words. As we will demonstrate in the next chapter, desired outcomes are also unique in that they are stable over time.

When executing the USFM, desired outcomes exist for each customer type that is involved in, or affected by, the strategy or plan that is being contemplated. Multiple customers typically exist. For example, the customers involved in formulating a company strategy may include the users of the company's products or services, suppliers, distributors, employees and stakeholders. As a second example, the customers involved in the development of a surgical system may include surgeons, nurses and support staff, the hospital administrators, internal company stakeholders and the manufacturer of the system. Whatever the situation, each customer type has its own unique set of desired outcomes.

Desired outcomes often include cost, time, quality and other performance or functional benefits. For example, each of the statements below are examples of desired outcomes on a surgical system—a system that enables surgeons to effectively perform surgical procedures. They represent a subset of all the desired outcomes on systems that are used to perform the process of surgery. Assume that there are only three customer types in this situation—doctors, stakeholders and the manufacturer—and that each customer type has only five desired outcomes. Of course, in a real world situation, there would be several more customer types, and each customer type would have dozens of desired outcomes.

In this example, doctors who use a surgical system desire certain outcomes from the system. They may want the system to:

1. Prevent the injury of healthy tissue.
2. Enable continuous, unobstructed vision of the field.
3. Minimize the amount of patient bleeding.
4. Ensure the complete destruction of unwanted tissue.
5. Prevent the formation of undesirable scaring.

Hospital administrators, who often make the actual purchase decision, have a different set of desired outcomes. They may want the surgical system to:

1. Require minimal effort to set up for different operations.
2. Experience minimal unexpected down time due to failure.
3. Reduce the frequency with which the device requires planned servicing.
4. Require a minimal amount of space.
5. Minimize the cost of upgrading to future levels of performance.

The manufacturer of the surgical system has yet another set of desired outcomes. The manufacturer may want the system to:

1. Require minimal test time.

2. Employ manufacturing processes that can be statistically controlled.

3. Minimize the dependence on skill-intensive manufacturing processes.

4. Reduce the manufacturing space required for production.

5. Minimize sensitivity to variations in the manufacturing process.


In this simplified example, the three customer types form what is called the customer set. Based on the experience of many consulting projects, we have established that between two to six customer types are typically included in a customer set when formulating a strategy or plan. It is common to obtain between 25 and 50 desired outcomes for each customer type, and, as a result, 50 to 300 desired outcomes can be expected in total.

Desired outcomes are one of the essential elements of strategy formulation. Without them an organization cannot expect to formulate a breakthrough strategy or solution. They must be captured and prioritized to understand what the various customer types value in a specific situation. When formulating a strategy, defining a plan or making a complex decision, the objective then becomes finding the solution that will satisfy the largest number of important desired outcomes. The concept of desired outcomes is described in detail in the next chapter. It will be demonstrated that most organizations fail to capture their customers' desired outcomes when they set out to capture customer requirements. We will further demonstrate that organizations rarely recognize that they have failed to capture what their customers truly value. We have discovered that this is the root cause of failure in most strategy formulation and planning processes today.


## CONSTRAINTS

Many organizations recognize that when formulating a strategy, it is not unusual to have constraints imposed on the solution. Constraints are typically imposed by individuals within the organization or by a third party. Constraints may be imposed by managers, employees, suppliers, customers, regulatory agencies or others. A constraint is a boundary condition that restricts or limits the number of options that are available for consideration when formulating a strategy or solution. A constraint restricts the number of solutions from which an organization may choose. Organizations must honor the constraints that are imposed on a solution. It is important to note that a constraint cannot be prioritized; it simply *must* be met.

Constraints are imposed for a variety of reasons. When applying pattern detection techniques to the process of strategy formulation, we recognized that constraints are often imposed as a result of:

1. Schedule, resource availability or financial limitations.
2. Cost, material or contractual issues.
3. Legal obligations or regulatory issues.

We also found that constraints exist in almost every situation in which a strategy is being contemplated. For example, when formulating a strategy to create a new surgical system or some other new product or service, an organization may impose constraints that denote that the solution must:

1. Be achievable by a certain date.
2. Meet a specific cost target.
3. Utilize a specific technology.
4. Be implemented using existing labor resources.
5. Honor patents that have been registered by competitors.
6. Limit development expenditures to a specified amount.
7. Meet a specific government regulation.

Each of these constraints will affect, shape and guide which solution is chosen. As constraints are imposed, the number of potential solutions that the organization is able to consider declines. Conversely, as constraints are removed, a wider range of potential solutions becomes available. Picture the universe of possible solutions contracting and expanding as constraints are added and deleted. The chosen concept, strategy or solution must honor any and all constraints. Therefore, if a proposed solution does not honor the stated constraints, it must be modified or dropped from consideration.

It is not unusual to have between 5 and 30 constraints imposed on a solution, but it is important to minimize the number of constraints that are imposed to increase the number of potential solutions that are available. All breakthrough ideas may be eliminated from consideration if a solution is over-constrained. In addition, an unnecessary or poorly conceived constraint may prevent an organization from achieving its growth and profitability objectives.

For example, an organization may constrain a solution by stating that the chosen company strategy must not require more than a $10 million capital investment and must produce a 15% return on investment in two years. Based on these constraints, if the organization came up with a strategy that could produce a 25% ROI in 18 months, but required an $11 million capital investment, it would be rejected. This may result in the loss of opportunity. For this reason, each constraint should be closely scrutinized. It is important to ask what would happen if a stated constraint is not honored. If the result is not debilitating, devastating or financially incapacitating, then the perceived constraint may not be a real constraint after all.

It is also important to note that as constraints are imposed on a solution, they may inhibit an organization's ability to satisfy one or more desired outcomes and may also make it difficult for an organization to achieve its desired competitive position. The organization may be forced to decide if it is more important to honor a particular constraint, satisfy a particular customer desired outcome or achieve the desired competitive position. This is a critical and expected part of strategy formulation. After all, as Michael Porter states in his article "What Is Strategy?" (1996), "strategy is making trade-offs in competing." Constraints are one of the essential elements of strategy formulation. To effectively formulate a strategy, they must be defined and documented by those involved in the strategy formulation process. Once a constraint is imposed, it must be honored. Therefore, it is important to ensure that each constraint is necessary and justifiable.

Ask yourself, when formulating a strategy, does your organization identify the constraints that must be honored? When are constraints defined? Are they defined before the first solution is evaluated or after the solution is selected? Although the concept of constraints is rather simple, it is amazing how often constraints are uncovered *after* a strategy or solution has already been selected, sometimes well after implementation has begun. This often forces an organization to make changes to the strategy and, if it is too late to make changes, it may simply degrade the amount of value that can be delivered by the chosen solution. Uncovering constraints before the strategy is chosen is consistent with the effective application of the USFM and Outcome-Based Logic. It is an essential step in the formulation of breakthrough strategies.

## THE DESIRED COMPETITIVE POSITION

Organizations want to choose and implement strategies and solutions that will continually move them or keep them at the forefront of the competition. When formulating strategies, the solution that is chosen is usually worth developing or implementing only if it places the organization in a favorable strategic position. Why would an organization intentionally and knowingly pursue a strategy or solution if a competitor was following a comparable or better strategy, and the strategy did not enable the achievement of a distinctive and sustainable competitive advantage? Clearly, it would not.

So, how does an organization determine the competitive position it wants to achieve? The determination must be made as an integral part of the strategy formulation process, and it must not be treated as an afterthought. To achieve a desired competitive position, an organization must first *define* the desired competitive position it wants to achieve. A well-defined competitive position will be both unique and valued. It will be unique in that it will enable the organization to satisfy select customer desired outcomes better than any other competing solution. It will be valued in that it will ensure the chosen solution satisfies desired outcomes that are important to the customer. The competitive position that is desired should also strengthen the organization's strategic position, enable it to deliver more or different value than its competitors and enable it to achieve a distinctive and sustainable competitive advantage.

When defining the desired competitive position, it is better to focus on achieving perfection over the long term than it is to focus on making incremental improvements over the short term. This often requires an organization to think differently about the concept of competitive analysis. Simply stated:

In order to effectively define the competitive position that is desired, an organization must decide to what degree it wishes to satisfy the customers' valued desired outcomes.

This degree of satisfaction may be established relative to competing solutions or relative to perfection. Once the organization decides on the degree to which it wants to satisfy the customers' desired outcomes, it must pursue the creation of the strategies and solutions that will enable the level of satisfaction to be achieved. Only certain solutions will enable it to achieve its desired competitive position, and very few, if any solutions will enable the achievement of perfection.

Expanding on the surgical system example, let's assume that we only want to consider the hospital administrator's desired outcomes and that the five desired outcomes obtained from the administrators are their most important desired outcomes as quantified through statistically valid research. In reality, of course, all customer types and many other desired outcomes would be considered. In this simplified illustration, the five most important desired outcomes are listed on the left in Table 3.1.

To define the desired competitive position, an organization must set the target values that define the level of satisfaction that they would like the chosen solution to deliver. The organization can set these target values relative to its competitor or relative to perfection. In the example given in Table 3.1, the organization is stating that it wants the chosen solution to satisfy the desired outcomes to the degree indicated by the target values found in the column on the right.

The values in the column on the right define the desired competitive position. If a strategy or solution is created that will enable these target values to be attained, then the organization will achieve its desired competitive position. The values stated should, at a minimum, place the organization in front of its competitors for the most highly valued outcomes. The idea then is to search out, create, innovate and discover the solutions that will make it possible for the organization to achieve this desired level of satisfaction. This is the essence of a unique approach to competitive positioning. Once an organization knows what defines the creation of value in a given situation—or in other words, which desired outcomes are most important—it can decide the degree to which to satisfy the outcomes based on its knowledge of the competition, its capabilities

**Table 3.1**
**Defining the Desired Competitive Position**

| Desired Outcome | Current Value for Organization | Current Value for Competitor 1 | Value That Achieves Perfection | Target Value Set by Organization |
|---|---|---|---|---|
| Require minimal effort to set up the system for different operations. | 3 minutes | 45 seconds | 0 seconds | 10 seconds |
| Experience minimal down time due to failure (unexpected down time). | 24 hours | 18 hours | 0 hours | 4 hours |
| Reduce the frequency with which the device requires planned servicing. | 4 times per year | 2 times per year | 0 times per year | 1 time per year |
| Require a minimal amount of space. | 800 cu. in. | 760 cu. in. | 0 cu. in. | 690 cu. in. |
| Minimize the cost of upgrading to future levels of performance. | 30% of initial cost | 25% of initial cost | 0% of initial cost | 10% of initial cost |

and its ability to achieve perfection. This approach to competitive positioning leads to the consistent creation of breakthrough strategies and solutions.

It is important to emphasize that the desired competitive position is something that is planned. When using Outcome-Based Logic, the desired competitive position is defined prior to the creation of the solution. It shapes, leads and guides the creation of the strategy or solution. The desired competitive position, once defined, dictates which desired outcomes the solution must satisfy and the degree to which they must be satisfied. It determines the level of satisfaction that the solution must deliver relative to competing solutions. The target values that are set establish the amount of value that the chosen solution must deliver.

The ability to define the desired competitive position is dependent on knowing the desired outcomes of the customers in the customer set. Without this knowledge, it is unlikely that a unique and valued position will be defined. Like desired outcomes, the achievement of the desired competitive position is also inhibited by constraints imposed on the solution. It may be necessary to remove or refine a constraint to achieve the competitive position that is desired.

## THE UNIVERSE OF POSSIBLE SOLUTIONS

When formulating a plan or strategy or making a complex decision, hundreds, thousands or even millions of potential solutions often exist. As demonstrated earlier, it is not uncommon to have as many as 40 million possible solutions from which to choose when formulating a company strategy. A large but finite number of potential solutions exist in every situation.

Solutions are the mechanism or means by which desired outcomes can be achieved or satisfied. A fundamental characteristic of a solution is that it must define *how* desired outcomes, constraints and the desired competitive position will be achieved. The solutions that are considered when formulating strategies and plans are often comprised of a combination of features, and those features can often be combined in various ways to form other solutions. These potential solutions form the universe of possible solutions.

The universe of possible solutions often contains millions of potential combinations of solutions that exist for a given situation at a specific point in time. The universe of possible solutions expands over time as new ideas and innovations are made practical and as new technologies become available. The advent of microprocessors, for example, expanded the number of potential solutions that were available to organizations that manufacture products for communications, data processing, scientific research and other markets. Technologies such as electronic books, DVD, digital imaging, neural networks, fuzzy logic, flat panel displays, anti-noise capability and others are expanding the universe of possible solutions for many other product and service industries. New ideas about management, organization, product development, manufacturing, marketing, positioning, competitive analysis and employee development are expanding the number of possible solutions an organization must consider when formulating a company strategy.

Organizations typically live in a Solution-Based world, so it is rarely difficult for them to define or uncover a variety of potential solutions. The difficulty often lies in sorting through all the potential solutions to determine which will deliver the most value in a given situation. It isn't always the solution that includes the latest and greatest technology that works best, it is often the solution that uses technology wisely that accelerates the creation of value.

## THE OPTIMAL SOLUTION

The optimal solution is the solution, from the universe of possible solutions, that: satisfies the largest number of important desired outcomes; honors the constraints that have been imposed on the solution; and enables the achievement of the desired competitive position. The optimal solution is the result of a well-executed strategy formulation process.

When contemplating a strategy, plan or decision, the principle objective is to create or discover the optimal solution. The optimal solution will deliver the greatest value to all those involved in, or affected by, the strategy or plan that is being contemplated.

## IMPOSING A MATHEMATICAL FRAMEWORK

We have defined the essential elements of strategy formulation as customer desired outcomes, constraints, competitive positioning data and the solutions that make up the universe of possible solutions. To simplify the understanding and execution of the USFM—especially among engineers, scientists and others with a background in mathematics—we often describe the essential elements of strategy formulation as constants and variables in a mathematical equation. This explanation implies the use of an imposed mathematical structure. This structure is only imposed to assist in the understanding and the execution of this advanced strategy formulation process.

Given that we impose this artificial structure, the elements of the equation must comply with the principles of mathematical problem solving—they must be defined and treated as either constants or variables. So, when formulating a strategy using the structure defined within the USFM, we treat the desired outcomes, constraints and competitive positioning data as constants in the equation. Each constant is assumed to be stable at the point in time at which the equation is being solved. The constants define the criteria that describe the optimal solution.

We treat the solutions in the universe of possible solutions as variables in the equation. The solutions are numerous and ever-changing. The objective, when solving this equation, is to determine which solution, from the universe of possible solutions, will enable the equation to close given the constants that have been defined in the equation. As you might guess, this requires some serious processing power.

When formulating a strategy, defining a plan or making a complex decision, an organization is attempting to solve what can only be described as a very complex equation. The organization is searching through the universe of possible solutions in an attempt to find the one solution that will satisfy the largest number of important desired outcomes given the internal and external constraints imposed on the solution and the competitive position that is desired. It is searching through the millions of variables—solutions—to find the one that will close the equation given the constants—outcomes, constraints and competitive position—that have been defined as important in a given situation.

The essential elements of strategy formulation, and the role they play as constants and variables in an imposed mathematical equation, are shown in Figure 3.2.

This equation is far more complex than a simultaneous equation found in most algebra classes. When contemplating a strategy, plan or decision, it is not unusual to consider between 50 and 300 constants and often as many as 40 million variables. Again, the constants include the desired outcomes, constraints and the values defining the desired competitive position. The variables include a large but finite number of possible solutions. To solve the equation, the information entered into the equation must be processed simultaneously.

When looking at this model from a mathematical perspective, once the constants in the equation have been established, the variables in the equation can be tested until the combination of variables that best fit the stated criteria is uncovered. In this case, that combination of variables represents the optimal

**Figure 3.2**
**Imposing a Mathematical Structure on the Universal Strategy Formulation Model**

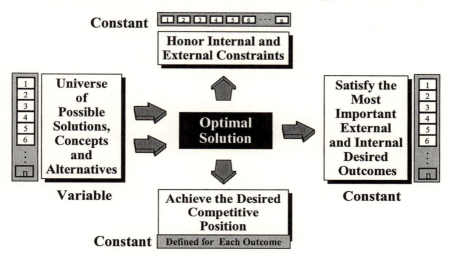

solution. This analogy often helps in understanding how the USFM is used as a structure for strategy formulation. The desired outcomes, constraints and desired competitive position are treated as constants for the point in time at which the equation is being solved. They are fixed; frozen at a point in time. The potential solutions that are, or will be, available at that point in time are then systematically tested within that framework until the solution that best solves the equation is discovered. That solution will be the optimal solution.

Based on research that we have conducted while executing dozens of consulting projects, we have concluded that between 8,000 and 40,000 decisions are typically required when attempting to uncover the optimal solution. Keep in mind that the human mind can effectively process only five to nine pieces of information at one time. Imagine attempting to solve such a complex equation in your head!

Ask yourself, how does your organization structure and process the information that is required to formulate an effective strategy? To what degree does it incorporate the essential elements of strategy formulation? What percent of the desired outcomes, constraints, possible solutions and positioning data are available when strategies, plans and decisions are typically contemplated? What percent of this information is used? How is it structured? What information is missing? What percent of the time is the optimal solution uncovered?

It should be mentioned again that although organizations may not always be aware of it, they are attempting to exercise the elements in the USFM when they contemplate strategies, plans and decisions. This model embodies a universal pattern, a pattern that describes how organizations are attempting to find the solution that will satisfy the largest number of important desired outcomes given the constraints imposed on the solution and the competitive position that is desired.

You may be wondering, to what degree would the quality of my strategies and solutions improve if I used the structure defined within the USFM when formulating strategies and solutions? To answer that question we conducted studies with organizations that have used both a traditional strategy formulation method and our advanced strategy formulation process. These studies were conducted with mostly *Fortune* 100 companies.

Quantitative methods integral to our process were used to evaluate hundreds of concepts proposed by dozens of organizations. We tested concepts derived from traditional methods that were proposed or implemented prior to the execution of our process. We also tested concepts that resulted from the execution of our process. The results of that research indicate that the *best* strategies and solutions resulting from the execution of traditional methods typically satisfied only between 5% and 15% of the targeted customer desired outcomes better than they were satisfied by the existing solution. It was also found that in some cases, the strategies chosen for implementation did not even satisfy the desired outcomes as well as the strategies and solutions that were already in place.

In contrast, when using our strategy formulation process, the same organizations often chose solutions that satisfied as many as 80% of the targeted desired outcomes better than the existing solution. On average, this process produced strategies and solutions that satisfied between 50% and 60% of the targeted desired outcomes better than existing solutions. This is a ten-fold improvement over what most organizations experienced when using their traditional methods. As a result, the uncovered solutions are often thought to be breakthrough solutions.

## A VISUAL INTERPRETATION OF THE MODEL

For those of you who are more visual, we like to describe the execution of the USFM using a series of filters that filter out all other solutions until only the optimal solution remains. Using this analogy, assume that we start with the universe of possible solutions. As we search through all the solutions, we filter out or eliminate the solutions that do not satisfy the customers' desired outcomes. This, of course, dramatically decreases the number of possible solutions that remain. We then filter out the solutions that do not honor the stated constraints, eliminating many of the remaining solutions. Lastly, we filter out the solutions that do not enable the organization to achieve its desired competitive position. This often results in just a handful of remaining solutions. They are the only solutions that will fit through all the filters. From there, it is quite simple to select the optimal solution. This concept is shown in Figure 3.3.

Notice how the universe of possible solutions is reduced to the optimal so-

**Figure 3.3**
**Filtering Out the Optimal Solution**

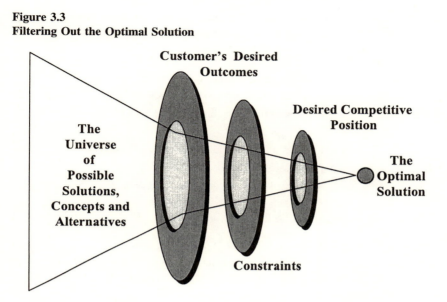

lution through this filtering process. This analogy often brings additional insight into how the USFM is executed to produce a breakthrough strategy.

## SUMMARY

We have discovered a universal structure for strategy formulation; a structure that any organization can use to effectively formulate a breakthrough strategy or solution in every situation. This structure resulted from years of research in which we applied pattern detection and modeling techniques that are often limited to physics, behavioral sciences and other non-business related disciplines. The application of these techniques led to the discovery of a pattern that was observed in every situation in which a breakthrough strategy was created.

This pattern defined how organizations were able to successfully formulate breakthrough strategies and solutions. The pattern that was identified is described as follows:

> In every situation in which an organization was successful at formulating a breakthrough strategy or solution, it had searched through the universe of possible solutions in an attempt to find the one solution that would best satisfy the largest number of important desired outcomes, given the constraints that had been imposed on the solution and the competitive position that was desired.

The discovery of this pattern led to the creation of a universal structure for strategy formulation called the USFM. This model describes a structure that addresses the complexity of strategy formulation, planning and decision making without generalization, deletions or oversimplification. The structure allows an organization to:

1. Determine what information is needed to create a breakthrough solution.
2. Organize information in a meaningful way, so that its role and purpose is understood.
3. Properly consider and process information brought forth by any individual.
4. Filter out information that is not required.
5. Organize the information into a format that is suitable for processing.
6. Use all pertinent information to reach a conclusion.
7. Agree on the criteria to be used to create and evaluate potential strategies and solutions.
8. Reach consensus using facts as the basis for agreement.

This structure also made it possible to define the essential elements of strategy formulation—desired outcomes, constraints, competitive positioning data and the universe of possible solutions. Each of these elements must be considered when formulating a breakthrough strategy or solution.

We imposed a mathematical framework on the USFM to explain how the model is executed. This mathematical analogy gives order to the elements in the equation as they are treated as either constants or variables. When using this mathematical framework, the overall objective becomes finding the solution—the variable—that will best solve the equation given the constants—desired outcomes, constraints and competitive information—that have been defined in the equation.

The USFM brings structure to the world of strategy formulation. The discovery of this structure provides a framework from which an organization can successfully formulate breakthrough strategies and solutions using Outcome-Based Logic. This structure also defines the essential elements of strategy formulation.

Once this discovery was made, we knew that we had to create and master the methods that would enable us to collect the information that is essential to the formulation of breakthrough strategies—desired outcomes, constraints and competitive data. We set out to create and master these methods. These efforts, as you will see, led to several other very important discoveries.

Chapter 4

# Desired Outcomes: Redefining the Concept of "Requirements"

In his book titled *Managing Customer Value* (1994) Bradley Gale writes, "If managers can't agree among themselves about the customers' desires, then it's unlikely they can achieve rapid progress toward fulfilling those desires." While using pattern detection techniques to study the process of strategy formulation, we found that managers engaged in the process of strategy formulation rarely agreed on what their customers valued. We found that their conflicting views were often dependent on which customers they had talked to and were shaped by their personal experiences, intuition and biases. We also found that even when managers did agree that certain customer requirements were important, they could not agree on which were most important.

Organizations have often used ineffective methods to help them understand and prioritize what their customers value. As a result, many misconceptions regarding the concept of customer requirements have been propagated throughout the years. Correcting these misconceptions is an important step in understanding the science of strategy formulation. For example, you may believe that customers do not know what they want or that customer requirements change quickly over time. Correcting these misconceptions will forever change the way you think about customer requirements and the role they play in the formulation of breakthrough strategies and solutions. Before we attack what is arguably the root cause of failure in most strategy formulation and planning processes, let us quickly review the ideas and concepts that have set the stage for this next important discovery.

We have established that organizations often lack the structure, information and the processing power that is required to formulate breakthrough strategies and solutions. We have demonstrated that the inherent use of Solution-Based Logic undermines the effective execution of most strategy formulation proc-

**Figure 4.1**
**Desired Outcomes in the Universal Strategy Formulation Model**

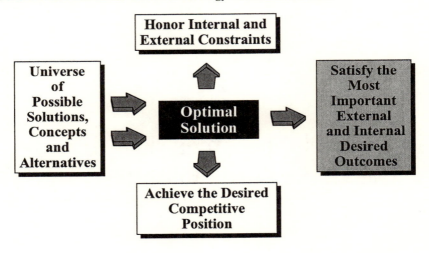

esses. We have introduced an alternative high-level thinking strategy called Outcome-Based Logic that transforms the way organizations approach the process of strategy formulation. We have introduced the Universal Strategy Formulation Model (USFM), a model that brings structure to the world of strategy formulation. The discovery of this structure provides a framework from which an organization can successfully formulate breakthrough strategies and solutions. This structure also defines the essential elements of strategy formulation, the types of information that are required to successfully execute the USFM. This information includes customer desired outcomes, constraints, competitive positioning data and solutions.

The next important step in unveiling this advanced strategy formulation process is to introduce the concept of desired outcomes. Because desired outcomes come from customers, many people want to conveniently classify them as customer "requirements." We will show that desired outcomes are unique and should not be confused with other types of requirements. Desired outcomes are incorporated into the USFM, as shown in Figure 4.1. The figure indicates, once again, that in any situation, the optimal solution must satisfy many important desired outcomes.

Organizations have long recognized the importance of understanding what their customers value. As a result, companies and consultants have developed dozens of techniques that are aimed at capturing customer requirements. Despite this fact, the methods used by most organizations today to gather customer requirements are ineffective at uncovering the customers' desired outcomes and, as we shall demonstrate, often preclude the discovery of the optimal solution.

In fact, an inability to effectively capture desired outcomes is the reason why most businesses fail in their quest to formulate breakthrough strategies and solutions. We will demonstrate that the methods typically used by businesses to capture customer requirements are the root cause of failure of most strategy formulation and planning processes around the world today.

It is interesting to note that many organizations are oblivious to the fact that they do not know what their customers value. In fact, many organizations are convinced that since they talk to their customers they must understand their customers' requirements. We quantified this fact in 1995 when we conducted 270 interviews with executives around the United States. The results showed that 71% of executives were very satisfied with their organization's ability to understand their customers' requirements. This was particularly intriguing because the research also showed that the same executives were very unsatisfied with their organization's ability to define the right products and services, target the most attractive segments, identify new market opportunities and select the best strategic direction.

The obvious question was, if organizations really understand what their customers value, then why are they struggling with these other closely related issues? Is it possible that many organizations believe they understand what their customers' value when in fact they do not? What is behind this paradox?

In this chapter we will describe the inefficiencies of traditional requirements gathering methods and explain what is behind this requirement's paradox. We will also explain the reasons why desired outcomes are often left out of strategy formulation and planning processes and how this prevents the formulation of breakthrough strategies. We will then show that incorporating desired outcomes into the strategy formulation process is a prerequisite for the formulation of breakthrough strategies and solutions. It will become apparent that the discovery of desired outcomes, a unique form of requirement, was a critical step in building the future of strategy formulation.

## THE REALITIES OF "REQUIREMENTS" GATHERING

Have you ever had the experience of gathering requirements from a customer or a group of customers? What happened when you asked them for their requirements? How did they respond? Did they give you vague, ambiguous statements? Did they go off on tangents, offering requirements on a multitude of subjects? Did their requirements conflict? Did they talk in terms of solutions? Did they give you all of their requirements? Did they respond with desired outcomes? Many difficulties can arise when attempting to capture customer requirements. Ask yourself the following questions. When gathering customer requirements:

1. What types of information are you trying to capture?
2. How do you plan to use the information?
3. What types of information do you end up capturing?
4. How do you end up using the information you obtain?

We have found that many organizations simply try to capture any statement that describes what is wanted or needed. They typically do not discriminate between the types of information they are receiving. They end up using whatever information they get to assist in the formulation of their strategies and solutions. What they may not know is that customers, when asked for their requirements, often respond with different types of information—most of which precludes an organization from understanding what its customers truly value and, therefore, inhibits the formulation of breakthrough strategies and solutions.

Based on over 1,000 interviews conducted over the past seven years, we have discovered that when asked for requirements, individuals will usually respond with one of three types of information. They will usually respond with solutions, vague statements or, sometimes, they will respond with desired outcomes. Let's profile each of these types of information in more detail.

1. *Solutions*: Solutions are the means by which desired outcomes will be achieved. A solution is a feature, mechanism or technology that delivers value and is usually tangible or physical in nature. A solution is treated as a variable in the USFM and belongs in the universe of possible solutions, the left side of the model. Based on over 1,000 interviews, we have determined that individuals, when asked for their requirements, will respond with solutions between 60% and 80% of the time.

2. *Vague Statements*: A vague statement is a word or phrase that can mean different things to different people. Easy-to-use, comfortable, durable and reliable are all commonly used words that form vague statements. Vague statements may also be partial solutions or partial desired outcomes. Individuals, when asked for their requirements, will respond with vague statements between 20% and 30% of the time.

3. *Desired Outcomes*: A desired outcome is a statement that describes an important benefit that an individual would like to receive from the strategy or solution that is to be implemented. A desired outcome is treated as a constant, must be free from solutions and, as we will demonstrate, is stable over time. Individuals, when asked for their requirements, will respond with desired outcomes less than 10% of the time.

It must be noted that from a technical perspective, a requirement could be a solution, a vague statement or a desired outcome. The word "requirement" is a vague statement itself, as it means different things to different people. A requirement is commonly defined as something that is wanted or needed. A solution, vague statement and a desired outcome all describe something that is wanted or needed, but desired outcomes and solutions play two very different roles in the optimization of strategies.

When attempting to formulate breakthrough strategies and solutions, it is imperative to be able to distinguish between the types of information that are captured from customers. Once the USFM was discovered, it became clear to us that when talking to customers, organizations needed to capture their desired outcomes, not their requested solutions.

In order to effectively execute the USFM, one must uncover the customers' desired outcomes and place them as constants, on the right side of the equation. Solutions that are captured from customers, or anybody else, are to be treated as variables and placed on the left side of the equation. The objective of executing the USFM is to find the solution that will satisfy many important desired outcomes.

The next several sections describe, in detail, what happens when solutions and vague statements are accepted as requirements. It will become apparent that accepting solutions and vague statements as requirements is the root cause of inefficiency and failure in most strategy formulation, planning and decision-making processes today.

## ACCEPTING SOLUTIONS AS REQUIREMENTS

Because most people intuitively use the high-level thinking strategy that we defined as Solution-Based Logic, we have found that most people think in terms of solutions, focus on solutions and respond with solutions when they are asked for their requirements. This type of response is common, because customers are typically trying to help you solve a problem. To make matters worse, quite often the person who is responsible for capturing the customers' requirements is also focused on obtaining solutions, because they do not know what types of information they should be looking for. To most people, dealing with solutions is natural, while dealing with desired outcomes is unnatural. Many requirements gathering sessions are not initiated with the intent of capturing desired outcomes. Typically, an organization engages in conversation with a customer without knowing what types of information they are looking for and without knowing the difference between solutions and desired outcomes. As a result, the individuals involved in the process instinctively talk about what is most natural—solutions.

So what are the ramifications of individuals applying Solution-Based Logic when stating their requirements? When an organization interviews people in an attempt to obtain the information required for the right side of the USFM (desired outcomes) up to 80% of the time they are obtaining information that should be put on the left side of the model—solutions. Now this poses an interesting problem. If an organization is capturing solutions from customers, then from whom will it capture the customers' desired outcomes? We have discovered that when organizations capture solutions from customers, they often simply accept those solutions as customer requirements and do not capture desired outcomes

at all. That's right. As a result of this phenomena, organizations often fail to capture the customers' desired outcomes altogether.

What happens in your organization? Do you search out specific information from your customers? Do you discriminate between solutions and desired outcomes when capturing customer requirements? Do you capture mostly solutions? Do you accept them as your customers' requirements? Do you attempt to capture your customers' desired outcomes if you first capture solutions? Many organizations are satisfied to capture solutions and, knowingly or unknowingly, stop short of capturing desired outcomes.

As an example of this phenomena, consider the approach used in the past by one of our clients. Prior to working with us, a major computer manufacturer had asked several company employees, and an external consultant, to gather requirements from their customers. The objective was to capture requirements on a specific type of data processing device. They conducted customer interviews and concluded the assignment with a list of customer requirements. The requirements they collected were a list of solutions that included items such as hot-swap cards, a tape back-up, an internal modem, data encryption, a high-speed hard disk and dozens of other product features. The list contained only solutions. They were prepared to move forward without knowing their customers' desired outcomes. They later admitted that they did not know what types of information they should be capturing from customers and felt content in capturing their requested solutions. They then realized that they had routinely accepted solutions as requirements and consistently failed to capture desired outcomes from its customers.

This is a very common occurrence. Organizations often fail to capture their customers' desired outcomes and end up with lists of solutions that spark debate and drive the execution of Solution-Based Logic. As a result of this phenomena, organizations often fail to include a complete and accurate set of customer desired outcomes in the processes they use to formulate their company, product and operating strategies. Imagine contemplating a strategy, plan or decision without knowing all the desired outcomes that are to be achieved! It happens all the time. This sounds hard to believe, but it is true. Desired outcomes are often partially or completely left out of processes designed to formulate strategies, define plans and make complex decisions. They are often unknowingly replaced with solutions. Organizations often use these solutions as a guide in driving the formulation of their plans and strategies. This precludes the discovery of breakthrough solutions and results in ineffective strategies. A typical scenario is as follows:

An organization sponsors market research to uncover what customers value. They want to be customer driven and responsive to the needs of their customers. As part of the research activity, the participants are asked a variety of questions. It is often the case that both the interviewer and the participants do not know the difference between desired outcomes and solutions. The interviewer, who may be following a planned agenda, is often content to have the participants interact and respond to the pre-defined questions. The results of the interactions are usually statements, in the form of solutions, which describe what the participants want. Upon hearing and seeing the solutions coming from the participants, the solutions are often accepted as the customers' actual desired outcomes. The reality is, however, that the participants are stating solutions that they believe will best satisfy their desired outcomes. Their actual desired outcomes are often left unstated and are, therefore, not captured.

The real problem arises, because the organization now believes it knows what its customers value, when, in fact, it does not. It only knows what solutions customers are asking for at that point in time, not the desired outcomes they are trying to achieve in the future. This confusion is the cause of the requirements' paradox. Organizations believe they know what their customers value when, in fact, they only know their customers' requirements in the form of solutions. Organizations often react by delivering the solutions that are requested by customers. Once they are delivered, competitors are already offering better solutions—solutions that the customers hadn't requested or even thought of. The company providing the requested solution becomes frustrated, because it doesn't know where it went wrong; after all, it was listening to its customers.

Failing to discriminate between solutions and desired outcomes is the most common mistake made in requirements gathering. It is important to understand the difference between desired outcomes and solutions and the role they play in the process of strategy formulation. Confusion and inefficiency will often result when solutions are accepted as desired outcomes.

When a single solution is accepted as a desired outcome, and it is input into the USFM as a desired outcome, the universe of possible solutions contracts, and it precludes other solutions from emerging. Alternative solutions are eliminated from consideration, because the solution that was accepted as a requirement has already been assumed as a constant in the equation (i.e., it will be part of the overall solution). Accepting a solution as a desired outcome has the same effect as imposing a constraint on the solution, the request must be honored. For example, let's say that a computer manufacturer interviews users and is told that a tape back-up is required in future systems. Those interviewed may not be aware that a 100MB floppy drive provides much better back-up capability than a tape drive in many situations. If the manufacturer listens to their customers' requirements as stated, they would provide them with a tape back-up. A competitor, who captures desired outcomes and is not constrained by the tape back-up solution, may decide to include a 100MB floppy drive in their offering. This may better satisfy the customers' desired outcome to minimize the time it takes to back-up important information. As a result, they may end up with a solution that users find much more attractive. Accepting a solution as a requirement limits

**Figure 4.2**
**Partial Execution of the Universal Strategy Formulation Model**

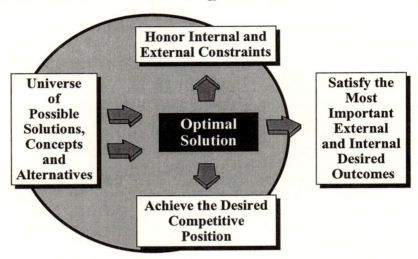

the chances of formulating a breakthrough strategy or solution. As a result, a sub-optimal solution is likely.

If many solutions are entered into the strategy formulation or planning process as desired outcomes, the problem becomes magnified. The potential solution becomes highly constrained. These constraints are often strongly debated, because they prevent the consideration of other solutions. This often leads to the debate, negotiation and compromise that are part of most strategy formulation and planning processes. People disagree over solutions, because their basis for agreement, desired outcomes, is missing. As a result, they become defensive and combative, following the patterns associated with Solution-Based Logic. Our experiences in many *Fortune* 500 companies indicate that this pattern is typically followed when organizations take part in strategy formulation activities.

When this occurs, strategies and solutions are evaluated for their ability to meet constraints and to achieve what can only be a poorly defined competitive position. This is only a partial execution of the USFM and results in less than optimal solutions. This partial execution of the USFM is illustrated in Figure 4.2.

Focus is often maintained only on how well the alternative solutions honor constraints and enable the achievement of the desired competitive position. As a result of executing a strategy formulation process without effectively considering the customers' desired outcomes, the degree to which the proposed strategies and solutions satisfy those outcomes cannot be determined.

It is important to remember that to effectively execute the USFM, one must uncover the customers' desired outcomes and place them, as constants, on the right side of the equation

Solutions that are captured from customers, or anybody else, must be placed on the left side of the equation and treated as variables. After all, the objective is to create or find solutions that will satisfy desired outcomes. An organization must understand the customers' desired outcomes before it can formulate strategies and solutions that will effectively satisfy those outcomes. Without desired outcomes, an organization is lacking the most important criteria by which to evaluate the potential of a proposed strategy or solution.

It may be obvious that the partial execution of this model will not produce the optimal solution. Despite this fact, many organizations attempt to formulate strategies and solutions without having a clear knowledge of the desired outcomes to be achieved. They often fail to discriminate between solutions and desired outcomes and rarely know what types of information to capture from customers.

Ask yourself, do you typically have a clear knowledge of the desired outcomes that are to be achieved when contemplating strategies, plans and complex decisions? Analyze your personal experiences gathering requirements. Have you ever attempted to capture requirements? What types of information were you trying to capture? Did you end up with solutions? Did you discriminate between solutions and desired outcomes? You may be thinking, "This subtle difference seems so trivial; how could this inability to discriminate between solutions and desired outcomes be the cause of such inefficiency in formulating strategies and solutions?"

If you cannot get the customers' desired outcomes from the customer, then you are forced to use the information they give you (solutions) as a basis for decision making. This makes it difficult, or impossible, to define the criteria by which to create and evaluate solutions and limits the possibility of creating the optimal solution. It forces and supports the use of Solution-Based Logic. It forces people to be defensive and argue about solutions.

Since most people intuitively use Solution-Based Logic, it is difficult for many to see the difference between using solutions and desired outcomes when contemplating strategies, plans and decisions. A focus on desired outcomes is counter-intuitive. Many well-known academics and strategists fail to discriminate between desired outcomes and solutions when discussing their theories on strategy formulation. For example, in Adrian Slywotzky's book titled *Value Migration* (1996), customer requirements are defined as "the benefits and features of products that customers would like to buy." We now know that benefits are synonymous with desired outcomes and that features are synonymous with solutions. Customer requirements then, as defined in *Value Migration*, include

**Table 4.1**
**Differences Between Solutions and Desired Outcomes**

| Solutions | Desired Outcomes |
|---|---|
| Change quickly over time | Stable over time |
| Technology dependent | Independent of technology |
| A means to deliver value | Describe an element of value that is desired |
| A physical or tangible item | A statement of benefit |
| Describe *how* to satisfy desired outcomes | Describe a benefit that a solution is to provide |

both desired outcomes and solutions—no discrimination is made between the two. Many people make the same mistake.

Consider the model that was created by Dr. Noriaki Kano, a professor at Tokyo Rika University. Dr. Kano developed the Model of Quality, which has become well accepted among product development consultants and individuals who utilize and teach Quality Function Deployment or QFD. Dr. Kano presented a paper titled "Attractive Quality and Must-Be Quality" at the 12th Annual Nippon Quality Conference in 1982. In this paper, Dr. Kano explained how customer requirements all become basic expectations over time as the initially unknown requirements, solutions, become requested by customers and eventually expected by customers as all competitors offer the same solutions or features. This model clearly shows that Dr. Kano refers to customer requirements as solutions. In fact, this model is built around the fact that customers talk about requirements in the form of solutions. The use of this model has made it difficult for those who use QFD to apply it effectively as a product planning process.

As a third example, in his book *Managing Customer Value* (1994), Bradley Gale shows how he aligns his "attribute life cycle stages" to the Kano Model. He shows that requirements are "attributes"—features or solutions—with a life cycle that begins with a latent attribute and ends with a basic attribute, following a similar model as Kano. He, like Kano, assumes that customer requirements are solutions. He too does not discriminate between solutions and desired outcomes when talking about customer requirements.

This lack of discrimination is common, even though the roles of solutions and desired outcomes in the strategy formulation process are distinctly different. A clear distinction is essential to effectively formulate a breakthrough strategy or solution. Several characteristics that help to discriminate between solutions and desired outcomes are listed in Table 4.1.

Solutions and desired outcomes are two distinctly different pieces of information. Recognizing the difference may require a transformation in logic. They must both be captured and classified appropriately to successfully formulate breakthrough strategies and solutions.

## ACCEPTING VAGUE STATEMENTS AS REQUIREMENTS

When asked for their requirements, individuals often respond with vague words or statements that can be interpreted in different ways by different people. As stated earlier, when asked for their requirements, individuals will respond with vague words or statements between 20% and 30% of the time.

Why do individuals state their requirements in the form of vague words or statements? It may be because they are trying to summarize their actual desired outcomes. As an example, when stating their requirements on a packaging design, rather than saying, "I want to minimize the effort required to locate the opening mechanism," or "I want to reduce the force required to open the package," an individual may say "I want the package to be easy to open." Easy is a commonly used word that creates a vague statement.

Treating a vague word or statement as a desired outcome and using it to execute a strategy formulation or planning process will inhibit the creation of the optimal solution.

As an example, assume that an organization accepted the statement, "I want the package to be easy to open," as a desired outcome. When this statement is passed along to the design team, the debate will begin—"what do they mean by easy to open?"

They could debate amongst themselves as to what this means, interpret it in their own way, and implement a solution that will enable the user to hold the package steady while they open it. This implemented solution may make the package easier to open, but it would not satisfy the two desired outcomes that were stated above. If the actual desired outcomes are not known, they are certainly less likely to be satisfied.

To eliminate this problem, vague words must not be accepted in the description of a desired outcome. In one consulting project, 20 separate desired outcomes were captured, all describing different aspects of what it would take to make a specific product easy to use.

Other words and statements that are considered vague include:

| | | | |
|---|---|---|---|
| Reliable | Comfortable | Durable | Technology |
| High-quality | Cost-effective | Advanced | Efficient |

Each of these terms and statements mean different things to different people. Accepting vague statements as requirements will lead to confusion, inefficiency and possibly failure as, once again, the customers' actual desired outcomes are left uncovered.

A well-stated requirement must be free from words that have more than one meaning. Words that have different meanings in different situations or environments must be avoided. If a customer states they want a product to be reliable, their definition of reliable must be understood. Reliable may mean a product should operate in extreme ranges of temperature. It may mean a product should operate, without failure, throughout its product life. It may have dozens of other meanings. The meaning intended by the customer must be captured without ambiguity.

As a result of capturing mostly solutions and vague statements, many organizations formulate their strategies and solutions with little knowledge of their customers' actual desired outcomes. What kind of result would you expect to get from a strategy formulation or planning process if up to 90% of the customers desired outcomes were not properly captured or considered? You could only expect to formulate strategies and solutions that satisfy between 5% and 15% of the targeted desired outcomes better than the solution they are looking to replace. It is no coincidence that this is what typically happens. This is the amount of incremental value typically created by strategies and solutions derived through the use of traditional strategy formulation and planning methods.

The processes used by organizations to capture requirements must ensure that solutions and vague statements are eliminated from requirements as they are transformed into desired outcomes. This creates a foundation from which breakthrough solutions can be discovered.

## ACCEPTING DESIRED OUTCOMES AS REQUIREMENTS

In addition to responding with solutions and vague statements, when asked for their requirements, individuals do respond with desired outcomes about 10% of the time. A desired outcome is a statement made by an individual involved in, or affected by, a strategy, plan or decision that describes an important benefit they would like to receive from the strategy, plan or decision that is being contemplated.

To ensure that each desired outcome is entered into the equation as a constant, it must meet several unique criteria. Each desired outcome must be:

1. Free from solutions or any references to technology or time-dependent solutions.
2. Free from specifications such as numbers or colors.
3. Free from vague words that could make the outcome ambiguous.
4. Stable over time, meaning it had to have been desired in the past, it must be desired today and it must be desired in the future.
5. Defined in a statement that includes what is desired.
6. Capable of being measured to ensure its satisfaction has been achieved.

A specialized requirements gathering process is used to capture desired outcomes that meet this criteria. This process, which we created as we evolved this advanced strategy formulation process, eliminates many of the problems and inefficiencies associated with traditional requirements gathering methods. This method is described in Appendix A.

**Table 4.2**
**Differences Between Solutions and Desired Outcomes for a Data Processing Device**

| Solution | Desired Outcome on a Data Processing Device |
|---|---|
| Hot-swap card | Allow dynamic changes to be made to the device without interrupting its operation. |
| Tape back-up device | Minimize the time it takes to protect against the loss of data. |
| Internal modem | Minimize the time it takes to access data that is stored in a remote location. |
| Data encryption | Prevent unauthorized access to data during a data transmission. |
| High-speed hard disk | Minimize the time it takes to retrieve archived data. |

To capture desired outcomes, one must be able to discriminate between a desired outcome and a solution. This is not as easy as it sounds. In fact, this difficulty, as mentioned earlier, is the root cause of many problems encountered by organizations when they attempt to execute their strategy formulation and planning processes. Capturing desired outcomes in the format stated above is essential to the formulation of breakthrough strategies and solutions. Let's look at a couple of examples that show the format in which desired outcomes should be captured.

We mentioned earlier that a major computer manufacturer attempted to capture customer requirements on a specialized computing device and ended up with a list of solutions. They had subsequently asked us to obtain requirements from a similar customer sample. We focused on capturing desired outcomes, not solutions. We captured approximately 40 desired outcomes in total using the techniques described in Appendix A. The desired outcomes corresponding to five of the initially stated solutions were included in the outcomes that we captured. Both the initial solutions that were captured by employees and the external consultant and the corresponding desired outcomes that we captured are shown in Table 4.2.

Note the differences between the desired outcomes and solutions. It is important to recognize that a high-speed disk, for example, is only one way to minimize the time it takes to retrieve archived data. Solutions are a means to satisfy a desired outcome at a point in time. A solution's value is dependent on the degree to which it satisfies one or more desired outcomes. Solutions are focused on technology, desired outcomes are focused on what it is the customer wants to achieve.

To clarify several other points regarding the collection of desired outcomes, let's pretend that it is 1975 and you are avid users of music media, or records as they were called. As you take yourself back to that unforgettable time period, pretend that I was hired by a music media manufacturer to capture your requirements on music media. Think about the types of statements that you would respond with once I began asking you for your requirements. As I began the

**Table 4.3**
**Differences Between Solutions and Desired Outcomes for Music Media**

| Requested Solution: I want ... | Desired Outcomes on Music Media |
| --- | --- |
| A larger record that will hold more songs | Provide access to a large number of songs |
| A thicker record that will not warp | Play without distortion over time |
| A harder material that will prevent scratches | Resist damage during normal use |
| The record to fit in my record case | Require minimal storage space |
| Stereo sound | Reproduce the music experience as if it were live |

interview, you probably would have made statements like, ''I want a larger record that will hold more songs,'' or ''I want a thicker record that won't warp over time.'' Let's assume that I captured the first five statements that you made, all of which included or implied solutions. Knowing that I could not accept solutions as requirements, I also used the methods we created to transform these statements into desired outcomes. After some additional questioning, you provided me with not only the list of five initially proposed solutions, but also with a list of five desired outcomes that corresponded to those solutions. The captured solutions and desired outcomes are shown in Table 4.3.

Notice that the statements on the left reflect what may have been requested initially, and the statements on the right reflect the actual desired outcomes that you were likely trying to achieve. For example, you may have initially said, ''I want a larger record that will hold more songs,'' but it is likely that you wanted music media that would provide access to a large number of songs. You may have said, ''I want a thicker record that won't warp over time,'' but it is likely that you wanted music media that would play without distortion over time. You may have said, ''I want stereo sound,'' but it is likely that you wanted music media that would reproduce the music experience as if it were live.

Notice that the statements on the right, the desired outcomes, are stable over time. They are valid today, they were valid in 1975, and they will be valid into the future. Notice that the items on the left—solutions—are far less applicable today than they were in 1975.

What if the statements on the left were accepted as the customers' requirements and used by the music media manufacturer to formulate their product strategies? If an organization made a larger or thicker record as their customers had asked for, where would they be today? They would be out of business. They would have ignored technologies such as the compact disc that promised to deliver more value—technologies that ultimately proved to deliver vastly improved versions of music media. Organizations that are focused on solutions often miss major market opportunities and become the dinosaurs of the industry.

Let's quickly review what we have covered. Thus far, we have described several important factors surrounding the concept of requirements gathering and desired outcomes. We have identified that many organizations:

1. Do not seek to capture specific types of information from customers and use whatever information they get to assist in their strategy formulation processes.
2. Fail to discriminate between desired outcomes and solutions.
3. Knowingly or unknowingly accept solutions as requirements.
4. Fail to formulate breakthrough strategies and solutions.

We have also demonstrated that:

1. Desired outcomes are one of the essential elements of strategy formulation.
2. Solutions and desired outcomes play distinctly different roles in the execution of an effective strategy formulation process.
3. Desired outcomes can be captured from individuals once the extraction of desired outcomes becomes a priority.

There may be several other important questions on your mind that have not yet been addressed. For example, you may be wondering, when gathering requirements, how do you know you have captured all the desired outcomes? Or do new desired outcomes come about over time? Because solutions are not finite in number and new solutions can become available over time, many individuals assume that desired outcomes have the same characteristics, but they do not. Although these questions are addressed in more detail in Appendix A, it is important to point out one very important discovery that we made regarding the practice of gathering desired outcomes.

> We found that there are a finite number of desired outcomes on any subject and that, statistically speaking, over 96% of those desired outcomes can be captured using the techniques described in Appendix A.

This discovery is important in that we can be certain that we know today virtually all the desired outcomes that will potentially be considered important in the future. This fact sets the stage for other important discoveries that will be introduced as we continue to build the future of strategy formulation.

## REQUIREMENTS-GATHERING MYTHS

There is a good chance that you have heard a co-worker or a manager make one of the following two statements. We have heard these statements hundreds, if not thousands, of times in small, medium and large businesses across dozens of industries around the world. Many individuals across all levels of management believe that:

1. Customers do not know what they want, and/or
2. Customer requirements change quickly over time.

It has been established that when most organizations are gathering requirements, they are actually gathering solutions, not desired outcomes. People who
believe these statements to be true routinely accept solutions as requirements.
Because we recognize the importance of discriminating between solutions and
desired outcomes when formulating strategies, we have been able to disprove
these two myths surrounding customers and their requirements.

### Myth 1: "Customers Do Not Know What They Want"

This myth is perpetuated by articles such as the one published in the May 1,
1995 issue of *Fortune* which is titled, "Ignore Your Customers." In this article,
Justin Martin states that listening to customers can "actually lead you astray. It
may cause you to create new offerings that are safe and bland." He goes on to
say, "Customers can be wildly un-imaginative. The roster of items that met
with initial customer naysaying—fax machines, VCR's, Federal Express and
CNN, to name a few—reads more like a hall of fame of business innovation."
He suggests that you should, "Ignore your customers. They will thank you for
it in the end."

As Justin Martin suggests, organizations that provide solutions suggested by
their customers often do find themselves chasing the competition. Solutions suggested by customers tend to be technologically challenged, as customers can
only request solutions of which they are aware. They may not be aware of
emerging technologies and pending breakthroughs. This, however, is not because customers do not know *what* they want. It is because they may not know
*how to best achieve* what they want.

Customers may not be able to identify a breakthrough technology or know
which solution will be optimal, but why should they? This is not their responsibility. Most customers are not technologists, engineers or strategists. The best
solutions often lie in the creative minds of company employees and other trained
experts. Placing the responsibility of creating new solutions and strategies in the
hands of the customer is a risky proposition. Soliciting and accepting their solutions as requirements, in essence, puts this responsibility in their hands. Just
imagine, by accepting solutions as requirements, many companies may be relying on the inputs of untrained, unqualified individuals—customers—to shape
their company's future.

In spite of their inability to effectively perform their externally imposed roles
as designers, engineers and strategists, customers do know, with certainty, what
desired outcomes they want to achieve. They may not know they want a microwave oven, especially if they don't even know what a microwave is. They
do know, however, that they want to minimize the time it takes to prepare a
meal and reduce the number of pans, plates, and utensils that must be cleaned
after a meal is prepared. They may not know they want a fax machine, especially
if they are not sure what a fax machine can do. They do know that they want
to minimize the time it takes to send important documents to other locations

and minimize the time required to receive important documents from other locations.

Customers do know what desired outcomes they want to achieve. We have confirmed this fact time and time again as we have captured desired outcomes on composite materials, medical devices, aircraft instrumentation, switching equipment, portable radios, mobile radios, pacing systems, consumer products, water filtration equipment, storage devices, banking services, technology centers, energy sources, mailing systems, surgical systems and other products and services that individuals use or desire to use. We have captured desired outcomes on improving the product development, manufacturing and ordering processes and on formulating distribution, pricing and marketing strategies. Generally speaking, from external customers, we have collected desired outcomes on dozens of companies, products and services, and from internal customers we have captured desired outcomes on many operating, support and management processes.

Since 1991, we have conducted over 1,000 interviews involving these and other subject matters. Each of these interviews has produced the customers' desired outcomes. It is the responsibility of the organization to capture their customers' desired outcomes and then let their engineers, technologists, strategists and management determine which solutions will best satisfy those desired outcomes. After all, the trained experts will more likely come up with a breakthrough solution.

Customers may not know what solutions they want, but they do know what desired outcomes they want to achieve. Creating the solutions that satisfy the customers' desired outcomes is the responsibility of those who are attempting to create value.

### Myth 2: "Customer Requirements Change Quickly Over Time"

Solutions—not desired outcomes—change quickly over time as new technologies and processes are developed and commercialized. In some industries, such as computers and communications, technology is moving so fast that new solutions are available every few months.

Desired outcomes, on the other hand, are stable over time. This stability is a fundamental characteristic of a desired outcome. A desired outcome, in its proper format, was desired 10 years ago, is desired today, and will be desired 10 years from now. For example, as long as music media has been around, individuals have wanted music media that would:

1. Provide access to a large number of songs.

2. Play without distortion over time.

3. Resist damage during normal use.

**Table 4.4**
**Satisfying Stable Outcomes over Time**

| Desired Outcome: Quickly communicate with others that are in a different physical location. ||
|---|---|
| 1820 Solution | The horse and buggy |
| 1860 Solution | The telegraph |
| 1930 Solution | The telephone |
| 1985 Solution | The cellular phone |
| 1995 Solution | The internet |
| 1999 Solution | Satellite communications |

4. Require minimal storage space.

5. Reproduce the music experience as if it were live.

Were these desired outcomes on music media valid 20 years ago? Are they valid today? Will they be valid for the foreseeable future? These have been, and will continue to be, desired outcomes on music media; they are stable over time. What does change over time is the level of importance that individuals place on each outcome and the degree to which the outcome is perceived to be satisfied. The methods used to determine which desired outcomes are most important are described in Appendix A.

As another example, Table 4.4 illustrates how solutions that satisfy an individual's desire to "quickly communicate with others that are in a different physical location" have changed over time. Notice that the desired outcome has remained the same, but the solutions have changed over time as new technologies have been developed and introduced.

As a third example, shown in Table 4.5, notice how solutions that satisfy an individual's desire to "participate in a business meeting in a distant location" have changed over time. Again, the desired outcome has remained the same, but the solutions have changed over time as new technologies have been developed.

As a result of studying the requirements gathering process, we have discovered and verified that solutions change over time and that desired outcomes are stable over time; in fact, they are stable over many years, even decades. The ramifications of this reality are far reaching. For example, when using the USFM with desired outcomes that are stable over time, an organization has the means

**Table 4.5**
**Satisfying Stable Outcomes over Time**

| Desired Outcome: Participate in a business meeting in a distant location. | |
|---|---|
| 1820 Solution | The horse and buggy |
| 1860 Solution | The train |
| 1920 Solution | The automobile |
| 1950 Solution | The prop-plane |
| 1975 Solution | The jet |
| 1999 Solution | Video conferencing |

to know today which strategies and solutions will deliver the most value in the future. As you will see, this is an important discovery, as this mechanism not only enables an organization to accurately predict the potential of alternative strategies and solutions, but it also ensures that they will select and pursue only those strategies and solutions that deliver breakthrough results.

## TRANSFORMING THE PROCESS OF STRATEGY FORMULATION WITH DESIRED OUTCOMES

Let's review the characteristics of desired outcomes and the role that desired outcomes play in the process of strategy formulation.

1. By definition, desired outcomes are statements that describe what outcomes customers want to achieve given a specified situation or mission. The mission may relate to formulating a company strategy, a product or service strategy or strategies that are designed to improve a company's operating, support or management processes.

2. Desired outcomes are free from solutions, specifications and vague statements.

3. Desired outcomes are stable over time. They describe the customers' perception of value in the past, now and in the future.

4. The desired outcomes for a given situation or mission can be captured from external and internal customers who are involved in or affected by that mission.

5. A set of desired outcomes, properly captured, will include over 96% of all the outcomes that are desired by the customers affected by the mission. This finite number of desired outcomes often falls between 50 and 300 outcomes for a given mission

with 25 to 50 desired outcomes coming from each customer type that is considered in the mission.

The role that desired outcomes play in the process of strategy formulation will be fully explained throughout the remainder of this book. However, it is important to get a glimpse of that role, even though we have not fully defined the foundation upon which that role is built. For now, just imagine each of the following statements are true, and consider the ramifications that these truths may have on your ability to create breakthrough strategies and solutions.

1. Once desired outcomes are captured for a specific mission, they form a universal set of 50 to 300 desired outcomes. This means, for example, that all surgeons share the same set of desired outcomes on improving the process of surgery, and all designers share the same set of desired outcomes on the process of product development.

2. Although individuals involved in a specific mission may share a universal set of desired outcomes, many individuals will differ in the importance they place on each desired outcome and the degree to which they perceive each outcome to be satisfied. In other words, different desired outcomes are more important to some individuals than to others, and their levels of satisfaction differ as well. This is what makes every situation different and explains why one solution will not fit all situations.

3. Opportunity can be discovered by quantifying which desired outcomes are most important and least satisfied to an individual, group of individuals or a total population. This can be accomplished using statistically valid market research.

4. Value can be created by formulating and providing solutions that increase an individual's perceived level of satisfaction on one or more desired outcomes.

5. The degree to which desired outcomes are satisfied will change over time as new ideas and solutions are formulated and implemented.

6. Since desired outcomes are stable over time, it is possible to know today which desired outcomes people will value in the future. As an example, "preventing the injury of healthy tissue" has been a desired outcome on the process of surgery since surgery was invented. This desired outcome will continue to be a desired outcome on the process of surgery well into the future.

7. Knowing the customer's future desired outcomes makes it possible to determine today which ideas, strategies and solutions will be valued in the future. This determination can be made in advance of the actual development or implementation of a proposed idea, strategy or solution.

With this knowledge, an organization is able to focus its resources on only the activities that it knows will successfully create value for the organization and its customers. An organization can eliminate its participation in non-value producing activities. It can anticipate future opportunities and start today to prepare to deliver the optimal solutions of the future.

Think of the impact that the use of desired outcomes can have on your company's strategy formulation, planning and decision-making activities. How could this knowledge impact your company's ability to create value for the organization and others? How would this impact your ability to grow your business, increase your profits and reduce your expenses? The ramifications of being able to capture and use desired outcomes as you execute the USFM are dramatic and far-reaching.

With the use of desired outcomes, it is possible to know today how much value a particular solution will deliver in the future. This makes it possible for an organization to anticipate future opportunities and to make the trade-off and investment decisions that will strengthen its future strategic position.

Desired outcomes are one of the essential elements of strategy formulation. They are integral to the formulation of breakthrough strategies and solutions. They define the customers perception of value. They form the basis for creating customer-driven strategies. And as you will see, they provide a foundation from which an organization can define its desired competitive position.

In spite of their importance, organizations typically exclude up to 90% of the relevant desired outcomes from their strategy formulation and planning processes. They are often unknowingly supplanted with solutions. This is one of the main reasons that organizations fail to consistently create breakthrough strategies and solutions. It is the root cause of inefficiency in most strategy formulation processes. Before this can change, an organization must know how to discriminate between desired outcomes and solutions. They must possess the skills that are required to capture desired outcomes that are both free from solutions and stable over time. The organizations that possess this skill will undoubtedly enjoy a competitive advantage. Without this information, organizations will likely fail in their efforts to create breakthrough strategies and solutions.

## SUMMARY

Organizations have long recognized the importance of understanding what their customers value. As the USFM illustrates, successful organizations understand what their customers value, because they are capable of uncovering their customers' desired outcomes. They are subsequently effective at finding the solutions that best satisfy those desired outcomes.

Many companies, however, have not mastered the techniques that are required to capture their customers' desired outcomes. What many organizations do not realize is that customers unintentionally make it difficult for anyone to capture their desired outcomes. When asked for requirements, customers will respond with solutions between 60% and 80% of the time. They will respond with vague statements between 20% and 30% of the time, and they will respond with desired outcomes less than 10% of the time. This fact is the root cause of failure in many strategy formulation and planning processes around the world today.

The problem arises when organizations accept solutions as requirements rather than desired outcomes. Quite often the people who are responsible for capturing the customers' requirements do not know what types of information they should be looking for and routinely accept any information that describes what a customer wants or needs. Many requirements gathering sessions are not initiated with the intent of capturing desired outcomes. In fact, many organizations engage in conversation with a customer without knowing the difference between desired outcomes and solutions. As a result, the individuals involved in the process—often driven by Solution-Based Logic—instinctively talk about what comes naturally, solutions.

In the end, the organization ends up with a list of requirements in the form of solutions, and desired outcomes are often left out of the strategy formulation process altogether. This series of events drives the dynamics that are associated with the application of Solution-Based Logic. It results in the ineffective execution of the USFM and often precludes the formulation of breakthrough strategies and solutions.

Desired outcomes play an important role in the science of strategy formulation. The ability to capture desired outcomes is a prerequisite for the successful execution of the USFM. The methods that are required to capture desired outcomes have been created. Organizations must be able to recognize the importance of capturing desired outcomes and must be able to distinguish between desired outcomes and solutions before the methods can be mastered.

Once an organization can distinguish between desired outcomes and solutions, it will recognize that only organizations that accept solutions as requirements believe that customers do not know what they want and that requirements change quickly over time. Disproving these myths has played an important role in evolving the process of strategy formulation. Customers do know what they want and can express what they want in the form of desired outcomes. Their desired outcomes describe their perception of value. Desired outcomes, unlike solutions, are stable over time and can be treated as constants in the USFM. This stability lends itself to the systematic formulation of breakthrough strategies and solutions.

Using statistical principles we have proven that it is possible to capture over 96% of all the desired outcomes that exist on a specific subject of interest. Customers typically express between 25 and 50 desired outcomes on any subject related to the formulation of a company strategy, a product or service strategy or a strategy that drives an organization's operating, support or management processes. We have discovered that when all the desired outcomes have been captured on a specific subject, they form a universal set of desired outcomes, meaning they are the same desired outcomes that all individuals in that customer group—not just those interviewed—have on that subject of interest. What differs from person to person is the importance they place on achieving each desired outcome and the degree to which they perceive each desired outcome to be satisfied. These differences, as we will see, determine which solution will best deliver value in each unique situation.

Once we discovered the USFM, we set out to create and master the methods that would enable an organization to collect the information that is essential to the formulation of breakthrough strategies. We have demonstrated that the methods required to capture desired outcomes have been created and mastered. We will now set out to demonstrate how we use desired outcomes, combined with a thinking process called predictive logic, to form the basis for an advanced approach to competitive positioning.

Chapter 5

# Defining the Desired
# Competitive Position

In his article titled "What Is Strategy?" (1996), Michael Porter states that, "Strategy is the creation of a unique and valued competitive position." He and other experts in the field of strategy formulation agree that an effective strategy, a breakthrough strategy, must enable an organization to achieve both a unique and valued competitive position.

The Universal Strategy Formulation Model (USFM) includes the four essential elements of strategy formulation: desired outcomes, constraints, the desired competitive position and solutions. We have established that desired outcomes can be obtained from customers and that the methods required to capture them have been created. We have established that constraints, which often result from time, resource or capital limitations, can be imposed on a strategy or solution by the organization itself or by a third party. Solutions, as we have learned, come from many sources including customers, employees, managers, consultants, technologists and others. We now know how to obtain each of these essential elements of strategy formulation, but one question remains, how do we obtain the information that is needed to define the desired competitive position?

Before we begin to explain how this information is captured, let's define what we mean by the desired competitive position. We define the desired competitive position as a unique and valued position that an organization desires to achieve relative to its competitors. The organization's desired competitive position should be unique in that it should be different from the competitive position that is occupied by other organizations. It should be valued in that it should deliver value to the internal and external customers for whom the strategy is being devised.

As we applied pattern detection techniques to the process of strategy formulation, we found that breakthrough strategies and solutions invariably resulted

in the achievement of a unique and valued competitive position. We also made
one other important discovery.

> We discovered that the consistent formulation of breakthrough strategies
> and solutions is dependent on an organization knowing, in advance, what
> competitive position it wants to achieve and then being able to successfully
> find the strategy or solution that will enable it to achieve that desired
> position. This discovery is consistent with the concept of Outcome-Based
> Logic.

When executing the USFM, the objective is to define the competitive position
the organization wants to occupy and then set out to find the strategy or solution
that will enable it to occupy that position. The position that the organization
chooses to occupy should be unique from other competitors, and it should deliver value to the organization and its customers.

Many organizations have not yet made this realization and continue to use
traditional approaches when defining the competitive position they want to
achieve. Because many organizations instinctively apply Solution-Based Logic,
the first step they typically take when defining the desired competitive position
is to select the strategy or solution they are going to pursue. Then, after the
strategy or solution is selected, they attempt to determine what competitive position they want the strategy or solution to enable them to achieve. This approach
to competitive positioning is reactive, it is an attempt to position something that
already exists. It is too late to proactively determine the desired competitive
position. In actuality, the competitive position that will be occupied is determined when the strategy or solution is selected. The chosen solution effectively
determines what competitive position the organization is going to occupy,
whether it wants to occupy that position or not.

Because the competitive position is often considered after the strategy or
solution is selected, organizations are typically forced to position a strategy or
solution that has already been chosen. They do not have the option of modifying
the solution in an attempt to occupy the position they desire. When using this
approach, organizations will likely end up occupying a competitive position that
is neither unique nor valued. As a result, many organizations are forced to spend
time and money marketing and advertising the strategies and solutions they have
chosen in hopes of changing the customer's perception of value, just so they
can attempt to occupy the competitive position they desire. Many organizations
and academics refer to this common practice as positioning.

In their book titled *Positioning: The Battle for Your Mind* (1993) Al Ries and
Jack Trout state, "Positioning is what you do to the mind of the prospect. That
is, you position the product in the mind of the prospect." It is much simpler to
position a company, product or service in the mind of the customer if the company, product or service satisfies the customers' important desired outcomes. If
a strategy or solution does not satisfy important desired outcomes, then an

organization certainly cannot expect to occupy the optimal competitive position, no matter what it tells its customers.

As we will demonstrate, a reactive approach to competitive positioning is rarely effective. A successful organization must decide what competitive position it wants to achieve and then find the strategy or solution that will enable it to achieve that position. In this chapter, we will describe how an organization can effectively define what competitive position it wants to achieve.

First, we will introduce a measurement system that redefines how an organization should measure the satisfaction of desired outcomes. We will describe how we leverage the synergy between desired outcomes to effectively prioritize what criteria should be used to define the desired competitive position. We will demonstrate how the desired competitive position is tied to the satisfaction of the customers' desired outcomes. We will explain how an organization can consistently choose a competitive position that is both unique and valued before it sets out to formulate the strategy or solution that will enable it to achieve that competitive position.

## MEASUREMENT SYSTEMS

The success of a strategy or solution is often quantified by measuring a specific set of criteria or parameters after the strategy or solution has been executed or implemented. As a result of measuring these parameters, an organization can obtain the information that is required to determine the level of success that was achieved as a result of introducing that particular strategy or solution.

Measurements of this type often give a precise account as to how well a specific strategy or solution has performed. Examples of measurements taken after a strategy or solution has been introduced include:

1. Return on investment measurements.
2. Revenue measurements.
3. Market share measurements.
4. Quarterly earnings measurements.
5. Customer satisfaction measurements.

Financial measurements indicate the impact that a strategy or solution has had on the organization's bottom line over a period of time. Customer satisfaction studies often quantify a customer's perceived level of satisfaction with the products and services that are offered by the organization. The data resulting from financial and customer satisfaction measurements provides an organization with an indication as to how well it has satisfied the desired outcomes of its internal and external customers.

Unfortunately, the information resulting from financial and customer satisfaction measurements does not enable an organization to predict how a specific strategy or solution will perform over the next measurement period. It is a measure of what has happened, not what will happen. Using these measurements to measure past success is logical. Using these measurements to determine if a specific strategy or solution is going to generate value in the future is very unreliable and risky as they are after-the-event measurements.

Despite this fact, organizations often use information resulting from after-the-event measurements to plan their future. In their book titled *Outcome Management* (1995), C. Dan McArthur and Larry Womack agree that, ''Most companies still use past performance to measure success and to plan for the future. Some have become more sophisticated and use current performance as the measure of success and the basis of planning.'' Ask yourself, what types of measurements are taken and used within your organization to plan your company's future? What types of information are used when your organization is defining the competitive position it wants to occupy?

It is common to take measurements that answer the question, ''How did we do?'' It is often considered counter-intuitive to take measurements that answer the questions, ''How is this strategy or solution going to perform once it is introduced?'' Or, ''To what degree is this strategy or solution going to enable us to achieve our desired competitive position?'' To determine how a strategy or solution is going to perform before it is introduced, measurements must be taken prior to the actual implementation. We must know—in advance—what desired outcomes are going to be satisfied and the degree to which they are going to be satisfied by the proposed strategy or solution. We must know the degree to which that satisfaction will result in the achievement of the desired competitive position. Achieving these objectives requires the application of a different kind of logic.

## PREDICTIVE LOGIC

Predictive logic is characterized by thinking about what can be done now to ensure, or predict, that a desired outcome will be better satisfied by a strategy or solution in the future. Predictive logic requires an organization to think about the impact that its actions will have on the satisfaction of the customers' desired outcomes in the future. It also requires an organization to think about the degree to which it must satisfy the customers' desired outcomes to achieve its desired competitive position. In addition, predictive logic requires that an organization measure—before a strategy or solution is introduced—the parameters that predict the amount of value that a proposed strategy or solution will create. This requires a before-the-event measurement.

The difference between a before-the-event measurement and an after-the-event measurement is shown in Figure 5.1. It should be noted that an event is defined as the introduction of a specific strategy or solution.

When creating a before-the-event measurement, an organization must think about what can be measured now to ensure, or predict, that a desired outcome

**Figure 5.1**
**Before-the-Event vs. After-the-Event Measurements**

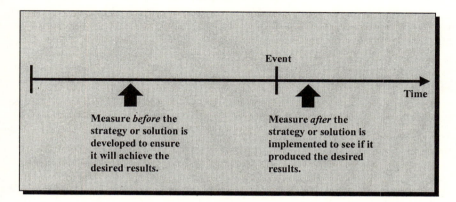

will be better satisfied in the future. For example, if the number of time consuming steps that exist in a manufacturing process are reduced, then that predicts that items can be manufactured more quickly in the future. If entry into a market segment requires a large initial investment, then that predicts that few competitors will be competing in that market. If the number of steps that are required to operate a piece of software are reduced, then that predicts the software can be operated with less effort. If the size of a device is reduced, then that predicts it will take up less space. If a strategy or solution satisfies a large number of important desired outcomes, then that predicts the strategy or solution will create customer value.

So, what is the advantage of using predictive logic? It enables an organization to define, in advance of introducing a strategy or solution, the criteria that are to be used as the basis for measuring the potential success of a strategy or solution. As a result, the use of predictive logic enables an organization to answer the question, "How is this strategy, solution, product, service or investment going to perform?" After all, if an organization can measure the parameters that predict the success of a proposed strategy or solution, they can then evaluate the likely success of their proposed strategies and solutions before they are introduced. In fact, they can evaluate the potential success of their proposed strategies and solutions before they are even developed. The question was posed earlier:

"If a solution can be classified as a failure after it is introduced or implemented, what is preventing an organization from knowing it is going to fail in advance of its introduction?" What criteria will be used to judge the success or failure of the strategy or solution after it is introduced? If that criteria were known in advance, and used to evaluate the potential of the concept to begin with, could its eventual failure be predicted in advance? Could the failure be avoided altogether?

We now know that desired outcomes, constraints and the desired competitive position define the criteria that are used to evaluate whether or not a breakthrough strategy or solution has been created. We can obtain, before a strategy or solution is generated, the desired outcomes that customers want to achieve. The customer's desired outcomes define how they will measure the success of a strategy or solution once it is introduced. We can obtain, before solutions are generated, the constraints that any proposed strategy or solution must honor. Also, as you will see, we can obtain the information that defines an organization's desired competitive position—before the first solution is generated.

Since this information can be made available before a strategy or solution is conceived, it can be used as the basis by which to measure the potential value of any proposed strategy or solution. It can be used to measure what outcomes will be satisfied and the degree to which they will be satisfied. It can be used to formulate a breakthrough strategy or solution. This is the philosophy behind Outcome-Based Logic.

The objective then, once the criteria are captured for a specific mission, is to determine which strategies and solutions, from the universe of possible solutions, will create the most value for the organization and its customers in the future. That determination can be made well before the first development activity is taken or investment dollar is spent, ensuring that an organization will not waste its time and resources pursuing activities that involve suboptimal strategies and solutions. As a result, an organization can ensure its activities are focused only on the strategies and solutions that will create the most value for the organization and its customers.

To enable an organization to quantify the degree to which a strategy or solution will deliver value, we have created a unique before-the-event measurement. This parameter is called a predictive metric.

## PREDICTIVE METRICS

A predictive metric is a parameter that when measured and controlled will predict the satisfaction of a desired outcome. A predictive metric is a before-the-event measurement. It states the parameter that must be measured and controlled, prior to the implementation of a strategy or solution, to predict if a desired outcome will be satisfied and to determine the degree to which it will be satisfied. Defining and using a predictive metric is often perceived as counter intuitive as it requires individuals to think in the future.

A predictive metric is a unique piece of information that is essential to the successful execution of the USFM. When executing this model, a single predictive metric is defined for each desired outcome. The metric must have a strong predictive relationship with that outcome. In other words, it must predict the satisfaction of that outcome. If the desired outcome contains a measurable parameter such as time, cost, weight, percent or foot-pounds, which we attempt to include where possible, then the metric will be stated just like the desired outcome. So, for example, when improving the manufacturing process, a desired outcome may be to minimize the cost of inventory. Since the cost of inventory can be measured in dollars, the predictive metric is simply a restatement of the outcome, and the metric is a method to minimize the cost of inventory.

If the desired outcome does not have a measurable parameter in it, then the outcome will be modified to include a measurable parameter such as time, cost, weight, percent, foot-pounds or some other unit of measure. This change will transform the desired outcome into a predictive metric. As an example, in the process of conducting surgery, a desired outcome of the surgeon is to "enable continuous, unobstructed vision of the field." To predict that a device or system designed to improve the process of surgery will enable continuous, unobstructed vision of the field, one could measure and control the *number of times and total time the visualization of the field is obstructed* by any proposed solution. The solutions that infrequently obstruct the visualization of the field, and do so for a minimal amount of time, will enable the surgeon to better achieve continuous, unobstructed vision of the field. The parameters that are measured predict the achievement of the desired outcome. "Reducing the number of times and the total time the visualization of the field is obstructed" is a predictive metric. It predicts that the desired outcome for continuous, unobstructed vision of the field will be satisfied and can be used to determine the degree to which it will be satisfied.

A predictive metric, when defined for a specific desired outcome, must meet a strict set of criteria. A predictive metric is a single statement that is:

1. One hundred percent predictive of satisfying the desired outcome for which it was created.

2. Capable of measuring the degree to which the desired outcome is satisfied.

3. Controllable in the design of the strategy or solution.

4. Measurable before the event, e.g., not an after-the-event indicator.

5. Appropriate for competitive benchmarking.

6. Descriptive of an activity that can be addressed to create value.

7. Free from solutions or any references to technology or time-dependent solutions.

8. Free from vague words such as easy, reliable, high-quality or comfortable.

9. Stable over time.

It should be noted that when a desired outcome is not properly defined, it becomes difficult or impossible to define a predictive metric that will meet the stated criteria. The methods used for capturing desired outcomes and defining their corresponding predictive metrics have been precisely defined to enable the

**Table 5.1**
**Desired Outcomes from Hospital Administrators**

| Desired Outcome | Corresponding Predictive Metric |
|---|---|
| The Ideal Surgical System would … | |
| Require minimal effort to set up for different operations. | Reduce the **time/steps** required to set up the system for different operations. |
| Experience minimal down time due to failure. | Reduce the **time** required to repair an unexpected failure. |
| Reduce the frequency with which the device requires planned servicing. | Reduce the **frequency** with which planned servicing is required. |
| Require a minimal amount of space. | Reduce the **space** (cubic inches) required by the system. |
| Minimize the cost of upgrading to future levels of performance. | Reduce the planned **cost** to upgrade to new technologies in the future. |

successful creation of breakthrough strategies and solutions. Following are three examples of desired outcomes and their corresponding predictive metrics as shown in Tables 5.1, 5.2 and 5.3.

### Example 1

Five desired outcomes that came from hospital administrators, who are responsible for making the decision to purchase surgical systems, are stated in Table 5.1 along with their corresponding predictive metrics. The desired outcomes are stated on the left and the metrics are stated on the right. Notice that each predictive metric contains a measurable parameter such as time, steps, frequency, space or cost.

Each predictive metric predicts the satisfaction of its corresponding desired outcome. Notice that each desired outcome becomes more and more satisfied as its corresponding metric is driven toward its ultimate target value. For example, if a solution were to reduce the time required to repair an unexpected failure, then it would predict the system would experience less down time due to failure. If the repair could be made instantaneously, then down time would not be experienced at all—achieving the ultimate target value—and the desired outcome would be satisfied to the greatest possible degree.

### Example 2

Five desired outcomes that came from surgeons who use surgical systems are stated in Table 5.2 along with their corresponding predictive metrics.

Notice again that each predictive metric predicts the satisfaction of its corresponding desired outcome and that each desired outcome becomes more and more satisfied as its corresponding metric is driven toward its ultimate target value. For example, if a solution were to reduce the number of cells that are

**Table 5.2**
**Desired Outcomes from Surgeons Who Use Surgical Systems**

| Desired Outcome<br><br>The Ideal Surgical System would ... | Corresponding Predictive Metric |
|---|---|
| Prevent the injury of healthy tissue. | Reduce the **volume** of healthy cells that are contacted during the surgery. |
| Enable continuous, unobstructed vision of the field. | Reduce the **number** of times and total **time** the visualization of the field is obstructed. |
| Minimize the amount of bleeding. | Reduce the **time** between the cutting and the sealing of a vessel. |
| Ensure the complete destruction of unwanted tissue. | Increase the **percent** of unwanted tissue that is identified for destruction. |
| Prevent the formation of undesirable scaring. | Reduce the **number** of cells injured to gain access through the surface. |

injured when accessing the surgical site, then that would predict the formation of undesirable scaring would be lessened. If no cells were injured, achieving the ultimate target value, then no scaring would occur. If several potential surgical systems were being evaluated against this criterion, then the system that injures the smallest number of cells would be considered the best at satisfying this desired outcome.

## Example 3

Five desired outcomes that came from manufacturers of surgical systems are stated in Table 5.3 along with their corresponding predictive metrics.

Notice that a measurable parameter is contained within each predictive metric, and each metric is free from solutions and stable over time. Also note that each metric predicts the satisfaction of its corresponding desired outcome, can be controlled within the design of a surgical system, and can be benchmarked versus a competitor when attempting to define the desired competitive position.

## PRIORITIZING PREDICTIVE METRICS

We have established that desired outcomes define the customer's perception of value. We have defined a parameter (a predictive metric) that can be used to predict the satisfaction of desired outcomes. By definition, each predictive metric is created to strongly predict the satisfaction of its corresponding desired outcome. In most strategy formulation activities, an organization can expect to consider between 50 and 300 predictive metrics, one for each desired outcome. As we will soon demonstrate, when formulating strategies and solutions, predictive metrics are used as the basis from which to define the desired competitive position. First, however, we must explain how we determine which of the up to 300 predictive metrics will be used to define the desired competitive position.

**Table 5.3**
**Desired Outcomes from Manufacturers of Surgical Systems**

| Desired Outcome<br><br>The Ideal Surgical System would ... | Corresponding Predictive Metric |
|---|---|
| Require minimal test time. | Reduce the **time** required to test the system. |
| Employ manufacturing processes that can be statistically controlled. | Reduce the **number** of elements that cannot be built/tested in a controlled production environment. |
| Minimize the dependence on skill intensive manufacturing processes. | Reduce the estimated training **time** that is required for individuals to learn the manufacturing process. |
| Reduce the manufacturing space required for production. | Reduce the **area** required to manufacture the product. |
| Minimize sensitivity to variations in the manufacturing process. | Reduce the **number** of parts and assemblies that are sensitive to variations in the manufacturing process. |

Predictive metrics are prioritized using a two-step approach. First, we must establish the importance of each desired outcome. This is accomplished through the quantitative research methods that are defined in Appendix A. Simply stated, the customers for whom the strategy or solution is being devised or targeted are asked to quantify the importance of each desired outcome and the degree to which each outcome is currently satisfied. Through this effort, it is determined which desired outcomes are most important and least satisfied, thus uncovering areas of opportunity. The desired outcomes that are most important and least satisfied obtain the highest priority. Their corresponding predictive metrics, by default, share the same priority.

The second step in this prioritization process is based on the fact that a predictive metric, although defined to predict the satisfaction of one specific desired outcome, may also predict, to some degree, the satisfaction of one or several other desired outcomes. In this sense, certain predictive metrics represent activities that complement, reinforce and optimize other activities. This concept is grounded in the fact that the satisfaction of some desired outcomes will predict the satisfaction of other desired outcomes.

To illustrate this concept, consider again the predictive metrics for the desired outcomes that came from surgeons using a surgical system. Reducing the volume of healthy cells that are contacted during the surgery not only predicts the prevention of injury to healthy tissue, it also predicts, to some degree, that bleeding is minimized and that the formation of undesirable scaring is prevented. The relationships that this predictive metric has with each of these desired outcomes are shown in Table 5.4.

This predictive metric is said to have synergy with other desired outcomes. This concept of synergy is important as it forms the basis by which predictive metrics are prioritized. Some metrics may predict the satisfaction of only one desired outcome. Some metrics may predict the satisfaction of two desired out-

**Table 5.4**

**Types of Relationships Between a Predictive Metric and Desired Outcomes**

| Desired Outcome | Predictive Metric |
| --- | --- |
|  | Reduce the **volume** of healthy cells that are contacted during the surgery. |
| Prevent the injury of healthy tissue. | **STRONG PREDICTIVE RELATIONSHIP** |
| Minimize the amount of bleeding. | **MODERATE PREDICTIVE RELATIONSHIP** |
| Prevent the formation of undesirable scaring. | **WEAK PREDICTIVE RELATIONSHIP** |

comes. Other metrics may predict the satisfaction of several important desired outcomes. The metrics that predict the satisfaction of a disproportionate number of important desired outcomes are the metrics with the most synergy. The process of determining these relationships is often referred to as synergy analysis. Once the relationship between each predictive metric and each desired outcome have been established, the predictive metrics can be prioritized, in descending order, based on their level of synergy. A detailed explanation of the methods used to prioritize predictive metrics can be found in Appendix B. Simply stated, matrix analysis, one of the seven tools of quality, is used to assist in establishing the relationships that exist between the desired outcomes and predictive metrics. An advanced normalized importance algorithm is then applied. It uses the importance and satisfaction ratings associated with each desired outcome as a basis from which to mathematically prioritize the predictive metrics.

This analysis enables an organization to determine which metrics predict the satisfaction of the largest number of important desired outcomes. When predictive metrics are prioritized using this methodology, it is often found that as few as 30% of the metrics often predict the satisfaction of up to 70% of the desired outcomes. They are the metrics with synergy.

As a result of this prioritization, an organization can determine which predictive metrics to use to define the desired competitive position. The high priority metrics effectively and efficiently predict the creation and delivery of value. They complement, reinforce and optimize one another. As a result of this prioritization, an organization can focus on the few metrics or activities that really matter. This concept is illustrated in Figure 5.2.

Once the predictive metrics are prioritized, we know what we must measure and control to predict the efficient creation and delivery of value. We know what criteria we should use to compare the amount of value that strategies and solutions are creating in one organization versus another. We know what it takes to be competitive in that situation, and we know what criteria to use to define the desired competitive position.

Obtaining this information can provide an organization with an enormous advantage. If an organization were to focus its limited resources on the

**Figure 5.2**
**Leveraging the Use of Valued Information**

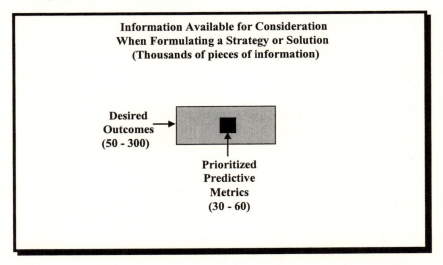

few metrics or activities that predict the satisfaction of 70% of the desired
outcomes, they could create solutions that would deliver the most value
for the smallest possible investment in time and resources. The benefit of
having and using this information cannot be overstated. This information
could provide those who use it with a tremendous competitive advantage.

During one consulting project, the metric that was at the center of the organization's attention turned out to be prioritized 67th out of 120 metrics. Although
it predicted one important outcome, it did not have synergy with any other
desired outcome, and other metrics predicted the satisfaction of its corresponding
desired outcome. This is a common cause of organizational inefficiency. By
focusing on the metrics with synergy, an organization can use its resources more
efficiently to strengthen its strategic position.

Which metrics predict the delivery of value in your organization? Are they
tied to the satisfaction of customer desired outcomes? Do they define the activities that will enable the organization to achieve a unique and valued competitive
position? Do they define the array of interlocked activities that will provide the
organization with a sustainable competitive advantage? Do they define the activities that complement, reinforce and optimize one another in a way that is
difficult for a competing organization to match?

It is rare that an organization has access to such powerful metrics. Their
creation is often inhibited by the use of Solution-Based Logic and after-the-
event measurements. In addition, the creation of a predictive metric is dependent

on an organization's ability to capture desired outcomes that are free from solutions and stable over time. Once these obstacles are overcome, an organization can gain access to the information that is required to define the organization's desired competitive position.

## THE DESIRED COMPETITIVE POSITION

The desired competitive position that is chosen by an organization should be unique from other competitors, and it should be valued by the organization and its customers. Predictive metrics, when prioritized, define the most efficient approach to the creation and delivery of customer value. They also identify the parameters against which a unique competitive position can be defined.

To demonstrate how predictive metrics are used as the basis from which to define a unique and valued competitive position, let's refer back to the music media example. This time, pretend we are executives in a music media manufacturing company and we are part of a team that is formulating a product strategy for the company. As part of our assignment, we are responsible for defining what competitive position we want the company to occupy. Let's assume we know what desired outcomes our customers value and the metrics that predict their satisfaction. Assume that the five predictive metrics stated in Table 5.5 are the top metrics as prioritized from a list of over 100 metrics. They are the metrics we will use to define our desired competitive position.

We begin this activity by establishing the competitive position our organization currently occupies along the stated metrics. For example, we determine that our company's music media is capable of storing 14 songs and that the diameter of the media is 3-1/2 inches. These current values are shown in Table 5.5. To understand where we stand relative to our competitors, we then set out to determine the competitive positions that are currently occupied by our top two competitors. We find, for example, that the music media produced by Competitor 2 is capable of storing 18 songs and that the music media produced by Competitor 1 is also 3-1/2 inches in diameter.

We know that a valued competitive position can only be obtained if our organization offers music media that delivers more value than the media offered by our competitors. As a result, we set the target values as shown in Table 5.5.

The target values reflect the organization's desired competitive position. They define what must be achieved to occupy a unique and valued competitive position. For example, if we know that Competitor 1 can store 14 songs and Competitor 2 can store 18 songs, then to be competitive, we know that we must be able to store at least 18 songs. But we must ask, "Will that allow us to achieve a unique and valued competitive position?" No it would not. In fact, it would place us in a "me-too" position, we would become just like our competitor, but no better. If we could store 32 songs, however, would that enable us to achieve a unique and valued competitive position? It certainly would. It would be a unique competitive position, because no other competitor would

**Table 5.5**
**Setting Target Values That Define the Desired Competitive Position**

| Predictive Metric | Current Value | Competitor 1 | Competitor 2 | Target Value |
|---|---|---|---|---|
| Increase the number of songs that can be stored. | 14 | 14 | 18 | 32 |
| Reduce the amount of distortion that is heard over time. | 8 decibels after 3 years | 6 decibels after 3 years | 10 decibels after 3 years | 2 decibels after 5 years |
| Increase the abrasion resistance of the material. | 55% | 65% | 75% | 85% |
| Reduce the size of the music media. | 3-1/2 inch diameter | 3-1/2 inch diameter | 3-1/2 inch diameter | 2-inch diameter |
| Increase the range of bandwidth over which the music sounds live. | 40% | 30% | 25% | 50% |

occupy that position. It would be a valued competitive position, because it would satisfy many important desired outcomes and deliver customer value.

If our organization could create music media that stored 32 songs, we would achieve our desired competitive position along that very important dimension. If our organization could create music media that was only 2 inches in diameter, we would achieve our desired competitive position along that very important dimension as well. If we could create music media that met the target values set for all the top metrics, we would achieve our desired competitive position across multiple dimensions. That would place us in a very unique and valued competitive position.

The important point is that we actually know which items to focus on to create value and to occupy a unique and valued competitive position. We know which metrics predict the creation and delivery of value. We know what competitive position we want to occupy. We know that if we find a solution that enables us to store 32 songs, then we will place ourselves in a unique and valued competitive position. Once the desired competitive position is defined, we can then set out to formulate a strategy or solution that will enable us to occupy that position. Other examples of how predictive metrics are used to define the desired competitive position are shown in Chapter 9 and in Appendix C.

## COMPETING AGAINST PERFECTION

In their book titled *Lean Thinking* (1996) James Womack and Daniel Jones state, "Although we gave a boost to the benchmarking industry with our previous book, *The Machine That Changed the World*, we now feel that benchmarking is a waste of time for managers that understand lean thinking. Our earnest advice to lean firms today is simple: to hell with your competitors; compete against perfection."

**Table 5.6**
**Setting the Ultimate Target Value**

| Predictive Metric | Ultimate Target Value |
|---|---|
| Increase the number of songs that can be stored. | 1,000,000 |
| Reduce the amount of distortion that is heard over time. | 0 |
| Increase the abrasion resistance of the material. | 100% |
| Reduce the size of the media. | 0-inch diameter |
| Increase the range of bandwidth over which the music sounds live. | 100% |

Competing with perfection makes far more sense than competing against a competitor. After all, simply beating a competitor does not guarantee that customers will be satisfied with a company's offering. It simply means the offering is somewhat better at satisfying a desired outcome than a competitor's offering. In reality, customers may be very unsatisfied with the performance of both offerings. In addition, when an organization gains a lead over a competitor, it often becomes complacent as it lacks both the motivation and direction to improve. Setting a clear direction for improvement, regardless of what competitors are doing, will guide an organization in its quest for continuous breakthrough improvement.

Prioritized predictive metrics define, over the long term, where improvements should be made to most efficiently and effectively create and deliver value. As a result, they can be used to systematically accelerate the creation and delivery of customer value, regardless of what a competitor is doing. This can be achieved through a continuous focus on the metrics that predict the satisfaction of multiple, important desired outcomes. Simply knowing which metrics to evolve over time often provides an organization with a competitive advantage. Organizations can leverage this knowledge by competing with perfection and only implementing the strategies and solutions that quickly evolve the high-priority metrics to their ultimate target values. This ensures that resources are applied to valued activities that might have otherwise been ignored. Conversely, it ensures the organization does not apply its resources to activities that do not create value.

The ultimate target values for the music media metrics are stated in Table 5.6. When competing with perfection, an organization is challenged to find the strategies and solutions that will enable it to achieve the ultimate target values for each of the top metrics. When the ultimate target value for a specific metric is achieved, perfection can be claimed because that predictive metric is at its fully evolved position. The objective is to reach this fully evolved position for each high-priority metric over time. The metrics, in their fully evolved position, define perfection in the eyes of the customer.

If an organization created music media that could store 1,000,000 songs, it is likely that customers would be completely satisfied along that dimension, as perfection has been achieved. If the music sounded live over 100% of the band-

**Figure 5.3**
**Systematically Accelerating the Creation of Customer Value**

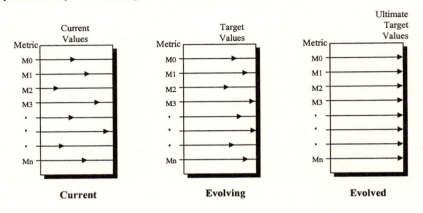

width, it is likely that customers would be completely satisfied along that dimension as well. As the ultimate target values are achieved for each predictive metric, the music media becomes fully evolved along that stated metric. Extending this logic to its natural conclusion, when a strategy or solution is capable of achieving all the ultimate target values, it is considered fully evolved. A graphical representation of this concept is illustrated in Figure 5.3.

The objective in any situation then is to uncover the strategies and solutions that will evolve the high priority predictive metrics to their ultimate target values over time. This, in essence, defines competing with perfection. Many incremental and breakthrough improvements may be required before the ultimate target values are achieved, but in each instance, the goal is to drive the top predictive metrics to their ultimate target values. It may take years to evolve all the top metrics to their fully evolved position. The degree to which the ultimate target values are achieved will determine an organization's ongoing competitive position. Knowing where to focus the company's resources will enable it to accelerate the creation of value and maintain a unique and valued competitive position.

An organization's products and services will evolve as new strategies and solutions drive the associated predictive metrics toward their ultimate target values. Music media, for example, has come a long way since the days of 33 rpm and 45 rpm records. It has evolved along multiple dimensions as it holds more songs, is smaller and more effectively resists damage. The technologies that will enable a music media manufacturer to achieve the stated ultimate target values will lead the ongoing evolution of that industry. Investing in value-generating technologies today will enable an organization to enhance its future market leadership position. A focus on perfection, rather than competitors, will accelerate that effort.

A focus on perfection will guide an organization as it makes investments in new technologies, equipment and people. It will guide an organization as it builds its core competencies, pioneers new products, services and technologies and forms new alliances. Organizations that rely on predictive metrics to compete with perfection can be assured that the activities and actions they are taking are focused on systematically accelerating the creation and delivery of customer value.

## OTHER APPLICATIONS OF PREDICTIVE METRICS

Predictive metrics predict the satisfaction of customer desired outcomes. They represent activities that are valued by the organization and its customers. In addition, they are measurements against which comparisons can be made and for which target values can be set. As a result, when executing the USFM, predictive metrics are used for a variety of purposes, all of which are geared toward the formulation of breakthrough strategies and solutions. As you will see later, in addition to using predictive metrics as the basis from which to define the desired competitive position, they are also used to:

1. Assist in the creation of alternative strategies and solutions.
2. Measure the value of a proposed solution in advance of its actual development or implementation.
3. Quantify the degree to which a solution satisfies a set of desired outcomes.
4. Compare the strengths and weaknesses of alternative or competing solutions.
5. Conduct competitive analysis.
6. Control the implementation of the solution.
7. Set a direction for continuous improvement.
8. Tie employee performance evaluation and reward systems directly to the satisfaction of customer desired outcomes.

Each of these applications will be described in more detail throughout the remainder of the book. For now, it is important to recognize the role that predictive logic and predictive metrics play in the definition of an organization's desired competitive position.

## SUMMARY

The desired competitive position is a unique and valued position that an organization desires to achieve relative to its competitors. An organization's desired competitive position should be unique—meaning it should be different from a position occupied by another organization; and, it should be valued—meaning it should deliver value to the internal and external customers for whom the strategy is being devised.

Many organizations attempt to position their strategies and solutions in the eyes of the customer after the strategy or solution has already been chosen and without knowing if the chosen strategy or solution will enable them to achieve their desired competitive position. This approach to defining the desired competitive position is reactive and often ineffective. We discovered that the consistent formulation of breakthrough strategies and solutions is dependent on an organization's ability to know, in advance, what competitive position it wants to achieve and then being able to successfully find the strategy or solution that will enable it to achieve that desired position. This discovery is consistent with the concept of Outcome-Based Logic.

To define a competitive position that is both unique and valued, an organization must focus on the parameters that predict the creation and delivery of customer value. For that reason, we created a parameter called a predictive metric that predicts the satisfaction of desired outcomes. The use of this parameter established the basis from which to define the desired competitive position. Predictive metrics, when prioritized, define an array of interlocked activities that complement, reinforce and optimize one another in a way that most efficiently predicts the creation and delivery of customer value.

It is rare that an organization has access to such powerful metrics. Their creation is often inhibited by the use of Solution-Based Logic and after-the-event measurements. In addition, the creation of a predictive metric is dependent on the ability of an organization to capture desired outcomes that are free from solutions and stable over time. Once these obstacles are overcome, an organization can gain access to the information that is required to define the organization's desired competitive position.

When defining the desired competitive position, it is often more effective if an organization competes with perfection rather than competing against other organizations. After all, simply beating a competitor does not guarantee that customers will be satisfied with a company's offering. It simply means the offering is somewhat better at satisfying a desired outcome than a competitor's offering. In reality, customers may be very unsatisfied with the performance of both offerings. In addition, when an organization gains a lead over a competitor, it often becomes complacent as it lacks both the motivation and direction to improve. Setting a clear direction for improvement, regardless of what competitors are doing, will guide an organization in its quest for continuous breakthrough improvement.

Prioritized predictive metrics provide that direction for improvement. They define where improvements should be made over the long term to efficiently create and deliver value. As a result, they can be used to systematically accelerate the creation and delivery of customer value, regardless of what competitors are doing. Simply knowing which metrics to evolve over time often provides an organization with a competitive advantage. Organizations can leverage this knowledge by competing with perfection and only implementing the strategies and solutions that quickly evolve the high priority metrics to their ultimate target values. This ensures that resources are applied to valued activities that might have otherwise been ignored. Conversely, it ensures the organization does not apply its resources to activities that do not create value.

An effective approach to defining the desired competitive position will guide an organization as it makes investments in new technologies, products, equipment and people. It will guide an organization as it builds its core competencies, pioneers new products, services and technologies and forms new alliances. Organizations that use predictive metrics as the basis from which to define their desired competitive position can be assured that the activities and actions they take are focused on systematically accelerating the creation and delivery of customer value and placing them in a unique and valued competitive position.

Chapter 6

# Integrating Structure and Information into a Process for Strategy Formulation

In his article titled "Killer Strategies" (*Fortune*, June 23, 1997), strategist Gary Hamel asks, "Can we do anything to increase the fertility of the soil out of which strategy grows? One good place to start is to develop a deep theory of strategy creation." Throughout the first five chapters of this book, we have provided the business world with a comprehensive theory of strategy creation.

We have established that organizations often lack the structure, information and the processing power that is required to formulate breakthrough strategies and solutions. We have demonstrated that the inherent use of Solution-Based Logic undermines the effective execution of most strategy formulation processes. We have introduced an alternative high-level thinking strategy called Outcome-Based Logic that transforms the way organizations approach the process of strategy formulation. When applying Outcome-Based Logic, an organization first defines the criteria that describes the optimal solution and then uses that criteria to create, evaluate and optimize alternative strategies and solutions until the optimal solution is uncovered.

We have introduced the Universal Strategy Formulation Model (USFM), a model that brings structure to the world of strategy formulation. The discovery of this structure provides a framework from which an organization can successfully formulate breakthrough strategies and solutions. We have shown that the USFM defines the four essential elements of strategy formulation—desired outcomes, constraints, the desired competitive position and solutions. We have established that desired outcomes can be obtained from customers and that the methods required to capture them have been created. We have established that constraints, which often result from time, resource or capital limitations, can be imposed on a strategy or solution by the organization itself or by a third party. Solutions, as we have learned, come from many sources including customers, employees, managers, consultants, technologists and others. We have also defined a means by which to define the desired competitive position before a strategy or solution is chosen.

We have combined these ideas and discoveries into a solid theory of strategy creation. Many of these ideas and discoveries have resulted from the application of advanced pattern detection techniques. Through these techniques, the secrets surrounding the formulation of breakthrough strategies and solutions have been revealed.

This book is written not only to provide the business world with a deep theory of strategy creation, but to also provide it with a process that enables the application of this theory—a process that integrates structure with information and facts with logic. The ideas and discoveries that support this theory of strategy creation have been integrated into a process that, when executed properly, will consistently produce breakthrough strategies and solutions. This process has been introduced as the Customer-Driven Mission Achievement Process or CD-MAP.

In this chapter, we will describe the step-by-step approach that is required to successfully execute this process, and we will explain how it is being used to formulate breakthrough strategies and solutions. We will describe how this process changes organizational dynamics, how it ensures that decisions are based on fact and how it prevents personalities, politics, personal agendas and gut-feel from negatively impacting the chosen strategy.

We will describe how it is designed to gain team, group and company consensus, and how it can be used to enable individuals throughout an organization to contribute their collective knowledge and wisdom to the formulation of breakthrough strategies and solutions.

When describing the execution of this process, we often analogize it to solving a complex simultaneous algebraic equation where you first define the constants in the equation and then work to solve the equation. As we explain how this theory of strategy creation is executed, we will apply the same analogy.

We will describe the execution of this process in two stages. The first stage is described as setting up the strategy formulation equation, or defining the constants in the USFM. The second stage is described as solving the strategy formulation equation or executing the model to uncover the optimal solution. It should be emphasized that the USFM is not actually a mathematical equation. It is only analogized as an equation to simplify the explanation of its execution.

## SETTING UP THE STRATEGY FORMULATION EQUATION

The CD-MAP process is defined in a series of 16 steps. The first nine steps are required to set up the equation or define the constants in the USFM. They are illustrated in Figure 6.1. Each step is required to define the criteria that are needed to create the optimal solution. The steps are listed in the order in which they are normally executed.

**Figure 6.1**
**The CD-MAP Process: "Setting Up" the Strategy Formulation Equation**

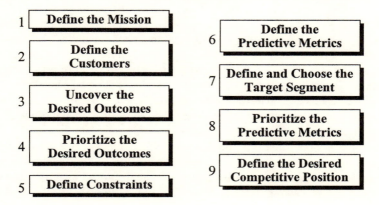

We will describe the actions that should be taken to ensure the successful execution of this process.

### 1. Define the Mission

Initiating this process often requires an organization to think differently about what it is trying to accomplish. Defining the mission involves defining what it is the company wants to improve or evolve. The boundaries of the mission must be clear and agreed upon. The mission itself must be concise and specific to ensure that the organization is focused on one mission at a time. Doing so will prevent irrelevant information from entering the strategy formulation process and ensure the desired results can be achieved.

It is often advantageous to define a mission in terms of improving or evolving a process, especially when using this process to formulate product and service strategies and strategies that drive an organization's operating, support and management processes.

It is important to note that if a mission assumes a solution to begin with, the process will optimize that solution; but, it may inhibit an organization from looking outside its current paradigm for a potentially better solution. For example, if an organization chooses to create an improved record, rather than an improved form of music media, the process would enable the organization to create an improved record. The problem, of course, is assuming a record as the solution will prevent the organization from discovering other solutions that utilize competing technologies. A project mission may be to create a better record, but that will prevent the discovery of the compact disc or DVD. It would be better to focus on improving music media.

This all gets back to the old question, "What business are you in?" An organization may be in many businesses. An organization must ask itself, "In each business, what process or processes are we attempting to evolve?" It must formulate a strategy to evolve each of those processes. A medical company may be in business to improve the process of pacing the heart or to improve the process of surgery. A two-way radio or cellular phone manufacturer may be in business to evolve the process of two-way communication. A storage device manufacturer may be in business to evolve the process of storing and retrieving information. A railway may be involved in the process of transportation. Defining the mission is a critical step in formulating a strategy. Assuming a solution in the mission statement can preclude the discovery of a breakthrough strategy or solution or prevent the discovery of an emerging market.

It should be noted that this strategy formulation process is also applicable to new or emerging markets—markets that are on the leading edge or bleeding edge. It is only applicable, however, if the organization knows which process or processes it is attempting to evolve as it moves into the emerging market. The microwave oven evolved the process of preparing a meal. The fax machine evolved the process of sending and receiving documents. The Internet evolved the process of obtaining information, of dispersing information, of business commerce and other processes. When defining a mission, think in terms of process, and set the bounds so as to encompass all the opportunities your organization is willing to pursue. A clear, agreed-upon mission statement must be in place before the process can successfully continue.

## 2. Define the Customers

To define the customers, an organization must identify the individuals, or groups of individuals, that are involved in, or affected by, the strategy, plan or decision that is being contemplated, given the stated mission. This discipline ensures that all the appropriate internal and external customers are considered in the strategy formulation process. A failure to include a customer could result in the rejection or failure of a strategy or solution.

The internal and external customer types included in the mission define the customer set for that specific mission. It is common to have between two and six customer types for any given mission. When defining the customers in the customer set, it is helpful to consider potential customer groups from the organization, the user community and any affected third party. If the mission were to improve the process of storing and retrieving information, then the customers may include the end user of the device, the systems integrator, the company stakeholders and the manufacturing personnel. If the mission were to formulate a company strategy, then the customers may include the users of the company's products and services, its distributors, suppliers and employees.

An organization may have to consider a new customer type when external changes have been made to the industry structure. In the medical industry, for example, hospital administrators are now responsible for making a large portion of the hospital's purchase decisions. Surgeons used to play a stronger role. The hospital administrators' desired outcomes must now be considered by medical device manufacturers when they formulate their company and product strategies.

In addition to defining the customers to be included in the strategy formulation process, the organization must also decide what weighting to give each customer in the customer set. This weighting reflects the importance of each customer type. If there are four customer types in a customer set, for example, each may receive a 25% weighting or two may receive a 30% weighting and the other two may receive a 20% weighting. Any combination of weighting is possible as long as they add up to 100%. It may be more important to satisfy the desired outcomes of one customer type than it is to satisfy the desired outcomes of another. As the weighting of a customer is decreased, the importance of the desired outcomes stated by that customer are decreased with respect to the other customers' desired outcomes. As a result, they play less of a role in the creation and evaluation of any proposed strategy or solution.

### 3. Uncover the Customers' Desired Outcomes

Customers unintentionally make it difficult to capture desired outcomes, because they are typically focused on solutions. We have developed the techniques that are required to capture desired outcomes even when customers offer statements that begin as solutions or vague statements.

The desired outcomes of each customer type are captured using the advanced requirements gathering techniques described in Appendix A. Desired outcomes are free from solutions, specifications and vague words such as easy, reliable, serviceable or comfortable. They are also stable over time. Approximately 25 to 50 desired outcomes are captured for each customer type in the customer set. Because there are typically between two and six customer types, it is common for between 50 and 300 desired outcomes to be uncovered for a specific mission.

Desired outcomes are captured in sessions that are conducted with customer types involved in or affected by the specified mission. The customers may be internal or external customers, depending on the mission that is being undertaken. The criteria that are to be used to select the customers that are to be interviewed are defined to ensure all pertinent customer types and segments are represented and also to ensure that a diverse set of customers are represented. It is common to interview between 30 and 40 individuals representing each customer type when capturing desired outcomes. A minimum of 30 interviews are required to ensure, statistically, that 96% of all the desired outcomes have been captured from each customer type.

### 4. Prioritize the Customers' Desired Outcomes

Once the desired outcomes are captured, quantitative research is conducted to prioritize the desired outcomes for each customer type in the customer set.

Typically, phone or personal interviews are conducted with a statistically valid sample of individuals representing each customer type. The research is conducted to quantify the importance of each desired outcome and its current level of satisfaction. The importance and satisfaction data are often captured from multiple target segments, as defined in the sample design. When conducting quantitative research, statistically valid sample designs and data collection methods must be used.

As a result of completing the quantitative research, areas of opportunity are uncovered. If a desired outcome is both important and unsatisfied, it represents an area of opportunity. With this knowledge, the desired outcomes are prioritized based on which offer the greatest degree of opportunity for the organization to create customer value. We use what we call the Opportunity Calculation to determine which desired outcomes are both important and unsatisfied. The calculation considers the importance (I) of each desired outcome and the difference between the importance (I) and satisfaction (S). Opportunity is calculated as $I + (I - S)$.

For example, if a desired outcome has an importance value of 9, on a scale of 1 to 10, and a satisfaction value of 7, its corresponding opportunity is calculated as $(9 + (9 - 7))$ or 11. If a desired outcome has an importance value of 9 and a satisfaction value of 2, its corresponding opportunity is calculated as $(9 + (9 - 2))$ or 16. The outcome that represents the largest opportunity receives the higher value and a higher priority. Statisticians from companies around the world have recognized that the Opportunity Calculation effectively enables an organization to quantify areas of opportunity. It should be noted, however, that organizations do have the option of prioritizing the outcomes based on importance only, if desired. The methods commonly used to prioritize desired outcomes are described in detail in Appendix A.

### 5. Define the Constraints Imposed on the Solution

Constraints that have been imposed on the solution by any individual, organization, or third party are defined and documented. Constraints often result from time, resource and financial limitations. They may also result from contractual issues, legal obligations or regulatory issues. It is not uncommon to have between 10 and 20 constraints imposed on a strategy or solution. Constraints do not have to be prioritized. They must simply be honored.

Each of the stated constraints will affect, shape and guide which solution is chosen. As constraints are imposed, the number of potential solutions that the organization is able to consider declines. Conversely, as constraints are removed, a wider range of potential solutions becomes available. The documentation of each constraint ensures that the organization is aware of any boundary condition that limits the selection of a potential strategy or solution. Proposed solutions that do not honor the stated constraints must be rejected when they are initially proposed or as they go through the evaluation process. The organization always has the option of modifying or deleting constraints or adding new constraints throughout the process.

## 6. Define a Predictive Metric for Each Desired Outcome

A predictive metric is a before-the-event measurement. It states the parameter that must be measured and controlled, prior to the implementation of a strategy or solution, to predict if a desired outcome will be satisfied and to determine the degree to which it will be satisfied. A single predictive metric is defined for each desired outcome. Each metric strongly predicts the satisfaction of its corresponding desired outcome. Individuals who are experts in their field often define the predictive metrics. Individuals who are experts at executing the CD-MAP process may also define them.

A well-defined predictive metric is 100% predictive of satisfying its corresponding desired outcome, controllable in the design of the strategy or solution, descriptive of an activity that can be addressed to create value, appropriate for competitive benchmarking, free from solutions and vague words and stable over time.

When executing this advanced strategy formulation process, predictive metrics are used for a variety of purposes, all of which are geared toward the formulation of breakthrough strategies and solutions. In addition to using predictive metrics as the basis from which to define the desired competitive position, they are also used to create alternative concepts, evaluate the potential of alternative concepts, set the direction for continuous improvement and tie employee reward systems directly to the creation of value.

## 7. Define and Choose the Target Segment

An organization must choose the segment of customers for which it will formulate a breakthrough strategy or solution. It may choose to target the total population or a segment of the population. When using traditional segmentation schemes, for example, an organization may choose to target a particular industry, business size, geography or age group.

An organization may also want to uncover and target segments that are unique to the industry in an attempt to gain a competitive advantage. To assist in achieving this objective, an advanced approach to segmentation is often executed as part of the CD-MAP process. Cluster analysis is conducted as part of the quantitative research to discover unique market segments. This approach to segmentation is unique from traditional cluster analysis in that desired outcomes are used as the basis for segmentation. The resulting segments contain homogeneous groups of individuals who value similar desired outcomes. Organizations often use these segments as a basis from which to create different solutions for various segments of the population. This method of segmentation is rare, because organizations typically fail to capture their customers' desired outcomes and are not able to use them as the basis for segmentation. This advanced approach to market segmentation is described in more detail in Appendix A.

When choosing which segments to target, a segment must be chosen for each customer type. For example, when formulating a company or product strategy, a segment of end-users, purchase decision-makers and internal company managers must be chosen. Each of them must represent the segments to be targeted with the strategy or solution that is to be devised.

When the organization selects which specific segments to target, the importance and satisfaction values given to the desired outcomes by individuals representing those segments are used to prioritize the desired outcomes. When using the Opportunity Calculation, the major opportunities are uncovered and documented for the target segment.

## 8. Prioritize the Predictive Metrics

Predictive metrics are prioritized using a two-step approach. Once the importance and satisfaction values for each desired outcome have been established, the priority order of the desired outcomes is determined. Their corresponding predictive metrics, by default, share the same priority.

The second step in this prioritization process is based on the fact that a predictive metric, although defined to predict the satisfaction of one specific desired outcome, may also predict, to some degree, the satisfaction of one or several other desired outcomes. In this sense, certain predictive metrics represent activities that complement, reinforce and optimize other activities. Some metrics may predict the satisfaction of only one desired outcome. Some metrics may predict the satisfaction of two desired outcomes. Other metrics may predict the satisfaction of several important desired outcomes. The metrics that predict the satisfaction of a large number of important desired outcomes are the metrics with the most synergy.

Matrix analysis, one of the seven tools of quality, is used to assist in establishing the relationships that exist between the desired outcomes and predictive metrics. The process of determining these relationships is often referred to as synergy analysis. Once the relationships have been established, an advanced normalized importance algorithm is then applied. It uses the importance and satisfaction ratings associated with each desired outcome as a basis from which to mathematically prioritize the predictive metrics. This calculation is used to prioritize the predictive metrics, in descending order, based on the importance of the desired outcomes and the synergy that exists between the predictive metrics and desired outcomes.

This analysis enables an organization to determine which metrics predict the satisfaction of the largest number of important desired outcomes. When predictive metrics are prioritized using this methodology, it is often found that as few as 30% of the metrics often predict the satisfaction of up to 70% of the desired outcomes. A detailed explanation of the methods used to prioritize predictive metrics can be found in Appendix B.

### 9. Set the Target Values That Define the Desired Competitive Position

The desired competitive position that is chosen by an organization should be unique from other competitors, and it should be valued by the organization and its customers. Predictive metrics, when prioritized, define the most efficient approach to the creation and delivery of customer value. They also identify the parameters against which a unique competitive position can be defined.

The desired competitive position is established by assigning a target value to each of the high priority predictive metrics. The target values that are assigned to the predictive metrics define the level of satisfaction that must be achieved by any proposed solution. Target values are set to define the desired competitive position and are then used as a guide to drive the creation of solutions that will achieve the desired competitive position.

In practice, the target values are often defined relative to a competitor's position. This approach is often taken to ensure that the resulting strategy or solution will enable the organization to occupy a competitive position that is superior to that held by its competitors. This technique enables an organization to position itself against its competitors along some meaningful set of criteria, before the strategy or solution is formulated.

Once the desired competitive position is defined, the organization is prepared to formulate a strategy or solution that will enable it to occupy that position. A solution that achieves all the assigned target values will enable the organization to occupy its desired competitive position. The steps taken to define the desired competitive position are described in more detail in Chapter 5 and Appendix C.

### SOLVING THE STRATEGY FORMULATION EQUATION

The first nine steps in the CD-MAP process are executed to set up the equation or define the constants in the USFM. Once completed, an organization has the facts it needs to systematically create customer value. Possessing this information often changes organizational dynamics as facts now exist that can expose individuals whose intentions are not focused on the creation of customer value. Politics and personal agendas quickly take a back seat to facts and logic.

Once the constants in the equation are defined, it is solved by stepping through a series of iterative steps that are designed to systematically create, test, recreate and retest alternative solutions. This iterative process is continued until the optimal solution is discovered. Process Steps 10 through 16 are illustrated in Figure 6.2. They are listed in the order in which they are normally executed.

Steps 10 through 14 are iterative in nature, meaning they are often performed

**Figure 6.2**
**The CD-MAP Process: "Solving" the Strategy Formulation Equation**

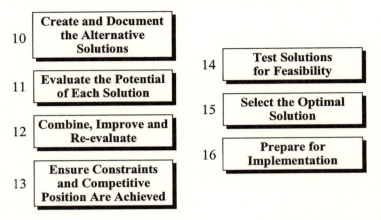

several times to uncover the optimal solution. Again, we will define the actions that should be taken in order to ensure the successful execution of this process.

## 10. Create and Document the Alternative Solutions

The prioritized predictive metrics, and their assigned target values, define what desired outcomes the optimal solution must satisfy and the degree to which they must be satisfied to occupy a unique and valued competitive position. They are the criteria that define the optimal solution and, as a result, are used to assist in the systematic creation of alternative solutions. Using the predictive metrics to assist in the creation of potential strategies and solutions reflects the philosophy that is embodied in Outcome-Based Logic. An organization first defines the criteria that describes the optimal solution and then uses that criteria as the basis for creating and evaluating potential solutions. The strategy or solution ultimately chosen should drive the predictive metrics to the levels of satisfaction that are required for the organization to occupy its desired competitive position.

To create a potential solution, features are first systematically created to address each metric in priority order across the total customer set. For example, one or more features are defined to address the first predictive metric, several features are defined to address the second metric and so on until a variety of features have been defined for the top 30 or so predictive metrics. Focusing on just one metric at a time makes it possible to channel and focus the organization's collective knowledge and wisdom on the systematic creation of value. This approach often leads to the creation of new ideas and discoveries.

Documenting these ideas is effectively an effort to document the universe of possible solutions. Building the universe of possible solutions using this technique is efficient and effective as it only addresses the features that are most appropriate for consideration when formulating a strategy or solution for the stated mission. Individuals do not have to waste their time and effort generating ideas and features that will not deliver value.

Once features have been defined for the top metrics, specific features are selected by the organization for inclusion into an overall concept. Alternative concepts are systematically created, as features are selected metric by metric. For example, an organization may create Alternative Concept 1 by deciding it wants to include Feature 4 to address Metric 1, Feature 2 to address Metric 2, Feature 8 to address Metric 3 and so on until features that address the top 30 or so metrics have been selected. The combination of features that are selected defines the complete concept, strategy or solution. After the first concept is defined, the same method is used to build Alternative Concept 2, Alternative Concept 3 and so on; only different features are selected for inclusion in the alternative concepts. It is common to create between three and eight alternative concepts at this stage of the process.

Concepts belonging to competitors, concepts that have been proposed in the past or concepts that were created using other methods are also documented at this time. The concepts must be documented in enough detail to discriminate them from other proposed strategies or solutions, and the features that are included in a concept must be mutually exclusive. The documented concepts often end up resembling a list of features that, when combined together, form a complete strategy or solution.

## 11. Evaluate the Potential of Each Solution

The prioritized predictive metrics that are used to create the potential solutions are also used as the criteria by which to evaluate each solution. Concept evaluations are commonly made using one of two evaluation methods. The first method involves comparing each concept against a baseline concept, or one of the stated concepts. The second method involves comparing each concept against a standard, which is defined as the fully evolved or theoretically perfect concept.

When evaluating each concept against a baseline concept, the objective is to determine if one solution is better than the other solutions at driving each predictive metric toward the target value that defines the organization's desired competitive position. Each solution is evaluated against the baseline concept to determine how well it performs relative to the top predictive metrics. It is common to use only between 30 and 60 metrics in the evaluation, as it is often the case that 30% of the metrics predict the satisfaction of up to 70% of the desired outcomes.

When using this evaluation method, the scores for each concept are calculated relative to the baseline concept. A concept may score between $-100$ and $+100$. A concept that receives a negative score should probably not be implemented, since a better solution is known to exist. A concept that receives a score of 5 to 15 offers incremental improvement over the alternative solution. A score in this range is typically achieved when an organization successfully applies Solution-Based Logic techniques to the process of strategy formulation. This is the world in which most organizations live today. A concept that scores over 50 typically delivers breakthrough improvements over the baseline concept. The objective of using this process is to create a concept that will score in this range.

The second method for evaluating the potential of a proposed strategy or solution involves testing the solution to determine the degree to which it has achieved a fully evolved position, in other words, testing it to determine how close it is to being the theoretically perfect concept. This method evaluates the potential for each solution to evolve each metric to its ultimate target value without requiring a comparison to other solutions or a baseline concept. This methodology requires an organization to rate the ability of a proposed strategy or solution to achieve the ultimate target value for each metric.

The use of this method enables an organization to determine how much better one concept is over another and the degree to which the theoretically perfect concept has been created. When using this method, a concept can obtain a score between 0 and 100, where 100 means the concept is fully evolved. A concept can only obtain a score of 100 if it drives every metric to its ultimate target value. If a solution obtains a score of 53%, that means the proposed solution evolves the product, service, process or subject of interest to 53% of its fully evolved position. If that were the case, then there would continue to be a considerable opportunity for improvement. If a solution obtains a score of 90%, then that means the proposed solution evolves the product, service, process or subject of interest to 90% of its fully evolved position, and only a small amount of opportunity for improvement remains.

Regardless of which evaluation method is used, it is important to note that the evaluation is taking place at the concept stage—at the time of conception. Having the ability to make this evaluation before the solution is actually designed, prepared, developed, prototyped or implemented saves an organization both time and money. It enables an organization to implement only the strategies and solutions that will create the most value for the organization and its customers. It enables an organization to effectively determine, plan and create its own future.

## 12. Combine, Improve and Re-evaluate Solutions

Two different methods are typically employed as part of this process to improve the highest scoring concepts after they have been initially evaluated. The first involves systematically analyzing and eliminating the weaknesses of the highest scoring solutions. The second involves the application of the Theory of Inventive Problem Solving, which is often referred to as TIPS, or TRIZ.

In the first method, improvements to the best solutions can be made by identifying and overcoming their known weaknesses with features that are recognized strengths in other solutions. For example, the highest scoring solution may have a weakness that is identified when the concepts are evaluated. Its weaknesses are identified when it is determined that the highest scoring solution did not score as well as another concept on a specific metric. The only way another concept can score better than the highest scoring concept on a specific metric is if it contains a feature that is not currently found in the highest scoring concept. The idea is to then take the feature from the lower scoring concept and determine if it can be included or modified for inclusion in the highest scoring concept. If the feature can be included in the highest scoring concept, then the highest scoring concept is improved through the elimination of one of its weaknesses. This activity produces new concepts that can then be evaluated. Multiple solutions may be created, tested, combined, improved and re-tested. After several iterations of improvement, the optimal solution is often identified. It should be noted that the optimal solution is not always the solution that utilizes the latest and greatest technology. It is often the solution that uses ideas and technology wisely to obtain the optimal results.

The second method that is used to improve the highest scoring solutions involves overcoming conflicts that specific solutions may have with different desired outcomes. It is often found that a proposed solution positively satisfies one important desired outcome, but negatively impacts other important desired outcomes. The creation of additional value may be dependent on an organization's ability to create solutions that allow the simultaneous achievement of seemingly contradictory desired outcomes. Doing so often takes time and effort. Prematurely accepting that a trade-off must be made may preclude an organization from discovering a new way of achieving the satisfaction of both desired outcomes.

As part of this process, the organization is presented with 88 inventive problem-solving principles that were derived from TIPS. The theory is based on research completed by Genrich Altshuller who worked in the patent office of the Russian navy during the 1940s. His research, which is highlighted in his book titled *40 Principles: TRIZ Keys to Technical Innovation* (1990), involved the analysis of thousands of patents. The patents were analyzed to determine if similar principles were used to achieve breakthroughs across various disciplines. The analysis resulted in the 88 TIPS principles. The principles represent patterns of invention that can be applied in many situations to overcome conflicts or contradictions. They are often used as part of this process to assist an organization in thinking of new ways to overcome a conflict without having to make a trade-off.

### 13. Ensure the Constraints and Desired Competitive Position Are Achieved

After completing steps 10 through 12, the solutions that satisfy the largest percentage of desired outcomes are known. The highly valued solutions are documented in detail. It must now be verified that the proposed solutions honor the constraints imposed on the solution and meet or exceed the target values that define the desired competitive position. If they do not, then the organization must decide whether to repeat steps 10 through 12 or modify the imposed constraints or the target values that have been set.

The best solution, at this point in the process, does not always enable the organization to achieve the target values that were set for every predictive metric. When an organization faces this scenario, it must decide whether or not to spend more time and effort devising features that will enable the target values to be achieved. It must know when to keep trying and when to move forward with implementation. As a general rule of thumb, we do not exit the iterative improvement phase of this process until a solution is formulated that satisfies at least 50% of the customers' desired outcomes better than the existing strategy or solution. Clearly, the objective is to formulate a breakthrough strategy or solution.

## 14. Test the Highly Valued Solutions for Feasibility

At this point in the process, an organization may have formulated two or three concepts that are shown to deliver similar amounts of value. So making the final selection may require further evaluation. As a result, the most attractive solutions are often evaluated for feasibility. The cost, risk and effort factors associated with the implementation of each solution are determined. Other feasibility factors are assessed as required.

Once the factors are established, the organization defines the feasibility values that are appropriate for the situation. The feasibility values range from 1.0 to 2.0. Using risk as an example, a value of 1.0 means the strategy or solution proposes no technical risk, and a value of 2.0 means the strategy or solution poses great technical risk. Values are established for each factor for the remaining concepts. An overall feasibility score is then calculated by dividing the concept evaluation scores by each of the feasibility values. The strategy or solution that delivers the most value for the least cost, risk and effort will likely be selected as the optimal solution.

## 15. Select the Optimal Solution

The final selection is based on all the evaluations that were previously conducted. Selecting the optimal solution becomes academic at this point in the process. A vast amount of data exists that enables an organization to select the strategy or solution that they will pursue. As the organization makes the final selection, it can be highly confident that it is selecting the optimal solution for the stated mission. After all, the desired outcomes, constraints and competitive positioning values are known and represent the criteria that have been used to create and evaluate the alternative strategies and solutions. The highest scoring solutions represent those that will create and deliver the most value.

The optimal strategy or solution can now be selected for implementation. The optimal solution is the one solution that satisfies the largest number of important desired outcomes, honors the stated constraints and enables the organization to achieve its desired competitive position. It is also the concept that delivers the most value for the least cost, risk and effort.

Unlike most strategy formulation processes, the use of this process allows an organization to determine when the optimal solution has been created. As a result, the user knows when to stop the iterative concept creation process and proceed with implementation. Based on post project evaluations, when using this advanced strategy formulation process, organizations agree that the optimal strategy or solution has been selected over 90% of the time.

## 16. Prepare for Implementation

The implementation of the optimal strategy or solution is planned and structured to ensure it is implemented in a way that will deliver the desired results. Predictive metrics describe the activities that must be completed to effectively deploy the chosen strategy or solution. The features comprising the selected strategy or solution are tied to the predictive metrics. This information is of value to those who are responsible for evolving the process, product, service or strategy of interest, and to those responsible for managing that evolution. Management often uses this information to achieve three major objectives.

First, this information is often used to prioritize the features within the chosen strategy or solution based on their value contribution. Using matrix analysis, the relationships between the features and the metrics are identified. The features that drive multiple metrics toward their stated target values often receive a higher priority than those that impact only one metric. The features with the most synergy are identified. Feasibility factors representing cost, risk and effort are then defined for each feature. Upon completing this activity, the organization knows which features are contributing the most value to the strategy or solution for the least cost, risk and effort. This gives the organization the information that is needed to determine where resources should be applied first. The features receiving the lowest priority, if left out of the concept, would have the least impact on the amount of value that is delivered by the chosen strategy or solution. The high-priority features are deployed to the individuals in the organization who are responsible for their implementation.

Second, the information is often used to drive an organization's continuous breakthrough improvement programs. The high-priority predictive metrics are deployed to the individuals in the organization who are responsible for defining, uncovering or inventing the features and technologies that will drive the deployed metrics to their ultimate target values over time. This ensures that company employees are focused on the creation of value well into the future and know where to focus their efforts to achieve continuous breakthrough improvements.

Third, this information is often used to measure and reward employee performance. When features are prioritized and deployed for implementation and the prioritized predictive metrics are deployed to drive continuous breakthrough improvement, employee performance and reward programs can be tied to the deployment activities. Doing so ties the reward system directly to the creation of customer value. As a result, reward and incentive programs are often tied to the measurements resulting from these feature and metric deployment activities.

## THE LINK TO QUALITY

In his book titled *Juran on Leadership for Quality* (1989), Joseph Juran states that ''quality planning can be produced through a road map; an invariable sequence of steps including:

1. Identifying who are the customers.
2. Determining the needs of those customers.
3. Translating those needs into our language.
4. Developing a product that can respond to those needs.
5. Optimizing the product features so as to meet our needs as well as customers' needs.''

The CD-MAP process supports Juran's theories on quality planning and provides a means by which to implement his theories in a practical manner. For years, organizations have been inclined to follow the advice of Juran and other leaders in quality planning. To date, they have not had the processes that are required to make this possible. The process introduced in this book is turning Juran's quality planning theory into a reality. Since quality can be defined as the degree to which the customers' important desired outcomes are satisfied, this strategy formulation process can be viewed as a quality tool for strategy formulation. It may be for this reason that it is common for an organization's quality management team to support the application of this process within an organization. Quality, however, continues to be the responsibility of all managers within an organization.

This process enables organizations to achieve many of its business and financial objectives. Strategy formulation is often an ongoing activity within an organization. The output of an organization's strategy formulation processes defines its future role as a competitor and a creator of value. Organizations can no longer afford to rely on gut-feel and intuition to determine their futures. They can no longer afford to let politics drive decisions that determine the amount of value they will create for the organization and its customers. Organizations now have a process that will enable them to participate in an Intellectual Revolution: a revolution in which organizations create their own futures, encourage change and focus on the creation of value; a revolution in which organizations understand what their customers value and use that information as the basis for their actions; and a revolution in which an organization of any size can possess the structure, information and processing power required to formulate strategies and solutions that will strengthen its strategic position.

## SUMMARY

Ideas and discoveries such as Outcome-Based Logic, the USFM, the essential elements of strategy formulation, desired outcomes, predictive logic and target values that define the desired competitive position have provided a strong foundation upon which to build a solid theory of strategy creation. Many of these ideas and discoveries have resulted from the application of advanced pattern detection techniques. Through these techniques, the secrets surrounding the formulation of breakthrough strategies and solutions have been revealed.

This book is written not only to provide the business world with a deep theory of strategy creation, but also to provide it with a process that enables the application of this theory—a process that integrates structure with information and facts with logic. The ideas and discoveries that support this theory of strategy creation have been integrated into a process that, when executed properly, will consistently produce breakthrough strategies and solutions. This process is called CD-MAP.

The execution of this process is often analogous to solving a complex simultaneous algebraic equation, where an organization first defines the constants in the equation and then works to solve the equation. The same analogy can be used when explaining the steps that must be taken to effectively execute this advanced strategy formulation process. As a result, the CD-MAP process is defined in a series of sixteen steps, broken into two stages. Stage one incorporates the first nine steps of the process. This stage is described as setting up the strategy formulation equation or defining the constants in the USFM. To execute the first stage of the CD-MAP process, an organization must:

1. Define the mission that is to be achieved.

2. Define the customers that must be satisfied.

3. Uncover the customers' desired outcomes.

4. Prioritize the customers' desired outcomes.

5. Define the constraints that are imposed on the solution.

6. Define a predictive metric for each desired outcome.

7. Define and choose the segment of individuals to target.

8. Prioritize the predictive metrics.

9. Define the organization's desired competitive position.

Each of these steps must be taken to define the criteria that are needed to create the optimal solution. Once completed, an organization has the facts it needs to systematically create customer value. Possessing this information often changes organizational dynamics as facts now exist that can expose individuals whose intentions are not focused on the creation of customer value. Politics and personal agendas quickly take a back seat to facts and logic.

Once the constants in the equation are defined, it is solved by stepping through a series of iterative steps that are designed to systematically create, test, recreate and retest alternative solutions to effectively execute the second stage of the CD-MAP process an organization must:

10. Create and document several alternative solutions.
11. Evaluate the potential of each alternative solution.
12. Combine, improve and re-evaluate the best solutions.
13. Ensure the constraints and desired competitive position are achieved.
14. Test the highly valued solutions for feasibility.
15. Select the optimal solution.
16. Prepare for implementation.

With the use of this advanced strategy formulation process, organizations have the power to consistently and effectively anticipate future opportunities, make value generating investment decisions and determine which products and service concepts to pioneer, which core competencies to build, which alliances to form, which activities to pursue and which trade-offs to make. The CD-MAP process is a systematic approach to the formulation of breakthrough strategies and solutions.

# Chapter 7

# Engaging in the Intellectual Revolution

The CD-MAP process is designed to enable an organization to achieve any mission in which a strategy, plan or decision is being contemplated. It is commonly used to formulate overall company strategies, product and service strategies and strategies that drive an organization's operating, support and management processes. It is often used to improve time-to-market and value-added processes, optimize investment and trade-off decisions, identify and select target markets, optimize product and service concepts, and execute other activities that impact customer and employee satisfaction. It is also used to help organizations overcome the challenges they face in manufacturing, development, distribution, pricing, promotion, billing, collections, advertising, planning, employee development, supplier relations and other areas of business.

This process can be used to formulate a strategy in any situation in which there are customers who have desired outcomes. In a broader sense, this process could be used to find ways to slow the effects of aging, improve the process of genetic therapy development or choose a candidate to run in a political party. It could be used to find solutions to crime, health care, welfare and other social issues.

The output of any process, however, is dependent on its inputs and the effectiveness of its execution. The effective execution of the CD-MAP process requires solid inputs and adherence to the steps that define the integrity of the process. The process will not result in a breakthrough strategy or solution if customers or their desired outcomes are ignored or if constraints go undefined. Breakthrough results cannot be expected if solutions are accepted as requirements or faulty quantitative methods are used to prioritize the importance of the desired outcomes. To ensure the effective execution of this process, an organization must ensure that it is executed correctly.

The steps that define the effective execution of the CD-MAP process have been defined. They can be carried out using a variety of methods, tools and technologies to assist in their execution. We will describe how an organization can use these methods, tools and technologies to engage in the Intellectual Revolution. We will first describe how a team approach to strategy formulation is often used in conjunction with executing this process. We will then define the mechanics of executing the process when using a team approach by explaining what activities should be taken over an appropriate time period to complete the process.

Next, we will describe how computer and software technology is providing the processing power that is required to formulate breakthrough strategies and solutions and is enabling organizations to overcome what used to be a natural barrier to success. In addition, we will describe how, over time, we discovered that the very nature of desired outcomes and predictive metrics lends itself to reusing much of the information captured for a specific mission in subsequent attempts to address or readdress the same mission. We will describe how this discovery—in conjunction with advances made in computer and software technology—has made it possible to simplify subsequent applications of the CD-MAP process for missions in which data has been captured.

Lastly, we will describe how advances in technology have made it possible to use this process across the entire enterprise to drive the creation of value. We will show how, by integrating important customer data and virtual libraries of alternative solutions into an integrated knowledge network, employees can use this technology to enable the consistent and ongoing formulation of breakthrough strategies and solutions.

## A TEAM APPROACH TO STRATEGY FORMULATION

When using this process for applications that cut across many organizations or across many functions within an organization, it is often best to consider a team approach to strategy formulation. We realize that a team approach to strategy formulation may not have worked in the past, as organizations routinely applied Solution-Based Logic when executing their strategy formulation processes. The advent of Outcome-Based Logic, however, has changed the dynamics of team interactions.

The drawbacks of a team approach to strategy formulation have been well documented over the past 10 years. In his book *Managing Customer Value* (1994), Bradley Gale summarizes several problems that are common to teams. He states, "Teams do not always unite to think through the problems of serving customers because:

1. Executives lack training outside their functional areas.
2. They do not share a common language or metrics of strategy.

3. The team rarely sees crucial non-financial information in a form that the members can understand and digest.

4. Organizations invest large amounts in market research, but few pull their market research and other non-financial data together in ways that enable them to act on it effectively.''

Many of the problems that are noted are directly related to the application of Solution-Based Logic. When executing the CD-MAP process, a team approach to the process of strategy formulation overcomes these and other related problems. The structure, information and processing power required to create a breakthrough strategy or solution is provided to the team. They share information and facts and focus that knowledge on the creation of value.

Several benefits of applying a team approach to the process of strategy formulation have been captured from organizations after they completed team-related CD-MAP projects. In post project interviews, individuals have stated that executing this strategy formulation process using a team approach has enabled them to:

1. Include individuals who will be impacted by the resulting strategy or solution in the strategy formulation process.

2. Make decisions that are focused on the creation of customer value.

3. Understand the rationale that is being used by other individuals as they make recommendations and decisions.

4. Prevent politics, gut-feel or other subjective factors from adversely affecting the selection of a strategy or solution.

5. Gain consensus and support for the resulting strategy or solution across the entire team.

6. Gain cross-functional and company-wide commitment to the resulting strategy or solution.

In addition to benefiting the organization as a whole, the execution of this process—according to team members—also offered benefits to the individuals participating on the team. In post project interviews, team members have stated that they believe the use of this process:

1. Improved their decision-making skills.

2. Enabled them to be focused and creative.

3. Empowered them to make decisions.

4. Assisted them in driving organizational change in a non-threatening manner.

5. Enabled them to become effective agents of change.

6. Improved the way they were able to interact with others.

**Figure 7.1**
**A Typical CD-MAP Project Time Line**

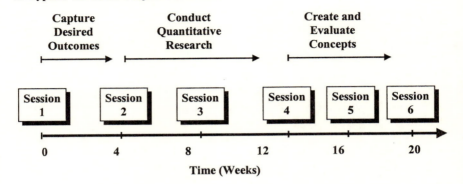

The CD-MAP process brings new dynamics to the process of strategy formulation. Once learned, the concepts that drive this process can be used by an organization on an ongoing basis to conduct many of its strategy formulation, planning and decision-making activities.

## THE MECHANICS OF EXECUTING A TEAM APPROACH TO STRATEGY FORMULATION

Executing this process using a team approach typically requires the involvement of a trained facilitator in addition to the team. A team typically consists of 6 to 10 individuals who represent various functions within the organization. They are responsible for creating, evaluating and often implementing the sought-after strategy or solution. Over a period of three to six months, the team can expect to meet between 5 and 25 non-consecutive days. The number of days is dependent on the complexity of the project, the mission, the amount of work assigned to the facilitator and the objectives associated with creating the team. The meeting days are often grouped together into sessions, and each session lasts between one and four days. All team members must be present when a session is in progress. The team is not required to conduct any activity prior to the first session.

It is common to conduct six team sessions, each requiring the completion of various activities that are essential to the successful execution of the process. The activities that are executed during these sessions typically follow the time line shown in Figure 7.1.

Slight variations in this time line are common, but the activities are typically the same from application to application. The description of each session will provide insight into how the process is structured and executed when using a team approach. It should be noted that the successful application of this process is dependent on its proper technical execution.

## Session 1

The first session typically extends between one and three days. The session begins by gaining team agreement on the mission and defining the scope of the project. Once agreement is obtained, the team is introduced to the CD-MAP process. The process and the theory behind it are explained in detail at this session. Education on each aspect of the process continues throughout the remainder of the project. It is important to educate the team on the process, so they will be comfortable with how it works, know what to expect upon completion and know what role they will play. After the initial education is complete, the team and the facilitator work together to:

1. Determine which customer types to include in the customer set.
2. Create a plan to obtain desired outcomes from each customer type.
3. Create a plan to quantify the importance and satisfaction of each desired outcome.
4. Agree on the project schedule for the remaining sessions.
5. Confirm the venue and facilities for the remaining sessions.

The most time consuming activity is typically creating the plan to obtain the desired outcomes from each customer type. This activity requires the team to decide where to conduct the qualitative research, who to recruit and what to include in the screener to ensure the appropriate individuals are recruited for the desired outcome gathering sessions. Because this information is needed to conduct the activities that are required before the next session is held, all these decisions must be agreed upon before the session concludes.

The second session is typically planned to take place four to six weeks after the first session. The time between sessions is used to capture the desired outcomes from each of the customer types in the customer set. The desired outcomes are captured through a series of customer interviews. The team members are expected to watch at least one of the outcome gathering sessions. Individuals who excel at gathering desired outcomes should be responsible for capturing the desired outcomes. Team members are not asked to capture desired outcomes as they are rarely trained to do so. Obtaining meaningful, actionable outcomes is the most important, and often the most difficult, aspect of this process. The techniques that are used to capture desired outcomes are discussed in Appendix A.

Once the desired outcomes are captured from multiple sessions, duplicate outcomes are removed from the resulting list and subsets and supersets are eliminated, where appropriate. This effort must be completed prior to the start of Session 2.

## Session 2

The second session requires between one and four days of team activity. The facilitator is responsible for presenting the results of the desired outcome gathering sessions to the team. The desired outcomes should be clear, concise and complete. Any questions regarding the resulting desired outcomes or how they were captured should be addressed with the team. It is important that the team members know what steps were taken to ensure that at least 96% of the customers' desired outcomes were captured. If the team does not agree with the desired outcomes or the methods used to capture them, then moving forward becomes a risky proposition. It is important to obtain team commitment to the results of each step of the process. At the second session, the facilitator and team work together to:

1. Review the customers' desired outcomes.
2. Finalize the questionnaires required to quantify the importance and satisfaction of each desired outcome.
3. Finalize the quantitative market research plan.
4. Complete the sample design.
5. Define the predictive metrics for each desired outcome.
6. Determine the relationships between each predictive metric and each desired outcome using matrix analysis.

Before this session is completed, the team must have a solid plan to conduct the quantitative research. They must agree on where (in what countries) to conduct the market research; what segments of the population to include as statistically valid cells in the sample design; how many interviews to conduct; whether or not to conduct Outcome-Based Segmentation; and what segment profiling questions to include in the questionnaire.

Immediately after this session is concluded, the questionnaires are finalized and the quantitative research begins. Quantitative research is required to obtain the importance and satisfaction data for the desired outcomes and to conduct an Outcome-Based Segmentation analysis where required. It typically takes between four and eight weeks to complete this activity. It is usually performed by a third party research firm and managed by the project facilitator.

Although the team typically begins to define predictive metrics for each of the desired outcomes at this session, they are not expected to complete this activity for all of the customer types. The team is not asked to conduct project work activities independently between sessions. This would likely undermine the team approach at this stage of the process.

## Session 3

The third session is typically conducted three to four weeks after the second session is completed. The third session usually requires between one and four days of team activity. The quantitative research is still in process and is not available to the team at this session. The facilitator and team use this session to:

**Figure 7.2**
**Executing the CD-MAP Process**

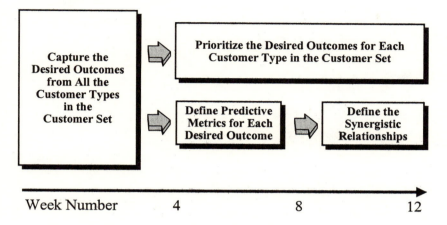

1. Complete the definition of predictive metrics for each desired outcome.

2. Complete the analysis of the relationships between each predictive metric and each desired outcome using matrix analysis.

3. Define any constraints imposed on the solution.

4. Prepare for concept creation.

The time and effort that is required to define the relationships between the desired outcomes and predictive metrics should not be underestimated. Not only is this activity time consuming, it is often mentally draining for the team members as well. Many short breaks are commonly taken as this activity is completed. As an option, we often recommend that a smaller team or the facilitator, if well trained, execute this part of the process and present the results to the remainder of the team.

The process steps that have been described thus far are illustrated in Figure 7.2. In summary, the desired outcomes are captured first. Once they are captured, they are quantified for importance and satisfaction. At the same time, the predictive metrics are defined and the relationships between the desired outcomes and predictive metrics are established.

It takes approximately 12 weeks to complete this portion of the process if external quantitative research is required; and it may take longer if a large number of interviews are required. It is common to conduct between 60 and 270 interviews per customer type. It is rare that larger samples are necessary. If external quantitative research is not required, this phase could be completed in as little as four to six weeks.

To ensure this process is executed effectively, it should be managed by a trained facilitator. It is not necessary for all the team members to become experts in the process, as their role is to participate in the process, not facilitate it. A good facilitator, however, is a prerequisite for success. To successfully execute Sessions 1, 2, and 3, the facilitator must be able to:

1. Provide the organization with the required education and training.
2. Set up the desired outcome gathering sessions.
3. Capture the desired outcomes.
4. Design the market research sample.
5. Design the questionnaire to be used for the research.
6. Manage the data collection activity.
7. Analyze the resulting data and analyze the results of the segmentation study.
8. Organize a team of experts for the purpose of defining and prioritizing predictive metrics.
9. Assist the team in defining the predictive metrics and defining the relationships between the metrics and the desired outcomes.

Several organizations have developed the internal expertise that is required to execute this process effectively. Others rely on the assistance of external facilitators or consultants to assist with the execution of the process.

### Session 4

Because the quantitative research is required for the fourth session, this session is typically scheduled to take place two to eight weeks after the completion of the third session. During this time period, the team is expected to start brainstorming features, ideas and concepts that address the predictive metrics with the most synergy.

The fourth session typically requires between one and four days of team activity. At this session, the facilitator presents the team with the results of the market research and segmentation analysis. Clustering techniques are used to segment the market. This methodology is described in Appendix A.

The research results are prepared for presentation by the facilitator prior to the team session. They typically include charts that show importance and satisfaction data, competitive analysis data, prioritized desired outcome data and prioritized predictive metric data. This information is available for various segments and clusters and for all customers in the customer set. If cluster analysis has been conducted, the facilitator may also include information regarding each of the resulting segments. That information may include segment size, profiling data, opportunity data and other information that will help the team decide whether or not to target any of the segments.

Once the research results are presented, the facilitator leads the team through the activities required to complete the definition of the criteria that will be used to define and evaluate alternative strategies and solutions. During the fourth session, the team is required to:

1. Analyze the completed market research results.
2. Determine which segment or segments to target.
3. Define the desired competitive position.
4. Review and complete the list of constraints that have been imposed on the solution.
5. Define any basic functions that customers expect any alternative strategy or solution to perform. They define the basic functions of the subject of interest. Functional tree diagrams are often used to define the basic functions.
6. Create concepts using the high priority predictive metrics as a guide.
7. Evaluate several concepts against the high priority predictive metrics.
8. Define features for each of the high priority predictive metrics.

In this session, the team often has the time to evaluate just one or two concepts. The objective of this session is to ensure that the team is prepared to create and evaluate concepts and to focus them on the metrics that will be used to create and evaluate the alternative solutions. After this session, the team knows where it needs to focus its attention to create a breakthrough solution.

During the two to four weeks leading up to the fifth session, the team is expected to work together or independently to define several features that would likely drive each of the high priority metrics to the target values, which define the organization's desired competitive position. They are effectively defining and documenting the universe of possible solutions from which the alternative strategies or solutions will be created. To make this process more efficient, the facilitator should ensure that the team members are only documenting features that will honor the constraints imposed on the solution. The team members should present the facilitator with their lists of features prior to the start of the next session.

## Session 5

At the fifth session, which also requires between one and four days of team activity, the facilitator and team work together to create and evaluate many other alternative concepts. The concepts are often created by systematically selecting the features, from the documented list of features, that will best drive the high priority predictive metrics toward their desired target values. Once several additional concepts are created, the team is asked to:

1. Complete the evaluation of any new concepts against the high priority predictive metrics.
2. Uncover the weaknesses in the most highly valued solutions and systematically eliminate them.

3. Evaluate solutions for feasibility.

4. Gain agreement on the optimal solution.

5. Select the features that make up the optimal solution.

When creating the optimal solution, the team may be required to modify or eliminate some of the constraints or alter the desired competitive position. When either of these constants are modified, the universe of possible solutions contracts or expands, and new considerations must be made.

This session typically ends in near final agreement as to which strategy or solution is to be selected. Since the optimal solution was likely created during this session, it is appropriate to let the team digest, analyze and get familiar with the favored strategy or solution over the following two to three weeks before the team meets again to reach a final conclusion.

### Session 6

At the sixth session, the team discusses and resolves any issues with the chosen solution. They have had two to three weeks to conduct any independent analyses they would like to perform prior to committing to the strategy or solution. If agreement is not readily obtained, then any newly suggested concepts are evaluated. During this session, which lasts between one and four days, the team and facilitator work together to:

1. Verify or gain agreement on the optimal solution.

2. Confirm the feasibility of the optimal solution.

3. Prioritize the features included in the optimal solution.

4. Create a plan for deploying and implementing the chosen strategy or solution.

Upon completion of this process, the team members should be committed to a specific strategy or solution and understand the process to the point where they can defend why that strategy or solution was chosen. It is prudent for the facilitator to conduct follow-up sessions on regular intervals to ensure the concept is being implemented as planned. To ensure Sessions 4, 5 and 6 are executed effectively, the facilitator must know how to:

1. Prepare the data resulting from the quantitative research study for team review.

2. Systematically create and document the universe of possible solutions.

3. Evaluate the potential of the alternative strategies or solutions.

4. Systematically eliminate any weaknesses from the best solution.

5. Gain team consensus on which strategy or solution to pursue.

6. Conduct follow-up activities.

A team approach to this process works best when a strong facilitator is leading a strong team through each step of the process. A question that typically arises is, "If more than one organization uses this process to formulate a strategy or solution relating to the same mission, would they reach the same conclusion?"

It is important to note that the solutions derived through the use of this process are dependent on the knowledge, skills and creative talents of those using the process. It is unlikely that any two organizations would reach the same conclusion. The final result is dependent on what an organization is able to include in its universe of possible solutions. This process is not a substitute for great people. It simply ensures that they are focused on the creation of value.

## PROCESSING POWER

Back in Chapter 1, we established there are three barriers that often stand in the way of formulating breakthrough strategies and solutions. They are structure, information and processing power. The first two barriers have been addressed, and one remains.

It takes more than the structure of the USFM and information in the form of desired outcomes, constraints and competitive positioning data to enable the creation of breakthrough strategies and solutions. The human mind is limited in its ability to simultaneously process the thousands of pieces of information required to formulate strategies, define plans and make complex decisions. This limitation is defined as the third natural barrier or obstacle that often precludes the creation of breakthrough strategies and solutions.

When contemplating strategies, plans and decisions, an organization must often consider between 50 and 300 desired outcomes, 10 and 20 constraints, 50 and 300 target values that define the desired competitive position, and thousands of potential solutions. We have calculated that over 40,000 independent decisions are often required to create the optimal solution. Given the fact that individuals can only process between five and nine pieces of information at a time, it is no wonder that the process of strategy formulation failed to evolve dramatically until computer and software technology brought processing power to the forefront of everyday business life. With the advent of personal computers, networks, Intranets and the Internet, the world of computing will never be the same, and neither will the process of strategy formulation.

Software technology is being used to assist in the execution of the CD-MAP process, enabling organizations to overcome what used to be a natural barrier to success. Software technology provides organizations with the power that is required to process critical information within the structure of the Universal Strategy Formulation Model (USFM). It enables an organization to overcome the natural processing limitations of the human mind. It enhances an organization's capacity to know, remember, process and apply the thousands of pertinent facts that are required to successfully formulate breakthrough strategies and solutions. Facilitators of the CD-MAP process routinely use software to store, retrieve and process:

1.  The desired outcomes of each customer type in the customer set.

2.  The importance and satisfaction ratings for each of the desired outcomes. The information is often stored for various segments, or target markets, for each customer type.

3.  The predictive metrics for each desired outcome.

4.  The relationships between all the desired outcomes and all the predictive metrics. This enables the automatic prioritization of the metrics given the importance and satisfaction ratings that have been assigned to the corresponding desired outcomes.

5.  Commonly encountered constraints.

6.  Features that define the universe of possible solutions.

7.  Detailed definitions of alternative concepts.

8.  Other information, calculations and algorithms that are required to execute the USFM and uncover the optimal solution.

Once this information is captured and embedded into a software tool, it can be used to assist the organization in creating and evaluating alternative strategies and solutions. It is often used to drive the discovery of the optimal solution.

After a project is completed, the software is often distributed to others in the organization—expanding the use of the project information beyond a single project team and across the entire organization. This enables the ongoing and widespread use of valuable information. Once the information is made available to others in the organization, they can use it to formulate strategies, define plans and make complex decisions relating to that mission. They can use it to evaluate new investment decisions, make trade-off decisions, anticipate future opportunities and accelerate the creation and delivery of customer value as it relates to that mission. They can use it on an ongoing basis, for many points in time, and in many situations.

Software technology is enabling the practical, widespread application of this advanced strategy formulation process. As a result, this process is driving an Intellectual Revolution in business: a revolution in which individuals are empowered—through structure, information and technology—to create breakthrough strategies and solutions.

## SIMPLIFYING THE ONGOING APPLICATION OF THE CD-MAP PROCESS

Over time, we discovered the very nature of desired outcomes and predictive metrics lends itself to reuse much of the information that is captured for a specific mission in subsequent attempts to address or readdress the same mission. After all, desired outcomes, predictive metrics and the relationships between them are stable over time. What changes from situation to situation is the importance of each desired outcome and the degree to which the outcome is currently satisfied. This discovery, in conjunction with advancements made in computer and software technology, has made it possible to simplify the subsequent applications of the CD-MAP process for missions in which data has already been captured.

As a result of this discovery, we set out to capture the information required to execute several missions that are universal across many organizations. We use these modules, as we call them, in our role as consultants to streamline the application of the CD-MAP process for the missions that have universal appeal. For example, the software modules contain the information that is required to help an organization:

1. Evaluate the attractiveness of a new business opportunity.
2. Evaluate the attractiveness of a specific market.
3. Evaluate the attractiveness of a specific market segment.
4. Formulate a strategy for introducing change into the organization.
5. Formulate a strategy to improve the product development process.
6. Formulate a strategy to improve the company/supplier relationship.
7. Formulate a strategy to improve the manufacturing process and related operations.
8. Formulate a pricing strategy.
9. Formulate a distribution strategy.
10. Formulate an overall company strategy.

The use of these software modules simplifies the application of the CD-MAP process for the facilitator and saves the organization a considerable amount of both time and money. The time required to execute the entire process can be reduced to between two and eight weeks. The condensed project time line is shown in Figure 7.3.

As a result of this breakthrough, many small- and medium-sized companies, who in the past could not afford the luxury of using advanced strategy formulation technologies, can now participate in the Intellectual Revolution with a process that consistently yields breakthrough results.

## APPLYING CD-MAP TECHNOLOGY AT THE ENTERPRISE LEVEL

Advances in technology have also made it possible to use this process at the enterprise level to redefine the way employees work and the way managers drive the creation of value in an organization.

Imagine an organization building virtual libraries of alternative solutions for the organization's key missions and placing them on an integrated knowledge network. Imagine all company employees contributing their ideas to this virtual

**Figure 7.3**
**A Condensed CD-MAP Project Time Line**

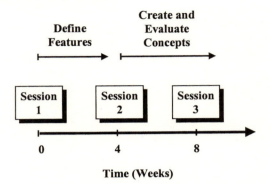

Time (Weeks)

library of alternative solutions, tapping the wealth of knowledge that exists within an organization. Then, through software that contains a series of advanced artificial intelligence algorithms, imagine individuals across the organization using that information to assist in the nearly automated execution of the CD-MAP process, resulting in the consistent formulation of breakthrough strategies and solutions.

This technology exists today. The software designed to achieve this objective performs the function illustrated in Figure 7.4.

The software acts like a series of filters—filtering out the solutions in the universe of possible solutions that do not satisfy important desired outcomes—while honoring constraints and enabling the achievement of the desired competitive position. The solutions that effectively pass through the filters are the most valued solutions.

Once such a network is in place, individuals throughout the company can use this technology to formulate breakthrough product and service solutions aimed at specific customer segments. They can use it to help the company define internal process improvement strategies that will reduce cost, improve time-to-market and improve employee satisfaction. They can use this technology to help the organization achieve a variety of missions and overcome many of its major business challenges, all of which will contribute to an Intellectual Revolution in business.

## SUMMARY

When using this process for applications that cut across many organizations or across many functions within an organization, it is often best to consider a team approach to strategy formulation. Many of the problems traditionally associated with the use of teams are directly related to the application of Solution-Based Logic. The use of Outcome-Based Logic, which is fundamental to the

**Figure 7.4**
**Filtering Out the Optimal Solution**

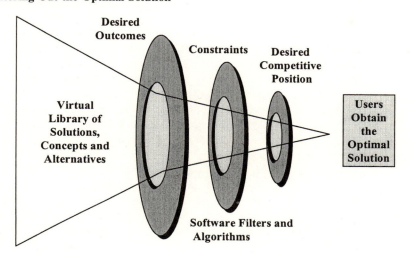

CD-MAP process, overcomes many of these problems. The dynamics of teams are changed when they are able to share information, facts and knowledge and focus on the creation of value.

When executing this process using a team approach, it typically requires the involvement of a trained facilitator in addition to the team. A team typically consists of 6 to 10 individuals who represent various functions within the organization. They are responsible for creating, evaluating and often implementing the sought-after strategy or solution. Over a period of three to six months, the team can expect to meet between 5 and 25 non-consecutive days. The meeting days are often grouped together into sessions, and each session lasts between one and four days. All team members must be present when a session is in progress. It is common to conduct six team sessions, each requiring the completion of various activities that are essential to the successful execution of the process. Over those six sessions, the process is executed, and the team concludes with the selection of what is typically considered a breakthrough strategy or solution.

Regardless of whether or not a team approach is used, computer and software technology are being used to assist in the execution of the CD-MAP process. This enables organizations to overcome what used to be one of the three natural barriers to success. Software technology provides organizations with the power to process critical information within the structure of the USFM. It enables an organization to overcome the natural processing limitations of the human mind. It enhances an organization's capacity to know, remember, process and apply the thousands of pertinent facts that are required to successfully formulate breakthrough strategies and solutions.

Over time, we discovered the very nature of desired outcomes and predictive metrics lends itself to reuse much of the information that is captured for a specific mission in subsequent attempts to address or readdress the same mission. After all, desired outcomes, predictive metrics and the relationships that exist between them are stable over time. What changes from situation to situation is the importance of each desired outcome and the degree to which the outcome is currently being satisfied. This discovery—in conjunction with advances made in computer and software technology—has made it possible to simplify the subsequent applications of the CD-MAP process for missions in which data has already been captured. This has made it possible to dramatically reduce the time and effort it takes to execute the CD-MAP process for missions that are universal across companies and industries.

In addition, advances in technology have made it possible to use this process at the enterprise level to redefine the way employees work and the way managers drive the creation of value in an organization. Imagine an organization building virtual libraries of alternative solutions for the organization's key missions and placing them on an integrated knowledge network. Imagine all company employees contributing their ideas to this virtual library of alternative solutions— tapping the wealth of knowledge that exists within an organization. Then through software that contains a series of advanced artificial intelligence algorithms, imagine individuals across the organization using that information to assist in the nearly automated execution of the CD-MAP process, resulting in the consistent formulation of breakthrough strategies and solutions. This technology exists today.

This advanced approach to strategy formulation provides organizations with the structure, information and processing power that is required to achieve many missions. Decisions that were once made subjectively and emotionally are now being made objectively and logically. Facts and logic are replacing politics, gut-feel and self-serving motivations as influences in the strategy formulation process. Traditional approaches to strategy formulation are giving way to new ideas and new technologies.

We have defined a solid theory of strategy creation and developed the structure, information and technologies that are required to support it. The process of strategy formulation is quickly evolving. The Intellectual Revolution has begun.

Chapter 8

# Case Studies and Evaluations

We have established that this strategy formulation process provides organizations with the capability to consistently formulate breakthrough strategies and solutions. It integrates the structure, information and processing power that is required to uncover the optimal solution in any situation. It is based on the application of Outcome-Based Logic. It considers the essential elements of strategy formulation and is supported by the structure of the Universal Strategy Formulation Model (USFM).

This process is being used by organizations around the world to effectively choose which markets, products, technologies, investments and activities to pursue. It is being used to formulate company strategies, product and services strategies and strategies that drive an organization's operating, support and management processes.

The financial benefits of using this process have been documented by several organizations. In many cases, dramatic financial improvements were obtained. For example, when using this process to improve the development of composite materials, a *Fortune* 100 company figured out how to reduce the cost of development by over 80% while reducing development time by nearly 75%. A cardiac pacing system company used this process to create a product that offered the same function as a highly valued competitive product, but at 40% of the cost. A manufacturer of industrial packaging used this process to create a strategy that increased their market share by 10% in an environment in which the top ten players had less than 50% market share. A medical device manufacturer used this process to create a line of angioplasty balloons that took them from less than 1% market share to a market leadership position in just two years.

Many organizations have used this process to formulate overall company strategies and product and service strategies that they believe will revolutionize their business. Many product and service concepts have been created as a result of using this process. Some are already on the market and others will be introduced by various organizations in the near future. The application of this process, regardless of the industry or company in which it has been applied, has consistently resulted in strategies and solutions that deliver up to 10 times more value than those created using traditional strategy formulation methods. In most cases in which this process has been applied, organizations have recognized gains in market share, revenue and profit while reducing their costs and cycle times.

Three organizations have given their permission to discuss the results of specific projects. The case studies describe the results that were achieved when using this advanced strategy formulation process to devise an overall company strategy, a product strategy and a strategy that was focused on the improvement of an internal company process.

The first case study describes how this process was used to formulate an overall business strategy for Southcorp, formerly a division of Gadsden Rheem. The second case study describes how this process was used to assist Cordis Corporation, now a division of Johnson & Johnson, in defining a strategy to develop and market a new line of angioplasty balloon products. The third case study describes how this process was used by Pratt & Whitney, a division of United Technologies, to formulate a strategy that was aimed at improving its manufacturing operation. In addition, this process has undergone evaluations at several organizations using various evaluation methods. The results of two of those evaluations, one made at Motorola and the other made at Hewlett-Packard, are also included in this chapter.

## CASE I: FORMULATING A DIVISION STRATEGY AT SOUTHCORP

In 1993, The Total Quality Group facilitated a consulting project for the Rigid Packaging Division of Southcorp, formerly Gadsden Rheem, in New South Wales, Australia. The general manager of the division was the sponsor of the project. The project mission was to develop and deploy a strategy aimed at improving the division's overall market share by 2%. It was believed that a 2% increase in market share was an aggressive goal in a market where the top 10 manufacturers controlled only 50% of the total market. A cross-functional team was formed representing all key areas of the business. They were responsible for participating in the process and implementing the resulting strategy.

The customers were defined as the users of the products and the stakeholders in the Southcorp organization. The facilitators and the team performed the activities required to define the constants in the USFM. Desired outcomes were captured from each customer type in the customer set. The team defined predictive metrics for each desired outcome and established the relationships between the metrics and the desired outcomes. At the same time, a questionnaire was developed and used to enable the quantification of the importance and satisfaction values for each desired outcome. Once the data collection was completed, cluster analysis was performed on the data using the desired outcomes as the basis for segmentation. Several uniquely defined segments were uncovered and subsequently targeted.

Once all the data was available and analyzed, the team used the data as the basis for formulating an overall division strategy. At this point in the project, the constants were defined and the ''equation'' was ready to be solved. The team worked diligently to create a strategy that would address the metrics predicting the delivery of value. After several days, a strategy was chosen. The chosen strategy satisfied over 50% of the desired outcomes better than their existing strategy. An implementation plan was defined using the predictive metrics as a guide. This enabled the systematic tracking of progress and the management of the strategy.

The strategy was implemented in late 1993. By 1996 Southcorp's market share had increased by 10% in a highly competitive market. Southcorp's management estimates that 7% of that increase was directly attributed to the implementation of the strategy resulting from this process.

This result was achieved by effectively enabling Southcorp to define a unique and valued competitive position and to determine which activities to pursue to achieve that position. Activities that complement, reinforce and optimize one another were uncovered; segment specific strategies were created; and their measurement system was tied directly to the creation of customer value.

## CASE II: FORMULATING A PRODUCT STRATEGY AT CORDIS CORPORATION

In early 1993, we were asked by Cordis Corporation, a medical device company located in South Florida, to help them devise a portfolio of products that would enable them to successfully enter a new market. At the time the project began, Cordis was a $223 million-a-year company, and their stock was valued around $20 per share. The vice presidents of operations and marketing co-sponsored the project. The project mission was to develop and deploy a product strategy aimed at making Cordis Corporation a major player in the angioplasty balloon market. At that time, Cordis had less than a 1% share of the angioplasty balloon market. The objective was to formulate a product strategy that would enable Cordis to achieve at least a 5% gain of market share as a result of this effort.

The cross-functional team involved in the project included individuals from engineering, marketing, regulatory, clinical, quality and manufacturing. The customers were defined as the cardiologists who use the products, the technical staff who assist and prepare the products during the procedure and the stakeholders within the Cordis organization.

The facilitator and team performed the activities required to define the constants in the USFM. Desired outcomes were captured from cardiologists, the technical staff and stakeholders. The team defined predictive metrics for each desired outcome and established the relationships between the metrics and the desired outcomes. Questionnaires were developed and used to collect the importance and satisfaction values for each desired outcome from a statistically valid number of individuals representing the target market.

Once all the data was available and analyzed, the team used the data as a guide in the formulation of an overall product strategy. At this point, the information required to create and evaluate potential concepts was defined. The team created a series of product concepts that addressed the metrics predicting the delivery of value. Many concepts were evaluated. Several initially favored concepts were shown to deliver little incremental value and were dropped from consideration. Each of the chosen product concepts satisfied at least 40% of the customers' desired outcomes better than the products they were benchmarked against. An implementation plan was defined using predictive metrics as the basis for deployment.

Over the next year, Cordis introduced 12 angioplasty catheters and saw its market share in interventional cardiology grow from less than 1% to nearly 10% in the United States. Its market share approached 20% in Europe, 30% in Canada and 18% in Japan. Net sales were up 30%, and the company's $50 million cash position enabled Cordis to expand into new markets. As stated by one Cordis team member:

> This process provided benefits beyond those typically measured in financial statements. As a team development tool, this process provided a platform to agree and disagree in a manner that enabled the selection of the best overall solution. This process drove the team to focus on real requirements rather than solutions, use unbiased measures and formulate product concepts that all could support. It also changed the views of project team members who were emotionally locked into a solution. They went on to create the products that the customer wanted and the team could deliver.

By mid-1995, Cordis gained a market leadership position. Their revenues for fiscal year ending June 1995 grew to $443 million. In February 1996, Johnson & Johnson acquired them for $109 per share.

Through the use of this process, Cordis Corporation was able to successfully anticipate future opportunities and make the trade-off and investment decisions that were required to accelerate the creation and delivery of customer value. They were able to identify the product features that delivered customer value and to deliver a series of products that placed them in a unique and valued competitive position.

## CASE III: FORMULATING AN OPERATING STRATEGY AT UNITED TECHNOLOGIES

In 1994, we were asked by Pratt & Whitney Aircraft, a division of United Technologies, to help them formulate a strategy to improve their manufacturing operation. The vice president of manufacturing sponsored the project. The project mission was to determine whether or not a proposed investment should be made to improve the manufacturing operation. Several individuals within the organization supported the investment that had been proposed. They were prepared to move forward with the investment. It should be noted top management proposed the investment that was to be evaluated, and many within the organization viewed our role as one of validating that management had made a good choice. It was known that this investment would cost the organization approximately $7 million.

Management wanted to be certain that any investment made in the manufacturing operation would deliver value to its customers. As a challenge to the team, they were not only asked to evaluate the potential of the investment under consideration, but to also come up with any other investment options that would deliver greater levels of value.

The cross-functional team involved in the project included individuals from all areas of the manufacturing organization. The customers were defined as the users of the manufacturing facility, the manufacturing personnel and the stakeholders in the manufacturing organization.

The facilitator and team performed the activities required to execute the process. Desired outcomes were captured from each customer type in the customer set. The team defined predictive metrics for each desired outcome and established the relationships between the metrics and the desired outcomes. A questionnaire was developed and used to collect the data needed to quantify the importance and satisfaction of each desired outcome.

Once all the data was available and analyzed, the team used the data as a guide to evaluate the investment decision. In the final analysis, the team concluded that the investment under consideration would enable the organization to better satisfy approximately 8% of the customers' desired outcomes. It was clear to the team that the proposed investment failed to address many of the customers' most important and unsatisfied desired outcomes. Taking on the challenge of coming up with a better investment strategy, the team went on to uncover a series of smaller investments that would enable the organization to satisfy over 70% of the customers' desired outcomes better than they were currently being satisfied.

The ability of the team to redirect its attention to the areas of opportunity led them to an investment strategy that delivered over 10 times more value than the investment strategy initially under consideration. As an added bonus, the cost of the chosen investment strategy was less than the cost of the initially proposed strategy. As a result of the project, management did not pursue the investment that was initially proposed. Instead, it made many of the investments proposed by the team.

By the end of 1996, the investments made by Pratt & Whitney management were shown to deliver a major increase, estimated around 35%, in overall customer satisfaction. In addition, the information resulting from the project has been used on numerous occasions to evaluate other investment opportunities. This has given management confidence in its ability to make investment decisions that deliver value to the organization and its customers.

This process enabled Pratt & Whitney to formulate a strategy that vastly improved its manufacturing operation. This result was achieved by effectively enabling the organization to make the trade-off decisions required to optimize their investment decisions.

## A QUANTIFICATION OF PROCESS BENEFITS AT MOTOROLA

In early 1995, a group of approximately 30 individuals involved in formulating a product strategy within Motorola were asked to evaluate the use of this process. They were first asked to state the desired outcomes they wanted to achieve from an advanced strategy formulation process. Approximately 25 desired outcomes were captured in total. Prior to executing this process with the team, they were asked to rate the degree to which their desired outcomes were satisfied with the methods they typically use for strategy formulation. They used a 5-point scale where 5 meant completely satisfied and 1 meant very unsatisfied. The results of that survey are documented in Table 8.1.

After the project was completed, they were again asked to rate their level of satisfaction, this time with our advanced strategy formulation process. They completed the evaluation using the same 5-point scale. The results for the top desired outcomes are documented in Table 8.1. The percent improvement is calculated in the column on the right.

The satisfaction levels of the desired outcomes shown here were improved between 150% and 293%. The team considered them to be dramatic improvements in satisfaction. Improvements such as these are possible as this strategy formulation process provides the structure, information and processing power required to overcome the traditional barriers that organizations face when formulating strategies and solutions.

## A QUANTIFICATION OF PROCESS BENEFITS AT HEWLETT-PACKARD

In another evaluation of this process, which was conducted in 1997, individuals involved in the formulation of a product strategy for a group within Hewlett-Packard compared the results obtained from their traditional strategy formulation methods with those produced by this advanced strategy formulation

**Table 8.1**
**Improvements Resulting from the Use of the CD-MAP Process**

| The Strategy Formulation Process Is to... | Traditional Method | Using CD-MAP | Percent Improvement |
|---|---|---|---|
| Support the results with documented facts. | 1.5 | 4.4 | 293% |
| Reduce overall program cycle time. | 1.6 | 4.0 | 250% |
| Deliver a prioritized set of customer "requirements." | 1.9 | 4.7 | 247% |
| Deliver an unambiguous, objective result. | 1.5 | 3.7 | 247% |
| Uncover areas of opportunity. | 2.1 | 4.6 | 219% |
| Reduce the expense of determining the value of a proposed concept. | 2.5 | 4.7 | 188% |
| Determine which features contribute the most value. | 2.5 | 4.7 | 188% |
| Ensure delivery on the proposed date. | 1.6 | 3.0 | 188% |
| Foster a customer driven culture. | 2.4 | 4.3 | 179% |
| Offer protection against high-risk technical solutions. | 2.1 | 3.7 | 176% |
| Identify unique market segments. | 2.7 | 4.6 | 170% |
| Determine common and unique requirements across segments. | 2.6 | 4.4 | 169% |
| Accurately evaluate the potential of new product concepts. | 2.6 | 4.0 | 154% |

process. It should be noted that this particular HP division, like other divisions, is focused on continuous improvement and strives to release product enhancements every six months.

Upon conducting the evaluation, it was found that the product enhancements created using their traditional strategy formulation methods typically satisfied about 6% of their customers' desired outcomes better than the previous product. At this rate of improvement, it took them approximately 30 months, or five product enhancements, to better satisfy 30% of the customers' desired outcomes.

In contrast, the use of this advanced strategy formulation process enabled them to formulate a product concept that could be delivered within six months and satisfied over 45% of the customers' desired outcomes better than the previous concept. It also enabled them to formulate a product concept that could be delivered within 12 months and satisfied over 70% of the customers' desired outcomes better than the previous concept. This is more than a five-fold improvement in the rate at which value is created. The contrasting rates of value creation are shown in Figure 8.1.

The comparison shows that the use of this process dramatically accelerates the rate at which customer value is created. As a result, the application of this process is enabling HP to leapfrog several generations of products that would deliver incremental value, and create product concepts that deliver breakthrough results. Their objective now is to achieve continuous breakthrough improvement.

**Figure 8.1**
**Using Advanced Strategy Formulation Technology to Accelerate the Creation of Value**

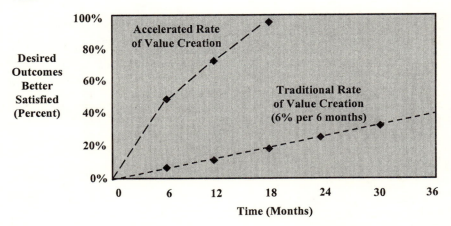

## ADVANTAGES AND DISADVANTAGES OF USING THIS PROCESS

Some of the more general benefits of using this process were captured over time from a cross section of individuals representing *Fortune* 100 companies and other smaller organizations that have used this process to achieve a variety of objectives. In their own words, users have stated that this process enabled their organization to:

1. Improve its ability to create value for the organization and its customers.
2. Increase customer satisfaction.
3. Consistently create breakthrough strategies and solutions.
4. Share knowledge and information company-wide.
5. Harness knowledge from across the organization and focus it on the creation of value.
6. Enhance its ability to reach a conclusion or consensus.
7. Develop a valuable core competency.
8. Incorporate new thinking into the organization.
9. Define the actions that enable the organization to achieve its objectives.
10. Decide how to allocate time and company resources.
11. Improve company policy.
12. Determine what the priorities of the organization should be.

As Peter Senge states in his book titled *The Fifth Discipline* (1990), ''In the simplest sense, a learning organization is a group of people who are continually enhancing their capability to create their own future.'' This process provides an organization with the structure, information and processing power it requires to create its own future. It enables it to focus on the metrics that predict the creation and delivery of customer value, and systematically use that information to accelerate the creation of value with breakthrough solutions. The execution of this process is designed to assist in the construction of a learning organization.

In addition to uncovering the recognized benefits of this process, we have also taken the time to understand why some organizations have been reluctant to use this advanced approach to strategy formulation.

First, the effective use of this process requires thought and discipline. This process provides everything that is required to create breakthrough strategies and solutions, but individuals or teams still have to put in the effort to create, evaluate, re-create and re-evaluate solutions until the optimal solution is discovered. This may take time, coordination and team effort. It also requires thought, discipline and creativity. Some organizations say they simply cannot find the time it will take to participate in this type of process. In reality, many organizations are often spending much more time and effort formulating their strategies and solutions than they would if they were to use this process. But because their activities are completed over longer periods of time, and often consist of uncoordinated activities that go untracked, they do not notice how much time they are actually spending on formulating their strategies and solutions. It is difficult for some organizations to recognize that this process will actually save them time and effort. In addition, it will deliver them a breakthrough strategy or solution, something that rarely results from the use of traditional strategy formulation methods.

Second, there are many steps associated with this process. They may not all be easy to understand and internalize. One objective of this book is to provide enough detail about each aspect of this process to make individuals feel comfortable with the concepts. If individuals are uncomfortable with any aspect of this process, they may be less willing to use it.

Third, this process often challenges well-established paradigms and often requires that individuals think differently about customer requirements, positioning and other elements of strategy formulation. Many individuals simply do not want to think differently about strategy formulation or learn a new process. This adversity to change is common and expected. Individuals who are adverse to change may not be overly interested in using this process.

Lastly, this process may be perceived to shift the balance of power within an organization as it provides workers and low-level management with a first-hand knowledge of the customers' desired outcomes and the ability to use that information to formulate breakthrough strategies and solutions. Not everyone views this in a positive light. Since the decisions and recommendations of workers and low-level managers using this process are based on fact, they may threaten others in the organization who use politically or personally motivated criteria to drive company activities. Others may perceive their span of control to be threatened. As stated by C. Dan McArthur and Larry Womack in *Outcome Manage-*

*ment* (1995), ''The organization's structure, infrastructure and activities must be driven by the needs of the customer and the business of the company, not by personal needs and ambition.'' Not everyone, however, prefers to act in accordance with this philosophy.

## SUMMARY

We have shown that this process is being used by organizations around the world to effectively formulate company strategies, product and services strategies and strategies that drive an organization's operating, support and management processes. We have documented several cases in which this process has produced breakthrough strategies and solutions.

For example, when using this process to improve the development of composite materials, a *Fortune* 100 company figured out how to reduce the cost of development by over 80% while reducing development time by nearly 75%. A cardiac pacing system company used this process to create a product that offered the same function as a highly valued competitive product, but at 40% of the cost. A manufacturer of industrial packaging used this process to create a strategy that increased their market share by 10% in an environment in which the top ten players had less than 50% market share. A medical device manufacturer used this process to create a line of angioplasty balloons that took them from less than 1% market share to a market leadership position in just two years.

In addition to documenting several case studies that demonstrate the successful execution of this process, we have also documented process evaluations that describe the amount of value this process has generated for two well-known companies.

One evaluation of this process, completed at Motorola in 1995, showed that many of the important desired outcomes they wanted to achieve from a strategy formulation process were far better satisfied through the use of this process than they were through the use of their traditional strategy formulation methods. This process was documented to deliver dramatic increases in the satisfaction of many of Motorola's most important desired outcomes relating to the process of strategy formulation. The satisfaction levels of many desired outcomes were improved by over 150%. Some satisfaction levels were increased by 293%, nearly a three-fold improvement.

In 1997, a process evaluation was completed at Hewlett-Packard. The evaluation showed that the use of this strategy formulation process accelerated the rate at which they could create value for their customers by a factor of 5.

Dramatic improvements such as these are possible, because this strategy formulation process provides the means by which to formulate breakthrough strategies and solutions. It enables organizations to overcome the traditional barriers they often face when executing the process of strategy formulation. It provides the structure, information and processing power that is required to accelerate the creation and delivery of customer value.

# Chapter 9

# Executing Concepts of Strategy

---

Organizations that are effective in using this advanced strategy formulation process are driving an Intellectual Revolution in business. They have the capability to effectively accelerate the creation and delivery of customer value. They are able to anticipate future opportunities, ensure their investments deliver value, occupy a competitive position that is both unique and valued and conduct other activities that determine an organization's strength as a creator of value. They are able to formulate strategies, define plans and make complex decisions that deliver up to 10 times more value than the strategies and solutions created by organizations that continue to use traditional strategy formulation methods.

This process enables organizations to think and act strategically. It enables motivated individuals to use the power of strategic thinking to overcome the challenges faced by their organizations and customers. It takes the mystery out of strategy and enables organizations to put into practice the theories that are supported by well-respected strategists, consultants and academics.

This chapter describes how this process is being used to address the important elements of strategy formulation as they are defined by one of today's leading strategists.

## SPECIFIC EXPECTATIONS OF STRATEGY

One insightful definition of strategy comes from Michael E. Porter, the C. Roland Christensen Professor of Business Administration at the Harvard Business School. In his article titled "What Is Strategy?" (1996), he describes *what* an effective strategy must deliver. He states that, "an effective strategy must enable an organization to:

1. Uncover a unique and valued position that involves a set of activities that are different than those taken by competitors.
2. Make all the required trade-offs, vis-à-vis competitors, to determine what activities should be pursued, and what actions should be taken.
3. Ensure the activities that are taken to execute the strategy fit together to create a distinctive and sustainable competitive advantage for the organization.''

It follows that a strategy formulation process used to create such a strategy must enable an organization to achieve these objectives. Using strategy formulation processes that apply Solution-Based Logic make it difficult to achieve these objectives for all the reasons that have been presented. For example, when using Solution-Based Logic, desired outcomes often go uncovered; predictive metrics are rarely used; the desired competitive position is often considered after the strategy or solution has been devised; and the process itself is often driven by politics, gut-feel and intuition rather than facts.

The ability to apply Outcome-Based Logic, use the structure of the Universal Strategy Formulation Model (USFM) and obtain information in the form of desired outcomes and predictive metrics enables an organization to achieve these and other expectations of strategy.

In this chapter, we will demonstrate how this advanced strategy formulation process could be used to enable an organization to achieve these strategic objectives. To demonstrate how they could be achieved, we will focus on a company that Michael Porter cites in his article ''What Is Strategy?'' as an organization that has been able to effectively achieve the three stated strategic objectives—Southwest Airlines. To make this demonstration effective, we have used the Southwest Airlines example in his article as the basis for our demonstration. But, we have fabricated a set of desired outcomes and predictive metrics and have assumed a set of values that define their importance. Although this demonstration does not reflect the completeness that accompanies the flawless execution of the USFM, it does offer some insight as to how this process can be applied to proactively formulate a breakthrough strategy. Please note that each time Michael Porter is referenced in this chapter, the reference is related to his article, ''What Is Strategy?'' (1996) unless stated otherwise.

## STRATEGY AS POSITIONING

As stated by Michael Porter, ''an effective strategy will enable an organization to uncover a unique and valued competitive position; one that involves a set of activities that are different than those taken by its competitors.'' To formulate a strategy that enables an organization to achieve this objective, the organization must be able to effectively determine:

1. What potential target markets exist, and which segments to target.
2. What activities are valued by that set of target customers.

3. How well each activity is currently performed by competitors.

4. What level of satisfaction must be achieved for each activity to occupy a unique and valued competitive position.

The demonstration that follows shows how to obtain this information and how an organization such as Southwest Airlines could have used this information to define the unique and valued competitive position they occupy today.

### Choosing the Target Segment

Historically, one of the most difficult aspects of occupying a unique and valued competitive position has been choosing which segment of customers to target. When selecting a target segment, organizations traditionally have a product or service in mind and then try to find the segment of the population that values that product or service. This approach is reactive and consistent with Solution-Based Logic. The organization has a solution and then determines whom to target with that solution. When using Outcome-Based Logic, the approach to choosing a target segment is different. An organization must be able to answer the following questions. What are we attempting to achieve as an organization? What segment of customers will allow us to get there? We will demonstrate how the use of Outcome-Based Segmentation, as we call it, enables an organization to select the target customers who will ensure the organization achieves its financial and strategic objectives.

The segmentation process begins by capturing the desired outcomes of a diverse set of airline passengers. The interviewed passengers represent business travelers, families, students and retirees. Individuals representing a variety of age groups and income levels are interviewed. We use our outcome gathering techniques to uncover between 25 and 50 desired outcomes from the 30 to 40 individuals that are interviewed. Once the desired outcomes are captured, their corresponding importance and satisfaction values are quantified across all potential segments using the market research methods described in Appendix A. In addition, Outcome-Based Segmentation is conducted to determine what segments exist. The organization then sets out to determine which segments are most attractive.

An attractive market segment often contains a homogeneous set of individuals whose most important desired outcomes are unsatisfied. By definition, such a segment would offer an organization a high degree of opportunity. Other criteria that are used to evaluate the attractiveness of a segment will vary from company to company and from situation to situation. Southwest, for example, may have been searching for a segment that:

1. Represents a sizable portion of the overall population.

2. Plays to the strengths of the organization.

3. Complements the organization's existing culture.

**Table 9.1**
**Quantifying the Importance and Satisfaction of the Passengers' Desired Outcomes**

| Passengers Desired Outcomes | Importance | Satisfaction | Opportunity I + (I - S)* |
|---|---|---|---|
| Minimize the passengers' cost of flying. | 9.7 | 3.4 | 16.0 |
| Minimize the time required to go between mid-size cities and large cities. | 9.5 | 2.8 | 16.2 |
| Ensure on-time departures. | 9.4 | 2.2 | 16.6 |

*I = Importance of each desired outcome; S = Satisfaction.

4. Lacks a strong competitor, or

5. Perceives the organization in a positive light.

An attractive market segment may also be required to satisfy other criteria that are important to the organization. When executing this process, these criteria are typically captured, prioritized and used to effectively choose which segment or segments to target. The segments that are chosen are the ones that best satisfy the segment selection criteria.

Because desired outcomes are used as the basis for Outcome-Based Segmentation, many segments are uncovered in which passengers value a unique set of desired outcomes. The segments are defined and profiled so the organization knows the makeup of each segment, its size and many other important factors that will help evaluate each segment against the stated attractiveness criteria.

As a result of the segmentation analysis, Southwest likely found a segment that met its attractiveness criteria. The passengers in this segment possessed a unique set of important, yet unsatisfied, desired outcomes. As documented in Table 9.1, the data resulting from the segmentation analysis showed that passengers in the target segment valued an airline that could minimize the passengers cost of flying, minimize the time required to go between cities and ensure on-time departures. The results also indicated that individuals in this segment are financially constrained. The importance and satisfaction values for each desired outcome were quantified in the segmentation study. The top three desired outcomes and their corresponding importance, satisfaction and opportunity values are shown Table 9.1. Keep in mind, in a real world study up to 50 desired outcomes may be considered in the segmentation formulation analysis. Much more information would be known about the target market than this example suggests.

It is shown that the passengers in Southwest's target segment find the desired outcomes stated above to be both important and unsatisfied. The fact that each passenger in this segment finds these desired outcomes both important and unsatisfied is the reason why they form a segment. It is this commonality that statistically brings them together. It is the discovery of this opportunity that enables an organization, such as Southwest, to create a strategy yielding a strong strategic position. Using this approach, an organization not only has the distinct advantage of knowing that this segment exists, but as a result of the research, they also know the size of the segment and what desired outcomes are valued by the individuals that are in it. Outcome-Based Segmentation enables organizations to uncover unique segments that are not constrained by artificial classifications or titles such as industry, business size or demographics. The organization can then evaluate each segment against the attractiveness criteria that has been defined as important by the organization and select the segment or segments that best meet the stated criteria.

## Determining What Activities Are Valued by the Targeted Customers

Once the target segment is chosen and the customers' desired outcomes are known and prioritized, the other customers in the customer set are considered. In the Southwest Airlines example, the other customers would likely include internal company stakeholders and company employees. The desired outcomes of these customer groups would also be captured and prioritized. Between 25 and 50 desired outcomes would likely be captured from each customer group, and the required research would be conducted to quantify which desired outcomes are most important and least satisfied.

When quantifying the importance of the stakeholders' desired outcomes, the stakeholders must take into consideration the segment the organization has chosen to target. Again, in a real world study up to 50 desired outcomes may have been included in the study. Let's assume that the stakeholders' top five desired outcomes and their corresponding importance, satisfaction and opportunity values have been uncovered. They are shown in Table 9.2.

The stakeholders' most important desired outcomes involve various aspects of reducing costs and increasing company profits. The research also enables the organization to uncover key areas of opportunity. The organization now knows what criteria a strategy must meet to create value for the internal company stakeholders.

Research would also be conducted with potential employees to uncover their desired outcomes. Once they are captured, a representative sample of potential employees would be interviewed to quantify which desired outcomes are most important and least satisfied. Again, up to 50 desired outcomes would likely be considered. Let's assume that upon completion of the research, the potential employees' top two desired outcomes and their corresponding importance and satisfaction values were uncovered. They are shown in Table 9.3.

The research shows that the potential employees want high levels of compensation and also want to share in company profits.

At this point in the process, a market segment with important and unsatisfied desired outcomes has been uncovered and targeted. The passengers' most important desired outcomes are known. In addition, the desired outcomes of internal company stakeholders and potential employees have been captured and prioritized. We know what is valued by each of the customer groups that would be affected by the strategy that is being devised. This information is required

**Table 9.2**

**Quantifying the Importance and Satisfaction of the Stakeholders' Desired Outcomes**

| Stakeholders' Desired Outcomes | Importance | Satisfaction | Opportunity I + (I - S)* |
|---|---|---|---|
| Minimize the cost of maintaining their airplanes. | 9.2 | 5.5 | 12.9 |
| Ensure the maximum daily use of their fleet. | 9.1 | 4.8 | 13.4 |
| Maximize the amount of daily profit that could be obtained. | 8.9 | 3.7 | 14.1 |
| Minimize the administrative costs associated with ticketing. | 8.8 | 5.0 | 12.6 |
| Minimize the cost of interacting with other airlines. | 8.6 | 3.3 | 13.9 |

*I = Importance of each desired outcome; S = Satisfaction.

**Table 9.3**

**Quantifying the Importance and Satisfaction of the Employees' Desired Outcomes**

| Potential Employees Desired Outcomes | Importance | Satisfaction | Opportunity I + (I - S)* |
|---|---|---|---|
| Ensure the employees receive high levels of compensation. | 9.5 | 3.3 | 15.7 |
| Enable the employees to profit from the airline's success. | 8.9 | 2.7 | 15.1 |

*I = Importance of each desired outcome; S = Satisfaction.

before an organization can determine which activities are valued by the targeted set of customers.

As the process continues, predictive metrics are defined for each desired outcome and are then prioritized. The methods used to define and prioritize predictive metrics are discussed in Appendix B. As a result of this analysis, the metrics with the most synergy are identified. For example, increasing the percent of departures that leave on time predicts that more flights will leave on time, and if this activity were performed well, it also predicts that the amount of profit obtained daily will be maximized and the daily use of the fleet will be optimized. This metric has synergy with other desired outcomes and, therefore, receives a higher priority. The metrics that predict the satisfaction of the important desired outcomes stated by the passengers, stakeholders and employees are stated in priority order in Table 9.4. The value that is shown in the column on the right is the normalized importance value associated with each predictive metric.

Notice that the predictive metrics define activities that must be performed to create value for the target customers in this situation. "Increasing the percent of departures that leave on time" is an activity. The airline performing this

**Table 9.4**
**Prioritized Predictive Metrics**

| Predictive Metrics | Customer Group | Value |
|---|---|---|
| Increase the percent of departures that leave on time. | Passenger | 21.2 |
| Increase the number of hours/day each plane is in flight. | Stakeholder | 17.4 |
| Reduce the cost of interacting with other airlines. | Stakeholder | 14.3 |
| Reduce the cost of airplane maintenance. | Stakeholder | 12.1 |
| Reduce the time required to go between mid-size cities and large cities. | Passenger | 9.7 |
| Increase the amount of profit that could be obtained per day. | Stakeholder | 7.6 |
| Increase the levels of compensation awarded to employees. | Employee | 7.1 |
| Reduce the administrative costs associated with ticketing. | Stakeholder | 6.4 |
| Increase the percent of profits that can be shared by employees. | Employee | 2.8 |
| Reduce the passengers' cost of flying. | Passenger | 1.4 |

activity in a way that enables it to always achieve on-time departures will undoubtedly enjoy a competitive advantage. Predictive metrics, by definition, are
descriptive of activities that must be addressed to create value. In order for
Southwest Airlines to create value for its targeted set of passengers, they must
be able to:

1. Increase the percent of departures that leave on time.

2. Increase the number of hours per day each plane is in flight.

3. Reduce the cost of interacting with other airlines.

4. Reduce the cost of airplane maintenance, and so on.

It is this set of prioritized activities that must be pursued to create value for
the customers in the target segment. They are the activities valued by the customers in the target market. They represent the array of interlocked activities
that complement and reinforce each other. They predict the creation and delivery
of value.

### Determining How Well Each Activity Is Performed

Once an organization determines which activities are valued by its target
customers, it can set out to determine how well each activity is being performed
by its competitors. Because the predictive metrics are defined as measurements,
an organization can accomplish this task by benchmarking the competitors of
interest. For example, through the mock benchmarking activity that is documented in Table 9.5, it can be determined how well Southwest's top two hypothetical competitors performed each of the important activities. The relative
strengths and weaknesses of the competitors can also be determined through
this analysis.

**Table 9.5**
**Using Predictive Metrics as a Basis for Competitive Analysis**

| Predictive Metrics | Current Value for Competitor 1 | Current Value for Competitor 2 |
|---|---|---|
| Increase the percent of departures that leave on time. | 83% | 85% |
| Increase the number of hours/day each plane is in flight. | 10 hours | 12 hours |
| Reduce the cost of interacting with other airlines. | $25/passenger | $28/passenger |
| Reduce the cost of airplane maintenance. | $7,000/flight | $7,500/flight |
| Reduce the time required to go between mid-size cities and large cities. | average of 3.6 hours | average of 2.8 hours |
| Increase the amount of profit that could be obtained per day. | $130/passenger | $127/passenger |
| Increase the levels of compensation awarded to employees. | $37K average | $36K average |
| Reduce the administrative costs associated with ticketing. | $26/ticket | $32/ticket |
| Increase the percent of profits that can be shared by employees. | 0% | 0% |
| Reduce the passengers' cost of flying. | $200/passenger | $212/passenger |

Let's assume the data shown in Table 9.5 is correct. The data shows the strength of Competitor 1 lies in its ability to reduce the costs associated with ticketing. The strength of Competitor 2 lies in its ability to reduce the time required to go between mid-size cities and large cities. The data indicates the competitors are not involved in performing many other activities in a way that is unique to their organization. The data also suggests that neither organization occupies what would be considered a unique and valued competitive position.

At this point in the process, the organization knows what activities its target customers value. It also knows how well each valued activity is being performed by its competitors. This information is critical to the formulation of an effective strategy and offers a basis for making strategic choices and decisions.

## Determining Which Level of Performance to Achieve

Once an organization knows what activities its target customers value and the strengths and weaknesses of its competitors, it may objectively decide how well each activity must be performed to achieve a unique and valued competitive position.

This is accomplished by first analyzing the passengers' perceived level of satisfaction with the solutions currently offered by Southwest's two hypothetical competitors. The satisfaction values would be obtained through the same market study that is conducted to quantify the importance and satisfaction values of the passengers' desired outcomes and to complete the Outcome-Based Segmentation study. Let's assume that the satisfaction values for the two competitors are accurately represented in Table 9.6.

**Table 9.6**
**Quantifying Levels of Satisfaction**

| Passengers Desired Outcomes | Satisfaction Competitor 1 | Satisfaction Competitor 2 |
|---|---|---|
| Ensure on-time departures. | 3.3 | 3.5 |
| Minimize the time required to go between mid-size cities and large cities. | 2.5 | 3.1 |
| Minimize the passengers' cost of flying. | 2.1 | 2.3 |

Southwest Airlines is now able to use this satisfaction data and the bench-marking data to determine how well each activity must be performed to increase the level of customer satisfaction to the degree that is required to secure a unique and valued competitive position. They may ask, ''What target values must we set and achieve before we believe a unique and valued competitive position is secured?''

As they define their desired competitive position, assume they set the target values stated in Table 9.7. The values indicate the levels of performance that Southwest believes must be achieved before the satisfaction levels are increased to the point where a unique and valued competitive position is attained.

It should be emphasized that in a real world situation, there are hundreds of activities that are associated with the operation of an airline. Southwest could have determined which activities were most important to its target customers and chosen to excel at those activities—capturing its desired competitive position. Let's assume that the target values shown in Table 9.7 for Southwest represent the competitive position they set out to achieve. Notice the levels of improvement that were desired for each of the valued activities. Many of the activities required performance improvements of between 50% to 100% for them to obtain the competitive position they wanted to occupy. It is this degree of improvement that is often required to obtain a unique and valued competitive position.

Based on the target values stated, it could be concluded that Southwest Air-lines decided to create a leadership position in each of the activities that were highly valued by its passengers, stakeholders and employees. They uncovered a unique and valued competitive position and chose to excel in a set of activities that are different than those aggressively pursued by their competitors.

When formulating a strategy, once the target values are set, the objective is to discover or create the strategy or solution which will enable the organization to achieve the target values that define the desired competitive position. If such a strategy can be formulated, its successful implementation often enables an or-ganization to attain a unique and valued competitive position. The target values define the level of performance that must be achieved to occupy that position.

To consistently occupy a unique and valued competitive position, an organ-ization must be able to successfully determine:

**Table 9.7**
**Setting Target Values to Achieve the Desired Competitive Position**

| Predictive Metrics | Current Value for Competitor 1 | Current Value for Competitor 2 | Southwest Airlines Target Value |
|---|---|---|---|
| Increase the percent of departures that leave on time. | 83% | 85% | 98% |
| Increase the number of hours/day each plane is in flight. | 10 hours | 12 hours | 16 hours |
| Reduce the cost of interacting with other airlines. | $25/passenger | $28/passenger | $0 |
| Reduce the cost of airplane maintenance. | $7,000/flight | $7,500/flight | $3000/flight |
| Reduce the time required to go between mid-size cities and large cities. | Average of 3.6 hours | Average of 2.8 hours | Average of 1.5 hours |
| Increase the amount of profit that could be obtained per day. | $130/passenger | $127/passenger | $150/passenger |
| Increase the levels of compensation awarded to employees. | $37K average | $36K average | $42K average |
| Reduce the administrative costs associated with ticketing. | $26/ticket | $32/ticket | $6 |
| Increase the percent of profits that can be shared by employees. | 0% | 0% | 6% |
| Reduce the passengers' cost of flying. | $200/passenger | $212/passenger | $180/passenger |

1. What potential target markets exist and which segments to target.

2. What activities are valued by that set of target customers.

3. How well each activity is currently performed by competitors.

4. What level of satisfaction must be achieved for each activity to occupy a unique and valued competitive position.

This process enables an organization to successfully achieve each of these objectives. A unique and valued competitive position is a prerequisite to an effective company strategy, and achieving such a position is undoubtedly an objective of most organizations. As stated by Michael Porter, "The essence of strategy is choosing to perform activities differently than rivals do." This demonstration was intended to show how this process can be used to choose these activities and determine the degree to which they must be performed to achieve a unique and valued competitive position.

## STRATEGY AS MAKING TRADE-OFFS IN COMPETING

Michael Porter also states that "the creation of an effective strategy requires that an organization be able to make all the required trade-offs, vis-à-vis competitors, to determine what activities should be pursued, and what actions should be taken." To achieve this objective, an organization must have the structure, information and processing power that is required to make a series of complex, interrelated trade-off decisions.

This advanced strategy formulation process is specifically designed to assist an organization in making these difficult trade-off decisions. We will first describe the methods that are used to assist an organization in determining what activities to pursue. The activities to pursue are directly related to the predictive metrics that are defined for each desired outcome. By definition, a predictive metric is descriptive of a valued activity.

We will then describe the methods embodied in this process that enable an organization to determine what actions to take. The actions that are taken by an organization constitute the plan of action or strategy that has been formulated.

## Choosing What Activities to Pursue

It was shown in the last section how this process could be used to determine what activities to pursue. In making that determination, many trade-off decisions were required. As stated by Michael Porter, "a trade-off, by definition, means that choosing more of one thing will necessitate less of another. An airline can choose to serve meals—adding cost and slowing turnaround time at the gate—or it can choose not to, but it cannot do both without bearing major inefficiencies."

Making the right trade-off decisions in a specific situation often determines an organization's ultimate success or failure. As demonstrated in the last section, to make effective trade-off decisions, an organization must know what desired outcomes are valued, which desired outcomes are not valued and how well each desired outcome is currently satisfied. It must also know the interrelationships that exist between desired outcomes and predictive metrics, and which metrics predict the satisfaction of the most important desired outcomes. Once all the required information is available, making the right trade-off decisions becomes academic.

The logic associated with choosing the best activities to pursue must be employed throughout the execution of an effective strategy formulation process. The logic and algorithms embedded into the execution of this process are designed specifically to enable an organization to identify which activities to pursue. Three examples of the trade-off logic that is employed in this process to ensure the most appropriate activities are identified and described as follows:

1. Trade-off logic is used to ensure that the chosen strategies and solutions drive the satisfaction of important and unsatisfied desired outcomes at the expense of satisfying less important or already satisfied desired outcomes. More specifically, when using this process, desired outcomes are prioritized using what we have defined as the Opportunity Calculation. This ensures the desired outcomes that are most important and least satisfied receive the highest priority. Conversely, the desired outcomes that are less important or already satisfied receive a lower priority. This leads to the identification of the high priority activities.

2. Trade-off logic is used to drive the pursuit of activities that satisfy many important desired outcomes at the expense of pursuing activities that satisfy only one important, or several relatively unimportant, desired outcomes. This logic is employed when the predictive metrics are prioritized. The high priority metrics, those with synergy, typically predict the satisfaction of multiple desired outcomes. The metrics that do not have synergy obtain a low priority. This leads to the direct identification of the high priority activities.

3. Trade-off logic is used also to drive the performance levels required to obtain a competitive advantage at the expense of achieving target values that produce a me-too competitive position. This trade-off logic is employed when target values that define the desired competitive position are set for the top predictive metrics. The target values are designed to specifically prevent an organization from formulating a strategy or solution that will leave them in a me-too or otherwise unfavorable competitive position. Knowing which activities to pursue and the degree of performance required drives the creation of strategies and solutions that yield a competitive advantage.

This is an example of the trade-off logic that is embodied in this strategy formulation process to ensure an organization selects the best activities to pursue. It is automatically applied as the process is executed. Its application requires an organization to define the relationships that exist between the predictive metrics and the desired outcomes and to prioritize the predictive metrics using the methods described in Appendix B.

This trade-off logic ensures the activities that deliver the most value are uncovered in priority order. The application of this logic ensures an organization will make the right trade-off decisions when choosing which activities to pursue.

### Choosing What Actions to Take

How did Southwest Airlines know they should eliminate baggage transfers, connections to other airlines and meals? Why did they decide to have a standardized fleet of 737 aircraft? What trade-off logic did they use? Could it be that they were attempting to formulate an overall strategy that would enable them to achieve the target values they set for each of the high priority predictive metrics?

Before an organization can determine what actions to take, or which strategy to pursue, it must know:

1. Which segments to target.

2. What activities are valued by that set of target customers.

3. How well each activity is currently performed by its competitors.

4. To what level of satisfaction each activity must be performed to achieve a unique and valued competitive position.

It has been demonstrated how this process can be used to obtain this information. Once this information is obtained, it can be used as the basis from which to make the trade-off decisions that are required to determine which actions to pursue. The logic and algorithms embedded into the execution of this process are designed specifically to enable an organization to identify which actions to pursue. After all, this is a strategy formulation process, and the actions to pursue define the chosen strategy. A strategy is a plan that describes the actions an organization will take to create value for the organization and its customers. This process is designed to uncover those actions.

Three different examples of the trade-off logic, which is employed in this process to ensure the best actions are chosen, are described as follows:

1. Trade-off logic is used to drive the pursuit of actions that enable valued activities to be performed at the expense of less valued activities. This is made possible because the actions have a numerical value associated with them and can be prioritized using that value. That value is tied back to the normalized importance value associated with the metric for which the action was defined.

2. Trade-off logic is used to drive the pursuit of actions that enable the achievement of the target values set for many highly valued activities at the expense of achieving the target value set for only one valued, or several relatively unvalued, activities. This logic is employed when the actions are prioritized. The high priority actions, those with synergy, typically drive multiple metrics toward their stated target values. The actions that do not have synergy obtain a low priority. This leads to the direct identification of the high priority actions.

3. Trade-off logic is used to drive the pursuit of actions that honor the stated constraints at the expense of all other criteria. This is accomplished by eliminating from consideration the actions that do not honor the stated constraints.

These are examples of the trade-off logic that is embodied in this strategy formulation process to ensure the efficient selection of what actions to pursue. It is applied automatically as the process is executed. The same methods that are used to prioritize the predictive metrics are used to prioritize the actions or features that are uncovered.

Let's look at how this trade-off logic could have helped Southwest choose which actions it should take to create value for its stakeholders, employees and customers. Let's assume that Southwest chose to take the actions that are stated in Table 9.8. Assume they were chosen because Southwest believed that by taking those actions they would be able to achieve the mock target values that defined a unique and valued competitive position.

Notice that several of the actions chosen helped them achieve the target values that were set for more than one activity. These actions have synergy with multiple activities. For example, the elimination of baggage transfers reduces the cost of interacting with other airlines, and it also increases the percent of departures that leave on time. It is important to notice how the actions stated in

**Table 9.8**
**Actions That Enable the Target Values to Be Met**

| Predictive Metrics (Activities) | Southwest Airline Target Value | Strategy (Actions To Be Taken) |
|---|---|---|
| Increase the percent of departures that leave on time. | 98% | 15-minute gate turnarounds. No meals. No baggage transfers. No connections to other airlines. Standardized fleet of 737 aircraft. |
| Increase the number of hours/day each plane is in flight. | 16 hours | Short-haul, Point-to-point routes between mid-size cities and secondary airports in large cities. Standardized fleet of 737 aircraft. 15-minute gate turnarounds. |
| Reduce the cost of interacting with other airlines. | $0 | No baggage transfers. No connections to other airlines. |
| Reduce the cost of airplane maintenance. | $3000/flight | Standardized fleet of 737 aircraft. |
| Reduce the time required to go between mid-size cities and large cities. | average of 1.5 hours | Short-haul, Point-to-point routes between mid-size cities and secondary airports in large cities. |
| Increase the amount of profit that could be obtained per day. | $150/passenger | High aircraft utilization. Frequent, reliable departures. Lean, highly productive ground and gate crews. No meals. Many of the other stated features. |
| Increase the levels of compensation awarded to employees. | $42K average | High compensation of employees. |
| Reduce the administrative costs associated with ticketing. | $6 | Automatic ticketing machines. No seat assignments. |
| Increase the percent of profits that can be shared by employees. | 6% | High level of employee stock ownership. Flexible union contracts. |
| Reduce the passengers' cost of flying. | $180/passenger | Very low ticket prices. Limited use of travel agencies. Limited passenger service. |

the column on the right drive the corresponding activities, or predictive metrics, to their stated target values.

Determining which actions are required to drive the corresponding predictive metrics to their stated target values is the essence of strategy formulation. The collective set of actions form the chosen strategy. The actions describe the features or the elements of the chosen strategy. Southwest's overall strategy is to offer short-haul, low cost, point-to-point service between mid-size cities and secondary airports in large cities. They avoid large airports and do not fly great distances. Making these choices enabled them to achieve the target values that defined what they believed to be a unique and valued competitive position.

Defining the fewest number of actions that will enable an organization to satisfy its customers' most important desired outcomes is the prime objective of strategy formulation. Defining these actions requires hundreds of trade-off decisions. These trade-off decisions can be made effectively using the trade-off logic that is integrated into this strategy formulation process.

As stated by Michael Porter, "Strategy is making trade-offs in competing. Trade-offs are essential to strategy. They create the need for choice and purposefully limit what a company offers." This advanced approach to strategy formulation enables an organization to effectively make the trade-offs that are required to determine what activities they should pursue and what actions they should take. It assists organizations in making the trade-off decisions that are required to achieve a sustainable strategic position.

## STRATEGY AS CREATING FIT AMONG A COMPANY'S ACTIVITIES

Michael Porter states, "The creation of an effective strategy requires that an organization be able to ensure its selected strategic activities fit together to create a distinctive and sustainable competitive advantage for the organization." In other words, the activities that an organization chooses to take must fit together such that they complement, reinforce and optimize one another, and the synergy between them must yield a sustainable competitive advantage.

Executing a system of interlocked activities is more likely to result in a sustainable competitive advantage than specializing in the execution of a single activity. The activities pursued by Southwest Airlines, for example, complement, reinforce and optimize one another. Their choice to eliminate meals, interline baggage transfers and seat assignments complement each other in ensuring on-time departures are achieved. These same choices reinforce Southwest's low cost positioning and optimize its ability to increase the number of hours per day each aircraft is in flight. As stated by Michael Porter, "positions built on systems of activities are far more sustainable than those built on individual activities."

To create a fit among a company's activities, an organization must be able to effectively determine which activities complement, reinforce and optimize the value delivered by other activities.

When using this advanced strategy formulation process, this set of relationships is determined when uncovering the synergy that exists between each predictive metric and each desired outcome. This is accomplished through the use of matrix analysis. When using this process, an organization can effectively determine which activities have a synergy with each desired outcome. This method is detailed in Appendix B. The questions are asked, "Which activities predict the satisfaction of each desired outcome? To what degree will these activities predict the satisfaction of each desired outcome?" The predictive met-

**Figure 9.1**
**Relationships Between Predictive Metrics and Desired Outcomes**

Synergy Analysis Legend
Strong Relationship ● 9
Medium Relationship ○ 3
Weak Relationship △ 1

| Desired Outcome | Reduce the cost of interacting with other airlines. | Increase the percent of departures that leave on time. | Reduce the administrative costs associated with ticketing. | Reduce the cost of airplane maintenance. | Increase the percent of profits shared by employees. | Increase the levels of employee compensation. | Increase the number of hours/day each plane is in flight. | Increase the amount of profit that could be obtained/day. | Reduce the passengers' cost of flying. | Reduce the time to fly between mid-size and large cities. | Importance | Percent Importance (%) |
|---|---|---|---|---|---|---|---|---|---|---|---|---|
| Minimize the passengers' cost of flying. | △ | △ | △ | △ | | | △ | | ● | | 9.7 | 10.6 |
| Minimize the time required to go between mid-size and large cities. | ○ | ○ | △ | | | | △ | | | ● | 9.5 | 10.4 |
| Ensure the employees high levels of compensation. | | | | | | ● | | △ | | | 9.5 | 10.4 |
| Ensure on-time departures. | △ | ● | △ | | | | | | | | 9.4 | 10.3 |
| Minimize the cost of maintaining their airplanes. | | | | ● | | | | | | | 9.2 | 10.0 |
| Ensure the maximum daily use of their fleet. | △ | ○ | △ | △ | | | ● | | | | 9.1 | 9.9 |
| Maximize the amount of daily profit that could be obtained. | △ | △ | △ | △ | | | △ | | | | 8.9 | 9.7 |
| Enable the employees to profit from the airlines success. | | | | | ● | | | | | | 8.9 | 9.7 |
| Minimize the administrative costs associated with ticketing. | △ | | ● | | | | | | | | 8.8 | 9.6 |
| Minimize the cost of interacting with other airlines. | ● | | △ | | | | | | | | 8.6 | 9.4 |
| **Normalized Importance** | 14 | 14 | 13 | 12 | 10 | 9 | 8 | 7 | 7 | 6 | | |

rics with the most synergy are those that predict the satisfaction of several important desired outcomes. They constitute the activities that most effectively drive the creation of value. In other words, the high priority predictive metrics represent activities that, when executed, will partially or completely assist in the execution of other activities. One activity may assist in the execution of several other activities. The top activities may assist in the execution of up to 70% of the other activities. This is what is meant by synergy.

In essence, the high priority predictive metrics represent a complex array of interlocked activities that complement, reinforce and optimize the other activities. The high priority metrics define the activities that, if action is taken, will result in a sustainable competitive advantage.

Figure 9.1 helps to explain how matrix analysis is used to prioritize the predictive metrics that have been defined in the Southwest example. The predictive metrics are shown along the top, and the desired outcomes are shown in the column on the left. The symbols in the matrix indicate where relationships exist and the strength of the relationship. The values in the right-hand column are associated with each desired outcome. They represent the weighted importance of each desired outcome. The values in the bottom row, the normalized importance row, reflect the percent of value contributed by each activity. This number is calculated using the mathematical calculation described in Appendix B. The activities with the highest normalized importance values contribute most to the creation of customer value. They partially or completely assist in the execution of multiple activities. They are the metrics or activities with synergy.

Notice that the high priority predictive metrics define the activities that complement, reinforce and optimize the satisfaction of the most important desired outcomes. The high priority metrics predict, to some degree, the satisfaction of multiple desired outcomes. Up to 300 predictive metrics are typically prioritized when applying this process to real world situations. Knowing which of those 300 predictive metrics have the most synergy with the desired outcomes enables an organization to determine which activities, if pursued, will complement, reinforce and optimize one another. The high priority predictive metrics define the system of interlocked activities that can be pursued to create a distinctive and sustainable competitive advantage.

As stated by Michael Porter, "The success of a strategy depends on doing many things well—not just a few—and integrating among them. If there is no fit among activities, there is no distinctive strategy and little sustainability." This advanced strategy formulation process is designed to enable an organization to define the activities that have fit and attain a strong strategic position.

## ADDRESSING THE EXPECTATIONS OF STRATEGY

In addition to enabling the achievement of the three important strategic objectives stated above, the process also enables organizations to:

1. Evolve their strategy formulation, planning and decision-making capabilities.
2. Understand their customers' perception of value.
3. Develop strategies and solutions that deliver many times more value than those previously created.
4. Systematically evolve the processes, products, services and strategies that affect their organization.
5. Increase the rate at which they create value for themselves and others.

As stated by Gary Hamel and C. K. Prahalad in *Competing for the Future* (1994), organizations "need a new process for strategy-making, one that is more exploratory and less ritualistic. They need to apply new and different resources to the task of strategy-making, relying on the creativity of hundreds of managers and not just on the wisdom of a few planners."

The CD-MAP process provides the structure, information and processing power that is required to formulate breakthrough strategies and solutions. It enables top management to communicate the customers' desired outcomes and the metrics that predict the delivery of value to employees throughout the organization. It enables hundreds of managers and other individuals to participate in and contribute to the formulation of breakthrough strategies. It enables individuals to focus on the achievement of the organization's strategic objectives.

This process can be integrated into an organization in many ways. Internal consultants can be trained, external consultants can be used and advanced technology can be used to make this process an integral part of the organization. For example, the tools that have been developed to support the application of this process can be used to create an integrated knowledge network. Such a network is capable of enabling an organization to define and organize the universe of possible solutions from which individuals throughout the organization can invent and discover. Individuals from across the organization can use this information to find the best strategies and solutions for a given situation. The tools are designed to enable users to quickly formulate the strategies and solutions that will satisfy the largest number of important desired outcomes while honoring any imposed constraints and enabling the achievement of the desired competitive position.

This process is driving an Intellectual Revolution in business—a revolution in which all organizations are empowered (have the power) to anticipate future opportunities, make value-generating investment decisions and determine which products and services to develop, which core competencies to obtain, which technologies to pioneer, which activities to pursue and which tradeoffs to make. In short, the process driving the Intellectual Revolution provides all organizations with the power to systematically accelerate the creation and delivery of customer value.

## SUMMARY

This process enables organizations to think and act strategically. It takes the mystery out of strategy and enables organizations to put into practice the theories that are supported by well-respected strategists, consultants and academics. As an example, it can be shown how this process is often used to address the important elements of strategy formulation as they are defined by one of today's leading strategists—Michael Porter.

In his article titled "What Is Strategy?" (1996), Michael Porter describes *what* an effective strategy must deliver. He states that "an effective strategy must enable an organization to:

1. Uncover a unique and valued position that involves a set of activities that are different than those taken by competitors.

2. Make all the required trade-offs, vis-à-vis competitors, to determine what activities should be pursued and what actions should be taken.

3. Ensure the activities that are taken to execute the strategy fit together to create a distinctive and sustainable competitive advantage for the organization."

To achieve the first strategic objective, an organization must be able to successfully determine:

1. What potential target markets exist and which segments to target.
2. What activities are valued by that set of target customers.
3. How well each activity is currently performed by competitors.
4. What level of satisfaction must be achieved for each activity to occupy a unique and valued competitive position.

This advanced strategy formulation process is often used to obtain the answers to each of these complex questions. Once the information is obtained, it is organized within the structure of the USFM. The information is then used to systematically formulate a strategy that places the organization in a unique and valued position. In addition, through the use of this process, an organization can be assured that its chosen strategy will involve a set of activities that are different than those taken by competitors.

The second strategic objective involves making the trade-off decisions that will enable an organization to determine what activities to pursue and what actions to take. Advanced trade-off logic is integrated into this strategy formulation process to enable an organization to determine what *activities* to pursue. The trade-off logic that is employed is used to:

1. Ensure that the chosen strategies and solutions drive the satisfaction of important and unsatisfied desired outcomes at the expense of satisfying less important or already satisfied desired outcomes.
2. Drive the pursuit of activities that satisfy many important desired outcomes at the expense of pursuing activities that satisfy only one important, or several relatively unimportant, desired outcomes.
3. Drive the performance levels required to obtain a competitive advantage at the expense of achieving target values that produce a me-too competitive position.

Advanced trade-off logic is also integrated into this process to enable an organization to determine what *actions* to pursue. The trade-off logic employed for this purpose is used to drive the pursuit of actions that:

1. Enable valued activities to be performed at the expense of less valued activities.
2. Enable the achievement of the target values that have been set for many highly valued activities at the expense of achieving the target value set for only one valued, or several relatively unvalued, activities.
3. Honor the stated constraints at the expense of all other criteria.

The third strategic objective involves choosing to execute activities that fit together to create a distinctive and sustainable competitive advantage for the organization. When executing this advanced strategy formulation process, the prioritized set of predictive metrics effectively defines the array of interlocked activities that complement, reinforce and optimize one another as they predict the creation and delivery of customer value. Prioritized predictive metrics drive the creation of a distinctive and sustainable competitive advantage.

This advanced strategy formulation process can be used to put into practice the theories that are supported by many well-respected strategists, consultants and academics. Although Michael Porter's view of strategy dominates much of today's thinking, many other theories exist. We have found that many of those theories, if sound, can be employed through the use of this process. It is the catalyst that is driving an Intellectual Revolution in business.

# Capturing and Prioritizing Desired Outcomes

## CAPTURING DESIRED OUTCOMES

Two of the most important factors associated with capturing customer desired outcomes are:

1. Recognizing that you are attempting to capture desired outcomes—not solutions, vague statements, antidotes, stories or other types of information.
2. Distinguishing between desired outcomes and solutions.

Customers unintentionally make it difficult to capture desired outcomes, because they are typically focused on solutions. We have developed the techniques that are required to capture desired outcomes even when customers offer statements that begin as solutions or vague statements.

Desired outcomes can be captured on a company, its products and services and its operating, support and management processes. Desired outcomes are captured in sessions that are conducted with customers who are involved in or affected by the specified mission. The customers may be internal or external customers depending on the mission that is being undertaken. The criteria that are to be used to select the customers are typically generated by a company consultant or by someone within the organization. The criteria are defined to ensure all pertinent customer types and segments are represented. A third-party research firm that specializes in recruiting is often used to recruit the individuals who will participate in the session. The participants are evaluated by that firm to ensure the individuals meet the specified screening criteria. The third-party firm also often provides the facility at which the interviews are conducted. The sessions are typically video recorded and taped. Although the environment is much like that of a traditional focus group, that is where the similarities end.

A session typically involves up to 10 participants and a desired outcome gathering expert. The advanced methods for gathering desired outcomes are based on a special application of Neuro Linguistic Programming (NLP). NLP is a behavioral science that is focused on modifying human response in a specific situation. As part of this science, the individuals undergoing treatment must convey their desired outcomes to a psychologist. We have studied the techniques that are used to capture a patient's desired outcomes and have modified them for use in capturing desired outcomes from customers.

As the session begins, the participants are introduced to the subject matter and are asked to introduce themselves. We then explain how the session will be conducted. The participants are aware that we are attempting to capture requirements in a specific format and that we may have to ask probing questions to get the information in the format we need it. One point should be made clear. We typically pay the participants anywhere from $75 to $250 to be there, and they are there for one purpose—so we can capture their desired outcomes— period. They are not there for us to entertain, or solicit for business or give the company a good spin. Everything we do is focused only on capturing their desired outcomes.

Desired outcomes are captured from individuals within the group in real time. The person gathering the desired outcomes typically types the customer's initial statements into a notebook computer and then begins the process of transforming them into desired outcomes. The solutions and vague statements that are initially received are used as a starting point from which to uncover the actual desired outcomes. The participants may be asked how a specific solution benefits them or why a stated solution is important. Each statement is scrutinized to ensure it meets a strict set of criteria. As the statements are transformed into desired outcomes, the interviewer is ensuring that each desired outcome is:

1. Focused on the subject of interest.
2. Free from any solutions and specifications.
3. Free from any vague words or ambiguous statements.
4. Stable over time.
5. Descriptive of what is desired.
6. Capable of being measured.

Once a desired outcome is captured in the required format, the interviewer reads the desired outcome back to the participants for clarification, verification and acceptance. If a desired outcome is not correct, it is addressed at that time. The session concludes with a list of desired outcomes that all the participants agree represent what they would like to achieve from the strategy or solution that is being formulated.

The techniques that we use to gather desired outcomes are more efficient, faster and less costly than methods that are traditionally used to capture customer requirements. They eliminate the need to go back to the individual for clarification as the desired outcomes are verified, in real time, with the customers during the session. There is no need for the organization to second-guess what the customers really meant. There is no need to get new or more requirements months later, as the desired outcomes are complete and are stable over time. This approach to requirements gathering enables organizations of all sizes to capture their customers' desired outcomes.

The objective of each session is to capture all the desired outcomes that the customers have on the subject of interest. It is important to note that desired outcomes are captured on one subject at a time. For example, if the objective is to capture desired outcomes on the process of storing and retrieving data, then desired outcomes on the process of distributing a storage system or on the sales representative selling the storage system are not accepted at that time.

Up to 70% of all the desired outcomes that will ever be captured on a subject are typically captured in a single session. To ensure all the desired outcomes are captured, multiple sessions are conducted. Each session is represented with individuals who have diverse views such that their experiences, user environments and demographics represent both extreme and mainstream views. This diversity ensures that even the most obscure desired outcomes will be captured.

It is important that we capture all the desired outcomes associated with a specific mission. This will ensure that opportunities are not missed. Fortunately, we do not have to capture thousands of desired outcomes. We have discovered that there are a finite number of desired outcomes on any subject and that, statistically speaking, over 96% of those desired outcomes can be captured using the techniques that we have developed. From a statistical perspective, if a large enough sample of individuals, representing diverse aspects of the subject of interest, are interviewed, then no matter how many additional individuals are interviewed, new desired outcomes will not be uncovered. Statistically speaking, when you interview 30 individuals, virtually all the desired outcomes that can be captured will be captured. It is this principle that guides the number of interviews that are conducted when we capture the customers' desired outcomes. John Hauser, a professor at MIT, and Abbie Griffin, a professor from the University of Chicago, discovered how this statistical principle applies to requirements gathering. Their research was documented in an article titled ''The Voice of the Customer'' (1993). Figure A.1, which summarizes their work, shows the percentage of desired outcomes that are captured as more interviews are conducted.

If four sessions are conducted, for example, 30 desired outcomes may be captured at the first session. At the second session, 30 desired outcomes may also be captured, but 21 of them may be the same as the desired outcomes captured in the first session. The total number of unique desired outcomes collected to that point is now up to 39. In the third session, 30 desired outcomes

**Figure A.1**
**The Statistical Foundation for Gathering Desired Outcomes**

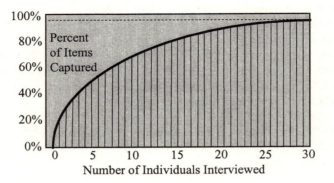

may also be captured, but 27 of them may have been captured in the previous two sessions. The number of desired outcomes now totals 42. In the fourth and final session, 30 desired outcomes may also be captured, but it would not be surprising if each of them were already captured in one of the previous three sessions. In total, 42 or so desired outcomes may be captured.

The 42 desired outcomes that may be collected represent all the desired outcomes that exist on that subject of interest for that customer type. The desired outcomes are mutually exclusive and collectively exhaustive. It is important to note that there are a finite number of desired outcomes on any subject of interest. Based on the projects we have completed, that number typically ranges between 25 and 50 desired outcomes for a given customer group.

It is also important to note that there are not a finite number of solutions that will exist over time. New solutions will be created over time as new ideas and technologies become available. The statistical principles described above, therefore, do not apply to the collection of solutions.

## PRIORITIZING DESIRED OUTCOMES

Once the desired outcomes are captured, we use traditional quantitative research methods to quantify the importance of each desired outcome and to determine the degree to which each outcome is currently satisfied. Traditional methods are used to acquire this information, but we do apply several techniques that are somewhat unique to the field of market research. We will describe the traditional methods that are used and then highlight the unique methods that we apply to obtain the required information without incurring excessive costs.

First, let's describe how the traditional quantitative market research is conducted. This process consists of several steps. They are as follows:

1. The customer types are defined. The organization must determine who the customers are given the specified mission. It is often the case that more than one customer group

is considered when contemplating a strategy, plan or decision. For example, computer users, company stakeholders and the manufacturer of a storage system may be identified as customers when formulating a strategy to improve a data storage device.

2. A questionnaire is prepared for each customer type. If three customer types exist, then three surveys are executed. Each customer type is asked to rate the importance and satisfaction for each of their desired outcomes. They only rate the importance of their desired outcomes. For example, the computer users rate only the computer users desired outcomes; stakeholders rate only the stakeholders desired outcomes and so on.

3. The customer segments from which data will be captured are defined in advance of administering the questionnaire. An organization may want several potential target segments to prioritize the importance of a specific set of desired outcomes. For example, a portable cell phone manufacturer may want policemen, boaters, factory workers and on-the-road executives to prioritize the desired outcomes they may have while communicating in transit.

4. A research sample is designed to ensure each customer type is interviewed in the appropriate proportions. The sample design must consider the overall size of the sample and the number of interviews that will be conducted in each cell or target segment. A minimum of 30 interviews per cell is required if variance is to be explained using normal distribution.

5. The questionnaires are administered. They are typically administered by a third-party research firm and are conducted via a phone or a phone/fax interview. We do not conduct mail-out research or any other form of research where the identity of the respondent is uncertain.

6. The results of the field-work are coded, tabulated and prepared for delivery to the organization sponsoring the research. A third-party research firm typically completes this activity.

7. The information is input into a database so the data can be viewed in the desired format.

One discovery that we made while executing many strategy formulation projects is—contrary to what most market research firms will tell you—an organization does not have to conduct a large number of interviews to obtain the information that is needed to formulate a breakthrough strategy. Many research firms will convince you that you have to complete over 1,000 interviews to obtain valid data. For this application, it is just not true.

Approximately 60 to 540 interviews are completed for each customer type. The number of interviews required is based on the objective of obtaining an error rate of plus or minus 6% at a 90% confidence interval for each data point. The size of the sample does not have to be very large to achieve these objectives. To reduce the error rate to plus or minus 3%, or increase the confidence interval to 95%, up to five times as many interviews must be conducted. This can more than triple the cost of the research. We are simply trying to find out which desired outcomes are most important and least satisfied. We do not need 1,000 interviews to obtain information with the accuracy that is needed to effectively

**Figure A.2**
**Diminishing Returns with Increasing Sample Size**

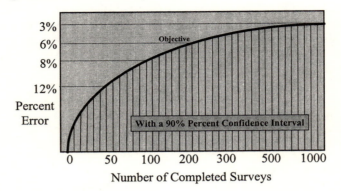

execute this process. When adding more interviews, you quickly reach a point of diminishing returns. This law of diminishing returns is illustrated in Figure A.2.

The sample size must increase geometrically to obtain small improvements in accuracy. For purposes of discriminating between the most and least important desired outcomes, a larger sample size is not necessary.

Once we receive the data from the research firm, we apply a technique developed to assist in ensuring that we obtain excellent discrimination between what is most and least important. Many organizations use means or averages—this usually produces poor discrimination. We take the percentage of individuals who rate a desired outcome a 4 or a 5—very important or critically important—and use that number in our rating. For example, if 89% of those surveyed rate the importance of an outcome a 4 or a 5—top two boxes—then we give that desired outcome a rating of 8.9—placing it on a scale of 1 to 10. The 8.9 is derived simply by dividing 89% by 10 to place it on the 1 to 10 scale. If only 23% of those interviewed rate the importance of an outcome a 4 or a 5, then we give the desired outcome a rating of 2.3. This technique enables us to obtain excellent discrimination along a 10-point scale, while ensuring that we are focused on what is clearly most important to those being surveyed.

We have developed one other technique that has assisted us in formulating breakthrough strategies and solutions. Once we have the raw data, we want to know where the greatest areas of opportunity lie. We know that if we can formulate a strategy or solution that will satisfy desired outcomes that are both important and unsatisfied, then we will likely formulate a breakthrough solution.

Although it is obvious that opportunity exists when a desired outcome is important and unsatisfied, it was somewhat difficult finding a mathematical equation that could be used to quantify opportunity. We wanted to be able to prioritize the desired outcomes based on the amount of opportunity that was associated with each one. We developed a calculation, called the Opportunity

Calculation, that enables the effective prioritization of desired outcomes based on opportunity. The calculation ensures that the high priority desired outcomes are those that are the most important *and* least satisfied. The equation is:

Importance Rating + (Importance Rating − Satisfaction Rating)

So, for example, if a desired outcome had an importance rating of 5 and a satisfaction rating of 2, it would receive a higher priority than an outcome that had an importance rating of 5 and a satisfaction rating of 4. The scores would be 8—5 + (5 − 2) for the first outcome—versus 6—5 + (5 − 4) for the second outcome. This technique is very effective in determining where the organization should focus to create the most value for the company and its customers.

All the research techniques used in this process have been developed and refined to specifically ensure the effective execution of the Universal Strategy Formulation Model (USFM). As a result, the research methods are both powerful and cost effective.

## USING DESIRED OUTCOMES AS A BASIS FOR SEGMENTATION

When executing this strategy formulation process, cluster analysis is often performed using the desired outcome numerical importance value as the basis for clustering. Computer software programs such as SPSS and SAS, which support cluster analysis, are used to perform this operation. This analysis is conducted to enable an organization to uncover market segments that are homogeneous. More specifically, it enables an organization to find or segment customers that value the same desired outcomes. This often greatly simplifies the formulation of company, product and service strategies.

When instructed to perform cluster analysis, the clustering program analyzes the importance ratings that each individual has given each desired outcome. It places the respondents that value the same desired outcomes into a cluster. Several clusters may exist—in fact the user can specify the number of clusters. In the end, all the individuals that are in a cluster are there because they rated the importance of the desired outcomes similarly. In essence, it finds and groups respondents that value the same desired outcomes. As illustrated in Figure A.3, the ratings a respondent gives to all the desired outcomes will give that respondent a numerical position in multi-dimensional space. The individuals positioned closely together form a cluster.

Individuals within each cluster have a homogeneous set of desired outcomes. Different desired outcomes are valued in each of the clusters. For example, the individuals in segment 1 above may value desired outcomes 1, 3, 7, 24 and 31. The individuals in segment 2 may value desired outcomes 2, 9, 15, 27 and 36.

**Figure A.3**
**Segments Generated Using Cluster Analysis**

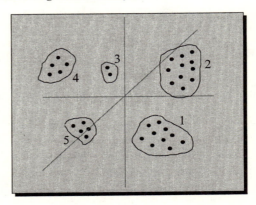

It is for this reason that they form separate clusters. The solutions that are required to satisfy the unique desired outcomes in each cluster may be different.

Exercising this aspect of the process provides an organization with a tremendous competitive advantage in the way they create, market and position their products, services and other solutions. Outcome-Based Segmentation, as we call it, provides a means by which to determine the similarities and differences of individuals within a market. This technique has been used by organizations to create and position products and services that meet the unique desired outcomes of customers in different market segments. In addition, it does not interfere with traditional segmentation schemes that may be used for financial, distribution or other purposes.

When applied to product and service development, Outcome-Based Segmentation enables an organization to determine which desired outcomes are valued across all market segments and to discover which desired outcomes are uniquely important to specific segments. This technique can lead to the creation of low cost product or service platforms that address the desired outcomes common to all market segments. It also enables an organization to develop unique offerings that address segment specific desired outcomes. This concept is illustrated in Figure A.4 for a situation in which three segments exist.

An ability to focus in this manner brings economies of scale and profit to a manufacturing or development organization. It drives the creation of a low-cost platform product that addresses the desired outcomes important across the total market. This platform product or service may be offered across all segments as a low-cost entry solution. In addition, it enables an organization to develop segment specific solutions. Customers within each segment are willing to pay a premium for that solution as it satisfies their unique desired outcomes. This methodology provides organizations with many advantages when creating and positioning its products and services.

**Figure A.4**
**Market Segmentation in Product and Service Development**

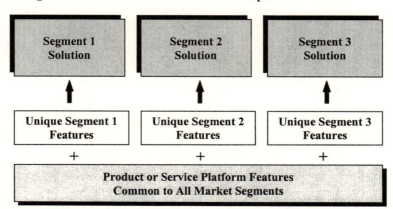

# Appendix B

# Prioritizing Predictive Metrics

As part of executing the Universal Strategy Formulation Model (USFM), a list of prioritized predictive metrics are used to achieve a variety of strategic objectives. The order in which they are prioritized is dependent on several factors. They include:

1. The number of relationships a predictive metric has with the desired outcomes.
2. The strength of each relationship.
3. The numerical importance value assigned to each desired outcome with which the predictive metric has a relationship.
4. The weighting given to each customer type in the customer set reflecting the extent of the role played by that customer type.
5. The weighting given to each customer type in the customer set to offset the differences in the number of desired outcomes that have been captured for each customer type.

The first three factors are combined into what is called a normalized importance calculation. The normalized importance of each metric is determined through the use of both matrix analysis and a mathematical formula. Matrix analysis is used to establish the predictive relationships that exist between each predictive metric and each desired outcome. Each metric is analyzed to determine if it predicts, to any degree, the satisfaction of each desired outcome. If a predictive relationship does not exist, then a value is not assigned. If a predictive relationship does exist, then a predictive value is assigned; this is a numerical value between one and nine. A weak relationship receives a numerical value of 1 and a strong relationship receives a value of 9. Other relationships receive values between 1 and 9. This analysis is completed for each customer type in

**Figure B.1**
**Prioritizing Predictive Metrics**

| | Predictive Metric 1 | Predictive Metric 2 | Predictive Metric 3 | Predictive Metric 4 | Importance (C1) | Percent Importance (C2) | Sum of Row (C3) | Percent Importance/Sum (C4) |
|---|---|---|---|---|---|---|---|---|
| Desired Outcome 1 | ● | | O | O | 5.0 | 29.4 | 15 | 1.96 |
| Desired Outcome 2 | | ● | △ | | 4.0 | 23.5 | 10 | 2.35 |
| Desired Outcome 3 | △ | | ● | △ | 5.0 | 29.4 | 11 | 2.67 |
| Desired Outcome 4 | O | | | ● | 3.0 | 17.6 | 12 | 1.47 |
| **Normalized Importance** | 24.72 | 21.15 | 32.26 | 21.78 | | | | |

Synergy Analysis Legend
Strong Relationship  ●  9
Medium Relationship  O  3
Weak Relationship  △  1

the customer set. Since each customer matrix may contain 50 desired outcomes and 50 predictive metrics, the analysis often requires the assessment of 2,500 relationships per customer matrix.

The use of the normalized importance calculation establishes a normalized importance value for each predictive metric. This value represents the amount of synergy that is associated with that metric, and is used as the basis by which to prioritize the metrics. To be more specific, the normalized importance value represents the percent of desired outcomes whose satisfaction is predicted by that metric. As an example, if a metric has a normalized importance value of 6.25, that means the satisfaction of 6.25% of the total number of desired outcomes is predicted by that one metric.

The calculation is best explained with the use of the information provided in Figure B.1. The four rightmost columns contain the data that is used to complete the calculation. The Importance column contains the importance rating assigned to each specific desired outcome. The Percent Importance column contains the weighted importance of each desired outcome. This value is obtained by summing all the importance ratings of the desired outcomes—5 + 4 + 5 + 3 = 17—and dividing the importance rating for each desired outcome by the total. For example, the first desired outcome has a percent importance rating of 5 ÷ 17 × 100 or 29.4.

The third column, Sum of Row, contains the sum of the predictive values for each desired outcome. For example, the first desired outcome has a strong relationship with metric 1, which has a predictive value of 9, and a moderate relationship with metrics 3 and 4, each of which have a predictive value of 3. The sum of the row is then 9 + 3 + 3 or 15. The sum of the row for Desired

Outcome 2 is 9 + 1 or 10. The fourth column contains a value that is calculated by dividing the Percent Importance, the value in Column 2, by the sum of the row, the value in Column 3. The value for the first desired outcome, for example, is calculated by dividing 29.4 by 15. This equals 1.96 as shown in Column 4.

With an understanding of how the values in the table are derived, let's now explain how the normalized importance value is obtained. We will first calculate the normalized importance value for Predictive Metric 2. The normalized importance value for Predictive Metric 2 is obtained by multiplying the value in Column 4, on the far right, by the predictive value that Predictive Metric 2 has with Desired Outcome 2. This becomes 2.35 × 9 or 21.15. This is the normalized importance value for Predictive Metric 2. Since Predictive Metric 2 has only one relationship with one desired outcome, the calculation is quite simple.

Calculating the normalized importance value for Predictive Metric 1 is slightly more complicated because multiple relationships exist. The normalized importance value for Predictive Metric 1 is obtained as follows.

For each desired outcome that has a relationship with Predictive Metric 1, you multiply the value in Column 4 by the predictive value that exists between the metric and the desired outcome. So, because a strong relationship exists between Predictive Metric 1 and Desired Outcome 1, we take 1.96 from Column 4 and multiply that by 9, the predictive value associated with a strong relationship. The product is 17.64. We then execute the same calculation for the other desired outcomes that have a relationship with Predictive Metric 1. For Desired Outcome 3, we multiply 2.67 by 1, the predictive value associated with a weak relationship, to obtain a product of 2.67. For Desired Outcome 4, we multiply 1.47 by 3, the predictive value associated with a moderate relationship, to obtain a product of 4.41. To obtain the normalized importance value we then add the three products together—(1.96 × 9) + (2.67 × 1) + (1.47 × 3). The result is a normalized importance value of 24.72. The number of products to be added together is dependent on the number of desired outcomes with which the predictive metric has a relationship.

Similarly, the normalized importance value for Predictive Metric 3 is obtained by adding (1.96 × 3) + (2.35 × 1) + (2.67 × 9). This totals 32.26. The normalized importance value for Predictive Metric 4 is obtained by adding (1.96 × 3) + (2.67 × 1) + (1.47 × 9). This totals 21.78.

Once the normalized importance values are calculated for each metric, the values are multiplied by two other factors to obtain the final prioritization that is carried forward through the process.

The normalized importance values are first multiplied by the weighting that is given to each customer type in the customer set to reflect the extent of the role that is played by that customer. For example, if two customer types exist in the customer set, one customer may be given a 60% weighting and the other may be given a 40% weighting. The normalized importance values for all the metrics in the customer matrix with the 60% weighting are therefore multiplied by 0.6. The normalized importance values for all the metrics in the customer matrix with the 40% weighting are multiplied by 0.4. This weighting adjusts the importance of the metrics so the most important customer type gains a stronger representation in the formulation of the strategy or solution that will result from the execution of the process.

The new values are then multiplied by one more weighting factor. This factor offsets the differences in the number of desired outcomes that have been captured for each customer type. If, for example, one customer matrix has 25 desired outcomes, and the second matrix has only 20 desired outcomes, then all the values for the predictive metrics in the matrix with 25 desired outcomes will be multiplied by .55 (25/45). The values for the predictive metrics in the matrix with 20 desired outcomes will be multiplied by .44; (20/45). This ensures that the results are not skewed due to differing numbers of desired outcomes in a matrix.

In a final calculation, the resulting numbers are recalculated as a percentage so they add up to 100%. This ensures that the final value represents the percent of desired outcomes whose satisfaction is predicted by each metric. This value then dictates the priority that is given to each predictive metric as it is carried forward throughout the process.

For more information regarding this subject, please reference the paper published by Robert Hales titled "Deployment Normalization." It was published in 1990 and is the property of International TecheGroup Incorporated in Milford, Ohio.

# Appendix C

# Using Predictive Metrics

## USING PREDICTIVE METRICS TO DEFINE THE DESIRED COMPETITIVE POSITION

One of the most important applications of predictive metrics is to use them to establish the desired competitive position. The desired competitive position is the unique and valued position that an organization desires to achieve relative to its competitors. To achieve the desired competitive position, the chosen solution or strategy must satisfy the customers' desired outcomes better than any competitive solution.

The desired competitive position is established by assigning a target value to each of the high priority predictive metrics. The target values assigned to the predictive metrics define the level of satisfaction that must be achieved by any proposed solution. Target values are set to define the desired competitive position and are then used as a guide to drive the creation of solutions that will achieve the desired competitive position.

The desired competitive position is not static. It is dynamic. As new ideas and technologies are introduced, it may be necessary to redefine the desired competitive position. The information collected as part of the process is often used by an organization to both define and maintain its desired competitive position. Target values are often set for multiple points in time to define the desired competitive position well into the future.

This point is illustrated in the following example. Target values for the predictive metrics that came from the hospital administrator in the surgical system example may be stated as in Table C.1 for various points in time.

Notice how the target values get more aggressive over time. An organization would like to define and achieve aggressive target values for the metrics that

**Table C.1**
**Target Values over Time**

| Predictive Metric | Target Value in 1 year | Target Value in 5 years | Target Value in 10 years |
|---|---|---|---|
| Reduce the **time** required to set up the system for different operations. | 3 minutes | 45 seconds | 10 seconds |
| Reduce the **time** required to repair an unexpected failure. | 24 hours | 18 hours | 4 hours |
| Reduce the **frequency** with which planned servicing is required. | 4 times a year | 2 times a year | 1 time a year |
| Reduce the **space** (cubic inches) required by the system. | 800 cu. in. | 760 cu. in. | 690 cu. in. |
| Reduce the planned **cost** to upgrade to new technologies in the future. | 30% of initial cost | 25% of initial cost | 10% of initial cost |

predict the satisfaction of the customers' most important desired outcomes. Identifying and prioritizing the desired outcomes, defining and prioritizing the predictive metrics and establishing the target values make it possible for an organization to define a unique and valued competitive position.

In practice, the target values are often defined relative to a competitor's position. This is often done to ensure that the resulting strategy or solution will enable the organization to occupy a competitive position that is superior to that held by its competitors. This technique enables an organization to position itself against its competitors along some meaningful set of criteria, before the strategy or solution is formulated.

As an example, documented in the worksheet in Table C.2 are the predictive metrics that came from the hospital administrator. They may be used by Company 1 as the criteria by which to establish a unique and valued competitive position over Company 2.

First, a measurement is taken to establish the current competitive position of each company. Next, Company 1 defines a future target value for each predictive metric. This future value describes the competitive position that is desired by Company 1 relative to Company 2. It describes their desired competitive position.

The future target value, once established, guides the quality of the solutions that are considered by Company 1 when they execute the Universal Strategy Formulation Model (USFM). If a proposed solution does not exceed the current value achieved by Company 2, then the company knows that the solution will not be competitive with the Company 2 offering along that dimension. For example, if a proposed solution does not enable the user to set up the system for different operations in less than 45 seconds, then the solution will not have a competitive advantage over the Company 2 offering. If a proposed solution meets the target value set by Company 1 (i.e., 10 seconds), then the company

**Table C.2**
**Defining the Desired Competitive Position**

| Predictive Metric | Current Value For Company 1 | Current Value For Company 2 | Target Value For Company 1 |
|---|---|---|---|
| Reduce the **time** required to set up the system for different operations. | 3 minutes | 45 seconds | 10 seconds |
| Reduce the **time** required to repair an unexpected failure. | 24 hours | 18 hours | 4 hours |
| Reduce the **frequency** with which planned servicing is required. | 4 times per year | 2 times per year | 1 time per year |
| Reduce the **space** (cubic inches) required by the system. | 800 cu. in. | 760 cu. in. | 690 cu. in. |
| Reduce the planned **cost** to upgrade to new technologies in the future. | 30% of initial cost | 25% of initial cost | 10% of initial cost |

knows that the solution will enable it to achieve a desired competitive position along that dimension.

Using this process to establish the positioning criteria has several advantages over traditional positioning techniques. The criteria, in the form of predictive metrics, are known to predict the delivery of value as perceived by the customer. Because they are in priority order, it is known which metrics predict the satisfaction of the majority of desired outcomes. As a result, the organization can use this information to make decisions that will enable it to strengthen its strategic position prior to formulating the strategy or solution.

Traditional approaches to positioning often require an organization to position a company, product or service after the strategy or solution has already been devised and implemented. This reactive approach to positioning is time consuming, costly and rarely effective. Breakthrough strategies and solutions result more consistently when an organization can first define the competitive position it wants to occupy, and then work toward formulating a strategy or solution that will enable it to occupy that position.

## USING PREDICTIVE METRICS IN THE CREATION OF STRATEGIES AND SOLUTIONS

Once the predictive metrics are defined and prioritized, they are used to assist in the creation of potential solutions. The potential solutions should drive the predictive metrics to the level of satisfaction required to achieve the desired competitive position. Using the predictive metrics to assist in the creation of potential strategies and solutions reflects the philosophy that is embodied in Outcome-Based Logic.

The use of Outcome-Based Logic requires that an organization first define the criteria that describes the optimal solution, the criteria by which a strategy or solution will be judged, and then use that criteria as the basis for creating and

**Figure C.1**
**Outcome-Based Logic**

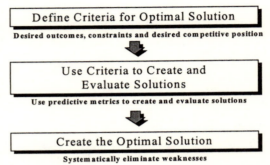

evaluating potential solutions. This concept is referenced once again in Figure C.1.

In executing the CD-MAP process, predictive metrics are used to drive the actual creation of a variety of potential solutions. They are the criteria that define the optimal solution and are used to create the optimal solution. Individuals sometimes tell us, "this is like cheating; you already know what the optimal solution is supposed to do." In one recent consulting assignment, when we reached this stage of the process and the team was evaluating a strategy they had conceived before the project had started, they realized that it did not impact many of the top predictive metrics. They said, "well, if we knew the solution had to drive this set of metrics, we would have defined the strategy differently." That is the whole point. If you know what the optimal solution must do, then it makes sense to use that information in an attempt to create the solution that will make it happen. After all, this is only made possible through the execution of this process. The time and effort has been put forth to define and prioritize the criteria that predict the delivery of customer value.

To create a strategy or solution using the metrics as a guide, it is best to systematically address each metric in priority order across the total customer set. As an example, assume that the predictive metrics (listed in Table C.3) for a system to improve the process of surgery represent the high priority predictive metrics across the appropriate customer set (i.e., surgeons, administrators and the manufacturer).

To create a potential solution, a feature is created to address each prioritized predictive metric. The combination of features becomes the total solution. Focusing on just one metric at a time when creating the total solution makes it possible to channel and focus the organization's collective knowledge and wisdom on one item at a time. In practice this proves to be a tremendous benefit. Individuals are able to focus on metrics they know to be important and predictive of success. They are willing to take the time to brainstorm solutions that will place the organization in its desired competitive position.

**Table C.3**
**Defining Solutions That Will Achieve the Target Values**

| Prioritized Predictive Metric | Target Value | Customer | Potential Solution |
|---|---|---|---|
| Reduce the **volume** of healthy cells that are contacted during the surgery. | 90% less healthy cells | Surgeon | Use minimally invasive fiber optic technology to deliver therapy. |
| Reduce the **number** of times and total **time** the visualization of the field is obstructed. | 0 number 0 seconds | Surgeon | Use fiber optic technology to enhance visualization. |
| Reduce the **time** required to set up the system for different operations. | 3 seconds | Admin | Integrate preprogrammed settings for all potential procedures. |
| Reduce the **time** required to repair an unexpected failure. | 15 seconds | Admin | Enable automatic detection and reroute of failures using modem connection and software. |
| Reduce the **time** required to test the system. | 60 seconds | Mfg. | Integrate a 100% self-test capability. |

When using traditional methods, organizations often go off in dozens of different directions not knowing which deserves the most attention. Individuals tend to brainstorm solutions that address isolated issues, satisfy the one or two customers with whom they have had contact or help them achieve their personal goals. Simply stated, they lack direction and tend to focus on what they believe to be important. The use of this advanced strategy formulation process enables an organization to stay focused on what is most important to the company's internal and external customers. Solutions can be systematically created, feature by feature, until the optimal solution is devised.

For example, in Table C.3, the features designed to address each predictive metric are listed in the column on the right. The company creates features for each metric, one at a time, using all available resources. Because individuals throughout the organization know what to focus on and the value it will provide, they are willing to dedicate their time and energy to executing the strategy formulation process. They are focused on the efficient and effective creation of customer value.

The combination of features listed on the right defines the total solution. It includes fiber optic technology, preprogrammed settings for procedures, failure detection and rerouting and self-test capability. The total solution can then be packaged and delivered as the optimal solution.

In a real world example, features are often created for the top 30 to 60 predictive metrics. Some features may impact several metrics and, as a result, it may not be necessary to define different features for each of the 30 to 60 metrics. In total, 10 to 30 features may define a complete solution. The features can then be prioritized using matrix analysis, if required, to determine which deliver the most value.

The features that are stated will, with certainty, deliver value to the customer set along the stated dimensions. This can be stated with certainty since the features that are created drive the metrics that predict the delivery of value. The features satisfy the most important customer desired outcomes. In fact, the features satisfy many of the other desired outcomes since the high priority metrics often predict the satisfaction of up to 70% of all the desired outcomes. The features that are defined using this approach are the features that most efficiently create value for the organization and its customers.

It should be noted that when creating potential solutions, all features included in the concept must be mutually exclusive of the other features. This means that a feature must not be an alternative to, or a replacement or substitute for, another feature that is listed as part of that concept. It is common to initially create up to six alternative concepts when using this process to formulate a breakthrough strategy or solution. Other concepts are devised after the alternative concepts have been evaluated.

## USING PREDICTIVE METRICS TO EVALUATE SOLUTIONS

The prioritized predictive metrics that are used to create the potential solutions are also used as the criteria by which to evaluate each solution. Concept evaluations are commonly made using one of two evaluation methods. The first method involves comparing each concept against a baseline concept or one of the stated concepts. The second method involves comparing each concept against a standard, which is defined as the fully evolved or theoretically perfect concept.

When evaluating each concept against a baseline concept, the objective is to determine if one solution is better than the other solutions at driving each predictive metric toward the target value that defines the organization's desired competitive position. Each solution is evaluated against the baseline concept for each of the top predictive metrics. It is common to use between 30 and 60 metrics in the evaluation.

When conducting an evaluation of a surgical system, as documented in the example found in Table C.4, the individuals involved in executing the process are asked if a proposed concept is better, worse or the same as the baseline concept at:

1. Reducing the volume of healthy cells that are contacted during the surgery.

2. Reducing the number of times and total time the visualization of the field is obstructed.

3. Reducing the time that is required to set up the system for different operations.

4. Reducing the time that is required to repair an unexpected failure.

5. Reducing the time that is required to test the system.

**Table C.4**
**Evaluating a Concept**

| Prioritized Predictive Metric | Normalized Importance Score | Evaluation of Proposed Concept |
|---|---|---|
| Reduce the **volume** of healthy cells that are contacted during the surgery. | 40.1 | Better +40.1 |
| Reduce the **number** of times and total **time** the visualization of the field is obstructed. | 25.3 | Better +25.3 |
| Reduce the **time** required to set up the system for different operations. | 15.4 | Same +0 |
| Reduce the **time** required to repair an unexpected failure. | 11.5 | Better +11.5 |
| Reduce the **time** required to test the system. | 7.7 | Worse -7.7 |
| **TOTAL CONCEPT SCORE** | 100% | 69.2 |

It should be noted that the concept against which all others are compared is often referred to as the baseline concept. When using this evaluation method, the scores for each concept are calculated relative to the baseline concept. If the proposed concept is better than the baseline or alternative concept at "reducing the volume of healthy cells that are contacted during the surgery," then the algorithm used to calculate the concept score adds the normalized importance value associated with that metric to the total score.

As stated earlier, the normalized importance value represents the percent of desired outcomes whose satisfaction is predicted by that metric. As an example, if a metric had a normalized importance value of 7.7 that means the satisfaction of 7.7% of the total number of desired outcomes is predicted by that one metric. The normalized importance values of all the metrics total 100%, as illustrated in Table C.4.

If the proposed concept is the same as the alternative concept, then the algorithm does not add or subtract the normalized importance value from the total score. If the proposed concept is worse than the alternative concept at "reducing the time required to test the system," then the algorithm used to calculate the concept score subtracts the normalized importance value associated with that metric from the total score. Each of these cases is illustrated in Table C.4.

The normalized importance value for each metric is added or subtracted to the score to obtain the total concept score. For example, the normalized importance values in the right-hand column are either added or subtracted to the score to obtain a total concept score of 69.2. A concept score of 69.2 indicates that 69.2% of the desired outcomes are better satisfied by the concept under evaluation that the concept it is being compared against. This score is calculated by simply adding all the evaluation scores for the stated metrics. For example, $40.1 + 25.3 + 0 + 11.5 - 7.7 = 69.2$.

The concepts could be tested against all the metrics, but as we know, the metrics are in priority order, and it is common to find that 30% of the metrics predict the satisfaction of up to 70% of the desired outcomes. For this reason, an evaluation against more than 30 to 60 metrics is rarely required, as doing so invokes the law of diminishing returns.

When using this evaluation method, a concept may score between $-100$ and $+100$. A concept that receives a negative score should probably not be implemented, since a better solution is known to exist. A concept that receives a score of 5 to 15 offers incremental improvement over the alternative solution. A score in this range is typically achieved when successfully applying Solution-Based Logic techniques to the process of strategy formulation. This is the world in which most organizations live today.

A concept that has a score of 50 or more offers breakthrough improvement over the alternative solution. The objective of using this process is to create a breakthrough solution. It is not uncommon to create a strategy or solution that scores between 50 and 80 when using this process. Possessing this capability provides the organization with a tremendous advantage. Improving the quality of strategies and solutions to this degree greatly enhances an organization's ability to create value for its customers and stakeholders.

One advantage of using this method to evaluate the potential of a solution is that it's fairly easy to identify if one concept is better than another along a specific dimension. Evaluations against a baseline concept can typically be completed in 20 to 30 minutes. The disadvantage is that, although you can determine which concept is better, you do not know the degree to which the solution is fully evolved. In other words, one concept may be better than another concept, but they may both be fairly ineffective concepts. This score will not enable you to make that determination. The other disadvantage is that although you know that one concept is better than the other concept, the score does not take into consideration how much better one concept is over another for each metric. As a result, we have developed a second evaluation method that overcomes these disadvantages.

The second method for evaluating the potential of a proposed strategy or solution involves testing the solution to determine the degree to which it has achieved a fully evolved position, in other words, testing it to determine how close it is to being the theoretically perfect concept. This method evaluates the potential for each solution to evolve each metric to its ultimate target value without requiring a comparison to other solutions or a baseline concept. This methodology requires an organization to rate the ability of a proposed strategy or solution to achieve the ultimate target value for each metric. The rating is established using a scale of 0 to 10, where 10 means the solution will move the metric to its fully evolved position and 0 means the concept has no impact on the metric. This rating, combined with the normalized importance value associated with the metric, is used in an algorithm to calculate the concept score. So, if a solution scores 53% for example, that means the proposed solution evolves the product, service, process or subject of interest to 53% of its fully evolved position. If that were the case, then there would continue to be a considerable opportunity for improvement. If a solution scores 90%, then that means the proposed solution evolves the product, service, process or subject of interest to 90% of its fully evolved position, and only a small amount of opportunity for improvement remains.

This method enables you to determine how much better one concept is over another and the degree to which the theoretically perfect concept has been created. When using this method, a concept can obtain a score between 0 and 100, where 100 means the concept is fully evolved. A concept can only obtain a score of 100 if it drives each metric to its ultimate target value. The disadvantage of using this method is that it may take more time than simply comparing a concept against a baseline concept. We have found that individuals typically find it slightly more difficult comparing concepts against the theoretically perfect concept than they do comparing them against other concepts.

Regardless of which evaluation method is used, it is important to note that the evaluation is taking place at the concept stage—at the time of conception. Having the ability to make this evaluation before the solution is actually designed, prepared, developed, prototyped or implemented saves an organization both time and money. It enables an organization to implement only the strategies and solutions that will create the most value for the organization and its customers.

## USING PREDICTIVE METRICS TO CREATE THE OPTIMAL SOLUTION

Once the solutions have been evaluated using either method, they can be improved through the use of an iterative technique. It is this technique that often leads to the creation of a breakthrough solution. This is the third step associated with the application of Outcome-Based Logic.

Improvements to the best solution are made by eliminating its known weaknesses and replacing them with strengths discovered in other solutions during the evaluation. For example, the highest scoring solution may have a weakness that is identified when the concepts are evaluated. Weaknesses are identified when it is determined that the highest scoring solution did not score as well as another concept on a specific metric. The only way another concept can score better than the highest scoring concept on a specific metric is if it contains a feature that is not currently found in the highest scoring concept. The idea is to then take the feature from the lower scoring concept and determine if it can be included in the highest scoring concept. If the feature can be included in the highest scoring concept, then you have just improved the highest scoring concept by eliminating one of its weaknesses.

This activity produces new solutions and concepts that are then evaluated. Multiple solutions may be created, tested, combined, improved and re-tested. After several iterations of improvement, the optimal solution is identified.

When using the evaluation method that compares concepts against a baseline concept, it is often best to change the baseline for comparison to discriminate between the differences in each proposed solution. As the top concepts emerge, it is best to compare them against each other rather than against a less valued alternative. For example, Concept A may have a rating of 42% and Concept B may have a rating of 41% when they are compared to Concept C. Such ratings indicate the two concepts deliver nearly equal value. When Concept A is compared to Concept B directly, it may be found that Concept A will obtain a rating of 20%. In conclusion, both Concepts A and B may appear to be equal when compared to Concept C, but Concept A may be found to be superior to Concept B when compared to it directly. Changing the baseline for comparison helps to create and uncover the optimal solution.

A question that typically arises is, "If more than one individual or organization uses this process to formulate a strategy or solution relating to the same mission, would they reach the same conclusion?"

It is important to note that the solutions derived through the use of this process are dependent on the knowledge, skills and creative talents of those using the process. Given that knowledge, skills and creative talents vary from organization to organization, it is unlikely that any two organizations would reach the same conclusion. The final result is dependent on what an organization is able to include in its universe of possible solutions. This process is not a substitute for great people. It simply ensures that they are focused on the creation of value.

## USING PREDICTIVE METRICS FOR MEASURING AND REWARDING IMPROVEMENT

Predictive metrics describe the activities that must be completed to effectively evolve the process, product, service or strategy under consideration. They are often assigned target values that define an organization's desired competitive position. This information is of value to those who are responsible for evolving the process, product, service or strategy of interest and to those responsible for managing that evolution.

Management may use this information to track the progress that is being made by the individuals who are responsible for achieving the assigned target values. Using this information to manage the evolution of a process, product, service or strategy ensures that workers are focused on the creation of value. Using this information to measure and reward employee performance ties the reward system directly to the creation of customer value.

As an example, the performance of individuals who are assigned the target values for the predictive metrics in Table C.5 may be tracked and rewarded, as appropriate.

**Table C.5**
**Tying Rewards to the Creation of Value**

| Predictive Metric | Target Value in 1 year | Target Value in 5 years | Worker | Reward |
|---|---|---|---|---|
| Reduce the **time** required to set up the system for different operations. | 3 minutes | 3 seconds | ACE | $X per 30-sec reduction |
| Reduce the **time** required to repair an unexpected failure. | 24 hours | 15 minutes | FAR | $X per 1-hour reduction |
| Reduce the **frequency** with which planned servicing is required. | 4 times a year | 0 times a year | AWL | $X per service reduction |
| Reduce the **space** (cubic inches) required by the system. | 800 cu. in. | 200 cu. in. | MIA | $X per 50 cubic inches |
| Reduce the planned **cost** to upgrade to new technologies in the future. | 30% of initial cost | 10% of initial cost | WOW | $X per 5% reduction |

Many employee performance measurement and reward systems are not tied to the creation of customer value, because the measures that predict the creation of value are rarely known. But, as stated by C. Dan McArthur and Larry Womack in *Outcome Management* (1995), ''If the company's current formal and informal reward system does not reward the kind of behaviors required to move the organization to a new level of performance, the reward system must be changed.'' Using predictive metrics as a basis for measuring employee performance ensures each employee is motivated to focus on the criteria that creates customer and stockholder value.

We often define quality as the degree to which all the customers' desired outcomes are satisfied given a specified mission. Successfully tying the employee reward system to the metrics that predict the satisfaction of customer desired outcomes will effectively drive employees to focus on quality. They will be focused on taking the actions that will deliver quality as defined by the customer.

So as we have demonstrated predictive metrics are used throughout the execution of this advanced strategy formulation process to achieve a variety of objectives—all of which are focused on the creation and delivery of customer value and all of which are focused on formulating breakthrough strategies and solutions.

# Glossary

*Accelerated Growth*: The enhanced, systematic evolution of a specific process, product, service, technology or organization.

*Assigned Values*: The numerical values, assigned to the weighting of a customer group, that weight the importance of that customer group relative to other customer groups in the customer set. The assigned values are based on best practices as determined through project experience.

*Baseline Concept*: The concept against which all other concepts are compared when conducting concept evaluation and testing.

*Basic Desired Outcome*: A desired outcome that has been so well satisfied or evolved by previous solutions that customers expect the same level of satisfaction from any future solution.

*Benchmark*: The process of comparing different products, technologies or organizations against a set of metrics to determine the relative competitive position of each. This is accomplished in this process by determining how well the competing items perform against a set of appropriate predictive metrics.

*Breakthrough Solution*: A solution or strategy that satisfies over 50% of the customers' desired outcomes better than an existing strategy or solution. Breakthrough solutions often deliver up to 10 times more value than commonly implemented solutions and enable an organization to leapfrog their competition. Breakthrough solutions also often provide an organization with a unique and valued competitive position.

*CD-MAP*: The Customer-Driven Mission Achievement Process (CD-MAP) is a process that enhances the ability of an individual or organization to formulate strategies, develop plans and make complex decisions. This process enables organizations to accelerate the evolution of their products, services, processes and strategies.

*CD-MAP Facilitator*: An individual trained in the execution of the CD-MAP process who works with a team within an organization to ensure the integrity of the process.

*CD-MAP Team*: A group of individuals within an organization who represent the functions required to execute the resulting strategy or solution. Team member selection is based on specific criteria, and team members are empowered to make decisions and take action.

*Cluster*: A group of individuals who are statistically similar in terms of which desired outcomes they value most. A cluster is derived through a computer analysis of the data received from appropriately conducted quantitative research.

*Cluster Analysis*: This is a multi-variant, statistical analysis technique that finds groups of customers who value the same desired outcomes. This technique is used in the CD-MAP process to conduct segmentation analysis using the desired outcomes as the basis for segmentation.

*Concept*: An idea, strategy or potential solution in its conceptual or theoretical stage.

*Concept Evaluation or Testing*: A method used to evaluate a concept's potential to deliver value to customers in a specified target segment.

*Concept Features/Elements*: The components or attributes of a concept that individually deliver unique value. Features are mutually exclusive components of a concept.

*Concept Optimization*: A method used to systematically create the solution that will deliver the most value to customers in a specified target segment.

*Concept Score*: A numerical value that quantifies the percent of desired outcomes that are better satisfied by the concept under evaluation than the concept it is being evaluated against.

*Constants*: Elements of the Universal Strategy Formulation Model (USFM) that are stable within the time period in which the mission must be achieved. The elements include customer desired outcomes, constraints and the desired competitive position.

*Constraint*: A boundary condition placed on the potential solution or strategy, which restricts freedom of choice. Constraints are typically imposed by an individual, the organization or by a third party. A constraint must be satisfied by the chosen solution.

*Customer*: An individual or group of individuals involved in, or affected by, the strategy, plan or decision that is being contemplated. As an example, if an organization wants to improve the process of surgery, the customers may include surgeons, support staff, hospital administrators, the manufacturer of the product and the individuals within the organization who are providing the solution.

*Customer Set*: All of the customer types that are involved in, or affected by, the decision, plan or strategy that is being contemplated. As an example, an end-user, decision-maker and distributor are customer types who combine to form a customer set.

*Customer Weighting*: The numerical value assigned to a customer type that defines their importance as a customer relative to other customer types in the customer set.

*Desired Competitive Position*: A unique and valued position that an organization desires to achieve relative to its competitors. To achieve the desired competitive position, the chosen solution must satisfy the most important desired outcomes better than any solution employed or planned by a competitor. The desired competitive position is established through target values that are defined for the most important predictive metrics.

*Desired Outcome*: A desired outcome is a statement, made by an individual involved in or affected by a strategy, plan or decision, that describes an important benefit they would like to receive from the strategy, plan or decision that is being contemplated. Desired outcomes are unique in that they are free from solutions, specifications and technologies, free from vague words such as "easy" or "reliable" and are statements that are stable over time.

*Desired Outcome Gathering Session*: Qualitative research conducted with individuals who are involved in diverse aspects of a specific process, product, service or organization. A session typically involves 10 participants and a desired outcome gathering expert. The participants are pre-screened to meet the specified target segment criteria.

*Direction of Improvement*: The direction in which a predictive metric is to be evolved or improved.

*Executable Plan of Action*: A series of actions carried out by individuals that satisfy a set of desired outcomes or execute a process. In an organization, this type of solution requires interaction between individuals.

*External Customer*: The individual or group of individuals external to the company who will receive value from the evolution of the process or the achievement of desired outcomes.

*Feasibility Factors*: Factors that must be considered to evaluate the feasibility of a specific concept. Feasibility factors usually include cost, risk and effort.

*Feature*: The components or attributes of a concept that individually deliver unique value. Features are mutually exclusive components of a concept.

*Implementation*: The execution of a plan or strategy.

*Importance*: The numerical value an individual places on a desired outcome that reflects the individual's desire to achieve that outcome.

*Importance and Satisfaction Data*: Quantified importance and satisfaction data that are obtained through statistically valid research. The data represent the importance and satisfaction that an individual places on a specified set of desired outcomes.

*Internal Customer*: An individual or organization engaged in the business of evolving a process or enabling the achievement of a set of desired outcomes.

*Lateral Thinking*: A method of thinking in which an individual searches across multiple disciplines, industries or cultures in an attempt to uncover the optimal solution.

*Matrix Analysis*: A tool that assists in identifying the relationships that exist between two sets of data. In the CD-MAP process, matrix analysis is used to identify the relationship between predictive metrics and desired outcomes. It is also used, in conjunction with the normalized importance algorithm, to prioritize the predictive metrics based on their predictive value.

*Mission*: A specific task or project with which an individual or organization is charged. A mission may be large or small in scope. When defining a mission, extending the focus of the mission past the existing boundaries of a stated process will often create new opportunity.

*Normalized Importance*: An algorithm that prioritizes the predictive metrics in the order of their predictive value. A high priority predictive metric will predict the satisfaction of several important desired outcomes.

*Opportunity*: Desired outcomes that an individual, segment or total population perceive to be both important and unsatisfied.

*Optimal Solution*: The one solution or strategy that will satisfy the largest number of important desired outcomes given the internal and external constraints imposed on the solution and the competitive position that is desired. The optimal solution will also be the solution that delivers the most value for the least cost, risk and effort. The optimal solution is typically a breakthrough solution.

*Outcome-Based Logic*: The logic that is used in the CD-MAP process to execute the USFM. Outcome-Based Logic is characterized as follows. First, all of the criteria to be used to evaluate any potential solution are defined and prioritized. Second, that criteria is used to drive the actual creation of a variety of potential solutions and evaluate the potential of each solution. Third, the results of the evaluation are used to assist in improving each solution by replacing its weaknesses with valued attributes from other solutions. After several iterations of improvement, the optimal solution is determined and selected.

*Outcome-Based Segmentation*: Quantitative market research that uses desired outcomes as the basis for segmentation. Cluster analysis is executed to create the segments. The segments are then profiled to determine their composition.

*Outcome Prioritization Method*: The numerical value or calculation that is used to prioritize the desired outcomes. The desired outcomes are typically prioritized by: their corresponding importance values; their corresponding importance and satisfaction values in a calculation that identifies opportunity; or their corresponding satisfaction values only.

*Positioning*: The process of comparing different products, technologies or organizations to determine the current competitive position of each and to establish a desired strategic position for the future.

*Predictive Logic*: Predictive logic is characterized by thinking about what can be done now to ensure or predict that a desired outcome will be better satisfied in the future.

*Predictive Metric*: A parameter that can be measured today to ensure its corresponding desired outcome will be achieved in the future. A predictive metric is measured and controlled in the design of the solution and predicts the solution will satisfy one or more desired outcomes. In the CD-MAP process, a single, strong predictive metric is defined for each desired outcome. A predictive metric may also be referred to as a predictive success factor.

*Predictive Value*: A numerical value that reflects the degree to which a predictive metric predicts the satisfaction of a specific desired outcome. Predictive values typically reflect a non-predictive, weak, moderate or strong predictive relationship with a desired outcome.

*Process*: A series of activities, actions or events that produce a desired result. Examples of processes include conducting surgery, manufacturing a product, making an acquisition, developing a product and formulating a strategy.

*Process Evolution*: Improving the degree to which the desired outcomes of a process, product, service or organization are satisfied. The evolution can be measured using the target values assigned to the predictive metrics.

*Product*: A device that is used by an individual or organization to assist in the execution of a process or to achieve a set of desired outcomes. User interaction with the device is characteristic of a product.

*Qualitative Research*: Market research that is conducted to uncover desired outcomes on the subject of interest. It is typically conducted as a group interview or personal interview. Qualitative research is conducted as part of the CD-MAP process to uncover desired outcomes.

*Quantitative Research*: Market research that is conducted to quantify the importance and perceived satisfaction level of each desired outcome.

*Sample*: A grid that defines the types and number of individuals who will be interviewed as part of quantitative market research. The sample is designed to represent all target segments within the population.

*Satisfaction*: The numerical value an individual places on a desired outcome that reflects the individual's perception of how well the desired outcome is currently satisfied.

*Scenario*: A situation that may currently exist, or potentially exist, that requires consideration.

*Screening Criteria*: Criteria used to ensure the customers interviewed for qualitative and quantitative research are representative of the target population.

*Segment*: A group of individuals who are considered a potential target market. A segment may include an industry, a business size, other convenient statistical classifications or clusters derived through segmentation analysis.

*Segmentation*: A method of finding individuals in a population who value the same desired outcomes. This is accomplished using a statistical technique called cluster analysis. When executing the CD-MAP process, desired outcomes are used as the basis for segmentation.

*Service*: A means by which desired outcomes are satisfied for an individual or organization by a third party. External customer interaction is common with the service provider, as the provider executes the process of interest for the individual or organization.

*Solution*: A specific set of features that form the basis of a plan or strategy, and define how the desired outcomes will be achieved. A proposed solution is often referred to as a plan or a strategy. Solutions are treated as variables in the USFM.

*Solution-Based Logic*: The logic pattern that is commonly used to formulate strategies. Solution-Based Logic is characterized as follows. First, individuals use various methods to think of several different solutions. The methods may include brainstorming, research or other methods. Second, individuals evaluate each of the proposed solutions to determine the best solution. The methods used to accomplish this task may include concept testing, conjoint analysis, quantitative research or other methods. Third, the best solution is selected based on the results of the previous steps.

*Stakeholder*: An individual or group of individuals who are responsible for the creation of a product service or strategy, or who must interact with those involved in a specific process.

*Strategy*: A strategy is a plan. It is an executable plan of action that describes how an individual or organization will achieve a stated mission.

*Strategy Formulation*: The process of creating a strategy.

*Strategyn*: An organization whose mission is to provide individuals and businesses with tools that evolve their ability to formulate strategies, define plans, make complex decisions and achieve their valued missions.

*Synergy Analysis*: A method for determining the relationships that exist between each desired outcome and each predictive metric. The relationships are uncovered using matrix analysis. Once the relationships have been established, the predictive metrics that have the most synergy can be determined.

*Target Segment*: The individual or group of individuals who the internal customers have chosen to serve.

*Target Values*: Values assigned to predictive metrics to guide the level of satisfaction that must be achieved by any proposed solution. Target values are set to ensure the final solution will enable an organization to occupy its desired competitive position.

*The Total Quality Group*: A consulting firm that specializes in the development and facilitation of the CD-MAP.

*Ultimate Target Value*: The target value that will drive a predictive metric to a fully evolved position. As each of the ultimate target values are achieved, the process, product, service or organization will be fully evolved along that stated dimension. When all the ultimate target values are achieved, the process, product, service or organization will be fully evolved.

*Universal Strategy Formulation Model (USFM)*: The USFM describes what organizations must do to formulate a breakthrough strategy or solution. The model can be explained as follows.

When formulating a strategy or solution, an organization must search through the universe of possible solutions in an attempt to find the one solution that will satisfy the largest number of important desired outcomes given the internal and external constraints imposed on the solution and the competitive position that is desired. That one solution is the optimal solution.

The USFM is designed to formulate strategies and plans using a mathematical structure. The model defines desired outcomes, constraints and the desired competitive position as constants in an equation and the universe of possible solutions as variables. Once the constants are defined, solutions are then evaluated until the optimal solution is found and the equation is "solved."

*Universe of Possible Solutions*: Any solution that could possibly improve or evolve the process, product, service or organization under consideration. When formulating a strategy or solution, there often exists hundreds or even thousands of possible solutions.

*User Environments*: Situations in which individuals desire to execute the process of interest.

*Value*: The degree to which a solution will satisfy a set of desired outcomes versus the cost of acquiring the solution.

*Value Creation*: Increasing an individual's perceived level of satisfaction on one or more desired outcomes.

*Variables*: Elements of the USFM that change over time. They include the features, concepts and ideas that form the universe of possible solutions. They change over time as new ideas evolve and new technologies become available. All potential solutions are treated as variables when executing the USFM.

*Weight*: A numerical value that reflects the perceived importance of a specific desired outcome or a customer type.

*Weighted Importance*: The importance assigned to a desired outcome given its numerical importance rating and the weighting assigned to that particular customer set.

# Bibliography

Altshuller, Genrich. 1990. *40 Principles: TRIZ Keys to Technical Innovation*. Worcester, MA: Technical Innovation Center.

Bailey, Robert W. 1989. *Human Performance Engineering: Using Human Factors/ Ergonomics to Achieve Computer System Usability*. 2nd ed. Englewood Cliffs, NJ: Prentice Hall.

Chandler, Alfred Dupont. 1962. *Strategy and Structure: Chapters in the History of the Industrial Enterprise*. Cambridge, MA: MIT Press.

Dilts, Robert. 1994. *Strategies of Genius: Volume II*. Capitola, CA: Meta Publications.

Gale, Bradley. 1994. *Managing Customer Value*. New York: Free Press.

Gardner, Howard. 1983. *Frames of Mind: The Theory of Multiple Intelligences*. New York: Basic Books.

Ghemawat, Pankaj. 1991. *Commitment: The Dynamic of Strategy*. New York: Free Press; Toronto, Canada: Maxwell Macmillan Canada; New York: Maxwell Macmillan International.

Griffin, Abbie, and Hauser, John R. Winter, 1993. ''The Voice of the Customer.'' *Marketing Science*, Volume 12, Number 1, pp. 1–27.

Gruenwald, George. 1992. *New Product Development*. Chicago: NTC Business Books.

Hamel, Gary. 1997. ''Killer Strategies.'' *Fortune*, June 23, pp. 70–84.

Hamel, Gary, and Prahalad, C. K. 1994. *Competing for the Future*. Boston: Harvard Business School Press.

Handy, Charles. 1989. *The Age of Unreason*. London: Business Books.

Henderson, Bruce D. November, 1989. ''The Origin of Strategy.'' *Harvard Business Review*, pp. 139–143.

Juran, Joseph. 1989. *Juran on Leadership for Quality*. New York: Free Press.

Kano, Noriaki. 1982. ''Attractive Quality and Must-Be Quality.'' Dissertation, Nippon Quality Conference 12th Annual Meeting, January 18.

Martin, Justin. 1995. ''Ignore Your Customers.'' *Fortune*, May 1, pp. 121–126.

McArthur, C. Dan, and Womack, Larry. 1995. *Outcome Management*. New York: Quality Resources.

Mintzberg, Henry. 1994. *The Rise and Fall of Strategic Planning*. New York: Prentice Hall.

Ohmae, Kenichi. November, 1988. ''Getting Back to Strategy.'' *Harvard Business Review*, pp. 149–156.

Ohmae, Kenichi. 1982. *The Mind of the Strategist*. New York: McGraw-Hill.

Porter, Michael. 1985. *Competitive Advantage*. New York: Free Press.

Porter, Michael. November–December, 1996. ''What Is Strategy?'' *Harvard Business Review*, pp. 61–78.

Ries, Al, and Trout, Jack. 1986. *Positioning: The Battle for Your Mind*. New York: McGraw-Hill.

Senge, Peter M. 1990. *The Fifth Discipline: The Art and Practice of the Learning Organization*. New York: Doubleday/Currency.

Slywotzky, Adrian. 1996. *Value Migration*. Boston: Harvard Business School Press.

Womack, James P., and Jones, Daniel T. 1996. *Lean Thinking: Banish Waste and Create Wealth in Your Corporation*. New York: Simon and Schuster.

# Index

**About the Author**

ANTHONY W. ULWICK is founder and President of the Total Quality Group, a consulting group that specializes in helping *Fortune* 100 companies formulate business strategies. He is also founder and President of Strategyn.com, a software and information technology cómpany that provides business and consulting firms with advanced strategy formulation technology.